Grabbing Tea:
Queer Conversations on Archives and Practice

Number 15 in the Litwin Books Series on Gender and Sexuality in Information Studies, Emily Drabinski, series editor.

GRABBING TEA:
QUEER CONVERSATIONS ON ARCHIVES AND PRACTICE

Shawn(ta) Smith-Cruz & Sara Howard, Editors

LIBRARY JUICE PRESS
SACRAMENTO, CA

Copyright respective authors, 2024

Published in 2024 by Library Juice Press

Library Juice Press
PO Box 188784
Sacramento, CA 95822

http://libraryjuicepress.com/

This book is printed on acid-free paper.

Cover image by Jasmine Smith-Cruz.

Publisher's Cataloging in Publication

Names: Smith-Cruz, Shawn(ta), editor. | Howard, Sara A., editor.
Title: Grabbing tea / Shawn(ta) Smith-Cruz and Sara A. Howard, editors.
Other titles: Queer conversations on identity and libraries. | Queer conversations on archives and practice.
Description: Sacramento, CA : Library Juice Press, 2024. | Series: Gender and Sexuality in Information Studies ; 14 (vol. 1) ; 15 (vol. 2) | Published in two volumes. | Include bibliographical references and indexes.
Identifiers: LCCN 2024931245 | ISBN 9781634001342 (v. 1; acid-free paper) | ISBN 9781634001359 (v. 2; acid-free paper)
Subjects: LCSH: Librarians – Interviews. | Archivists – Interviews. | Sexual minorities – Interviews. | Library science – Social aspects. | Archives – Social aspects.
Classification: LCC Z682.4.G39 G73 v.2 2024 | DDC 020.02--dc23
LC record available at https://lccn.loc.gov/2024931245

Table of Contents

Acknowledgements..vii

Foreword...ix

Introduction..1

Brewing Narratives

1. On New Orleans and Its LGBTQ Community: A Microcosm
Perry Brass and Frank Perez..21

2. Towards a Many Gendered Daughters of Bilitis
Megan Paslawski and Meg Metcalf...35

3. Ephemeral: Queer Felt Experiences in Archives
Xena Becker and Donna Langille..49

4. *Paint Me a Dangerous Woman*: A Conversation about tatiana de la tierra's Lesbian Poetics and Librarianship
Lizeth Zepeda and Liliana C. González...63

5. Memory Work: Archival Evidences at the Schomburg and the Forward
Bridgett Kathryn Johnson-Pride and Chana Pollack.................................75

Sipping Strategies

6. A Responsibility to the Future: Sending Along the Record of LGBTQI Lives
RL Goldberg and Gerard Koskovich..95

7. Lessons for Archival Practice from Queer Resistance: Care, Intimacy, and Slowness
Jehan L Roberson and Shannon O'Neill..111

8. Queer Tinge: Adjusting Archival Practice to Meet the Needs of Rural Communities
Emma Curtis and Nicole Martin 129

9. (In) Terms of Who We Are: The Homosaurus Board in Conversation
Marika Cifor, Jay L. Colbert, Clair A. Kronk, K.J. Rawson, and B. M. Watson 141

10. Preserving Our History, Building Our Futures: Design, Naming, and Queering Library Systems
Danielle Maurici-Pollock and W. Arthur Maurici-Pollock 167

Steeping in Community

11. Representing the Yoni, the Self-Naming & Signature Files
Polly Thistlethwaite and Morgan Gwenwald 183

12. *Are You Family?* Mapping the Genealogy of Black Queer Library Workers
Zakiya Collier and Steven G. Fullwood 199

13. "It's a Friendship, It's a Kinship, It's a Relationship"
Steven D. Booth and Tracy S. Drake 217

14. Moments of Complication: Navigating the Profession While Queer
Claudia Berger and Claire Fox 235

15. Queer Time in Libraries and Archives: Democratizing Personal and Historical Narratives
Julie Adamo and Tanya Pearson 247

16. Que(e)ry Inque(e)ry: Reflections on Ten Years of Fundraising for Queer Archives
M'issa Fleming and Matthew Haugen 259

Index 273

Acknowledgements

We'd like to acknowledge firstly, the Litwin Books/Library Juice Press Gender & Sexuality in Information Studies Series Editor, Emily Drabinski. Emily, we thank you for your advice, support and patience. We are so happy to acknowledge the many people that have contributed to this collection. We begin, of course, with the authors who have been so willing to share their stories, struggles, time, and insights into what a queer conversation could be. We were supported at the start by a few open sessions and express our gratitude to the folks who helped us launch this venture: Andi Johnson, Nicole D'Andrea, Elizbeth Verrelli, and Andrew Rarig who built us an amazing queer tea-cup logo. We have to acknowledge our fantastic copy editors: Aria Bracci, Bailey Anderson, Drey Jonathan, Eirini Melena Karoutsos, Justin Buss, and Talyor Cook. This project would still be in process without their labor. We would also like to thank the institutions that provided in-kind financial support: CLAGS: Center for LGBTQ Studies; New York University Libraries; Pratt School of Information and the Pratt Faculty Development Fund; Princeton University Library; and the Wesleyan Queer Studies Reading Group.

 Shawn wants to thank her daughter Joey, who went from toddler to a little talking one and has kept every zoom meeting over the course of the year filled with popsicles. Jasmine "Jaz" Smith-Cruz, her wife, who's slipped in sweet treats, too, but mostly for the time to get these drafts done. For her comrades in queer archives, many of whom are in this book, and also the coordinators of the Lesbian Herstory Archives who continually keep her on the ground and in action. Finally, to her living and ancestral family: Locario and Smith and Lambey and Cruz, Judy and Lloyd, and grandmas Cynthia and Mary. Thank you.

Sara wants to start by honoring the memory of her parents, Sondra and Robert, who provided her with love, support, and chutzpah, and the ultimate shout-out to her brother, David, who has been a constant source of support and a meticulous editor! Sara also wants to thank those who offer endless support and love: Edie Thomas-Chin, Rimma Aranovich, Lauren Feiring, Sarah Rolfe and Rosie. There are too many friends and lovers along the way to thank here, but thank you all! In closing, Sara dedicates her part in this book project to her niece and nephew, Nathaniel and Leia, who inspire her every day!

There are so many people for whom we cannot thank by name, our unending queer network, but still, we thank you!

Foreword

This lovely compilation of conversations, edited by Shawn(ta) Smith-Cruz and Sara Howard, captures the lived experiences of queer memory keepers and the following themes: community archives and access; metadata and the power of naming; the need to dismantle and reclaim safe spaces for healing; queer identities and representation; desire and pleasure; and queer ancestry and genealogy. After I read the conversations, or "platicas," in this book, I closed my eyes and saw the faces of queer youth, elders, and ancestors. Simultaneously, I experienced this immense wave of love, grief, urgency, and longing in my body. As queer people, our bodies and archives carry divine intergenerational and intersectional knowledge, trauma, and resilience from one generation to the next. When I reflect on our collective and personal experiences, I am reminded that we yearn to exist and find a queer home; we yearn to hold on to the past and nostalgia; we yearn to alter the present and future through radical acts of love and decolonizing.

In my recent publication "Community-Driven Archives: Conocimiento, Healing, and Justice,"[1] I share my personal experience as a Queer Latinx and archivist in academia. I share how my queer love and leadership helped establish ASU Library's Community-Driven Archives (CDA) Initiative. My team and I are transforming 21st century archives

---

[1]. Nancy Liliana Godoy, "Community-Driven Archives: Conocimiento, Healing, and Justice," in "Radical Empathy in Archival Practice," eds. Elvia Arroyo-Ramirez, Jasmine Jones, Shannon O'Neill, and Holly Smith, *Journal of Critical Library and Information Studies* 3, Special issue.

by dismantling power structures that dehumanize Black, Indigenous, People of Color (BIPOC) and the Lesbian, Gay, Bisexual, Transgender, and Queer (LGBTQ) community in Arizona. As an Associate Archivist and Director of CDA, I seek to decenter whiteness and change patterns of homophobia and transphobia, both products of colonialism, by embracing the theory of Queer BIPOC feminists like Gloria Anzaldúa. She proposes that "conocimiento," a Spanish word for knowledge, can be used to decolonize our minds, souls, and storytelling. Like Anzaldúa and many authors in this book, I believe our healing journey begins when we reject this world, reclaim queer narratives, and dedicate ourselves to self-reflection and honest multi-layered conversations. When we breathe, reflect, and speak, these actions awaken our minds and archival imagination.

For BIPOC and LGBTQ communities, an archive is a collection of feelings and sensations. It is a sacred space, more than a repository, where we heal and return home to our bodies and find wholeness. As archivists and community members, there is an opportunity to preserve archival collections and teach people how to process human emotions and historical trauma. The authors remind me that there is collective power, vulnerability, and intimacy when we share our memories, stories of survival, and vision for a liberated queer archive. Through memory work, we are creating safe spaces and building a bridge into the future with profound passion, tenderness, and desire. This book showcases how our communities, driven by justice and our dreams, move through time in a non-linear way to uplift the stories and lives of queer people.

Conversations also discussed the importance of queer visibility within history and the profession. For many, visibility can represent death, discrimination, freedom, or radical joy. In a few chapters, I saw a glimpse of the strength it takes to be yourself and become a queer elder. Growing old is a privilege BIPOC and Queer communities do not have. As a queer child, I never thought I would grow old or experience happiness in this world. As an adult and archivist, I am very transparent about my queerness and thankful my ancestors have kept me safe while showing me how to support future generations. If you are queer, especially if you are a young person, I hope you see that you come from a long line of courageous activists, archivists, and leaders. Historically and presently we lack the resources to fight against systemic inequities and injustice, but we have a rich legacy of collective care, service, and mutual aid within our community. After you read this, I think you will be inspired to listen more carefully; to love more deeply without fear; to preserve our history and be your true self; and to dedicate the rest of your life to helping our communities remember and resist.

Nancy Liliana Godoy
June 2022

Bibliography

Godoy, Nancy Liliana. "Community-Driven Archives: Conocimiento, Healing, and Justice." *Journal of Critical Library and Information Studies* 3, no. 2 (2021).

Introduction

Shawn: Are you drinking lemon ginger today or peppermint?

Sara: Honestly, I'm having a glass of red wine.

Shawn: Oh good, me too. Except mine is white, but I was pretending there was tea in my mug to stick with the theme.

Sara: Well, we can start there, with the theme.

Shawn: Yes, the theme of queer conversations, this book.

Sara: These two books!

Shawn: Two books—ha! Correction, two books, over forty conversations, and over ninety authors!

Sara: And don't forget all of the data, the process, the money, the time…

Shawn: Are you referring to the $3000 in grant money, the three years, the over 4000 pages of transcript, almost 5000 minutes of audio, and nearly forty gigabytes of space sitting on our laptops?

Sara: Exactly. It's not just two books, it's a whole project.

Shawn: Yes, the *Grabbing Tea* project.

Sara: Well, there's only one way to share this with the contributors, our colleagues, and the world.

Shawn: Oh yes, what way is that?

Sara: You know: in conversation!

Shawn: Of course, like this one we're having right now.

Sara: Precisely.

Shawn: Cheers to that.

The Meeting of Minds

We had our first meaningful conversation[1] while grabbing tea after the 2018 ACRL-NY Annual Symposium. We learned later that we were each running late; Shawn couldn't find a seat, scrambling instead to find the lactation room; Sara placed too much faith in New Jersey transit and was running through Penn Station as the conference was starting; she also could not find a seat. That year we both experienced a struggle to engage with the professional community, but despite that feeling of out-of-placeness, we each came with a mission to formally meet each other—a fellow librarian doing work in queer studies or as a queer

---

1. We were introduced initially through a Gale-sponsored panel in Charleston, South Carolina, titled, "Intersectionality: How the definition has evolved and how libraries can support the conversation." While in Charleston, we had dinner at a swank restaurant but otherwise didn't have one-on-one time to chat, because Shawn had her daughter (still nursing) and wife with her, and Sara was on a mission to have as much BBQ as possible. Shawn in NYC at the CUNY Graduate Center, and Sara at Princeton in New Jersey, we hadn't had the chance to connect otherwise. When presenting in Charleston, we discovered that we shared the same goals: to work with a queer collaborator who has an intersectional approach and considers gender and sexuality to be a core component of our personal and political lives as well as our librarianship.

identified queer library liaison. After being miffed by the symposium raffle and the stress of the start of the day, we decided a glass of wine was well deserved.

We finally found each other and sat down for a drink after ACRL (where Shawn was able to have a measured single glass of wine while her breasts turned into milky rocks). It was there, with our consumption of some mutual beverage, that our conversation began: one that investigated topics such as queerness and the profession; identity, community practice, and outreach; visibility and coming out or being outed in the library; the archive and the implications of race and sexuality in archival practice. The conversation was lubricated by the chance to sit and grab some tea, to release the questions and ponder the answers. It's a place where we all begin, we surmised—a place where we could give our full selves, as librarians, embodied with queerness.

We continued to have conversations via phone or google hangouts, with Sara almost always running two minutes late and texting or emailing, "be right there—grabbing tea!" And though we've presented multiple times together on sexuality and gender in libraries, this was the fabric of our conversations: timely, unstructured, and raw, without peer reviewed, cleaned up dialectics, but instead, as visceral, actual, and present experiences. These intentional conversations were so informative to our work that we found we wanted to not lose the method that kept us coming back to each other.

Why Conversations?

Conversation is queer. To bring a queer lens to our librarianship, we chose the Litwin Books "Series on Sexuality and Gender" as an appropriate place to submit a book proposal, since its catalog of titles has been hugely impactful to the communities of this project. Litwin Books is the leader within the sexuality and gender continuum for the most relevant content that directly speaks to LIS. They produce works that bring library issues into conversation with contemporary theoretical debates and practical approaches in feminist, queer, and gender studies in librarianship and archives. *Grabbing Tea: Queer Conversations...* will be in collaboration and, if we may, *in conversation,* with the titles of the Litwin catalog. In choosing Litwin, we aim to continue the rich lineage already so carefully curated by this great press and the voices of its contributors.

Conversation is switchy and penetrative—a method by which we take our whole selves, our entire range of self-hood, including our bodies and queer perspectives, and bring them to match with the entire range of self-hood of another person or peoples. By acknowledging our queer and racialized bodies, we knew the conversation was a birthing place for fertile ground in our field. To be active inside of a conversation, to not be passive, to inter-penetrate,[2] requires the opposite of inaction. The conversation allows us in the queer library and archives community to move inside of each other, to interoperably engross ourselves and be bound up with one another.

Conversation is a technology. Using the broad definition of technology as that which "encompasses the strategies and techniques" relating to a specific process "as well as the equipment and resources used to support it," technology in librarianship is very much grounded in our scholarly communication infrastructures.[3] The "conversation" was approached in this project as not only an alternative technological format with an aim to loosen the tight confines of the scholarly publishing landscape, but also as a queer response to the strictures of authority and format. We propose the conversation as a queer deconstruction of the inhibitive technology of scholarly publishing.

Through the application of queer conversations in this two-book series, a technological paradigm shift takes hold. We librarians and archivists, who have become beholden to the (self) manufactured processing

---

2. Mary Parker Follett, *The New State, Group Organization the Solution of Popular Government* (New York etc.: Longmans, Green and co., 1918), https://catalog.hathitrust.org/Record/100764889.

3. Susan Wallace, "Technology," in *A Dictionary of Education*, ed. Susan Wallace (Oxford University Press, May 21, 2015), http://www.oxfordreference.com/view/10.1093/acref/9780199679393.001.0001/acref-9780199679393-e-1018.

system of scholarly production, as producers, providers, and users of this scholarship, engage in the immediate curation and efficient output of scholarship at the initiation of a scholarly idea. Whereas the onus is traditionally placed on publishers, editors, and referees to determine the output of the scholarly landscape, a queer deconstruction repositions the author as creator to be in a unique role of reorienting the technology of scholarly communication itself. Similar to the community-focused history of lesbian presses, whose technological formation was reliant on a quest to communicate and document processes of formulated theoretics,[4] librarians are also considering how storytelling and narrative formation within the profession are integral to its growth.[5] Examples of this paradigm shift takes place across the field, including instances where "questioning the technology of a lecture" (as in USC Knowledge Schools)[6] overlap with shifts in pedagogical practice, information literacy critiques, and participatory learning as benchmarks for librarian integration into curricula.

Conversation is scholarship. This evolution of the conversation as a technology shift requires a means of distribution. Using the medium of the monograph (as opposed to a podcast, meme, television production, or radio interview), as a gentle shift from, but still within the confines of, traditional scholarship, allows for a widening of the friction-laden current model of scholarly contribution. The conversation, taking on the audacious task of acting not only as a technology but also as a scholarly contribution, then, *queers* scholarship, challenging its function to reach wider audiences, those beyond a functional peer-review model, and into the hands of any participant within the field - for any person can have a conversation, just as any person may have a gender identity or a lover

---

4. Kate Adams, "Built Out of Books," *Journal of Homosexuality* 34, no. 3–4 (January 9, 1998): 113–41, https://doi.org/10.1300/J082v34n03_07.

5. Emily Ford, "Tell Me Your Story: Narrative Inquiry in LIS Research," *College & Research Libraries*, March 5, 2020, https://doi.org/10.5860/crl.81.2.235.

6. Darin Freeburg and David Lankes, "Introduction from the Editors of the Special Issue," *Journal of New Librarianship* 4, no. Special (09-23 2019): 293–302, https://doi.org/10.21173/newlibs/7/1.

of the same or variant sex. There is no prerequisite to the conversation. There are no gate-keepers within the playing field of the conversation. We are instigating peer exchanges and not peer review by allowing the stakeholders/players/patrons into the conversation of how libraries and archives are managed, utilized, entered, accessed and experienced.

In library instruction, librarians utilize ACRL frameworks to promote the frame of "Scholarship as Conversation," which refers to the idea of sustained discourse within a community of scholars, researchers, or professionals, providing new insights and discoveries occurring over time as a result of competing perspectives and interpretations.[7] This approach to the conversation as a scholarly endeavor further distinguishes conversation as a tool for teaching and learning, but does not interpret the conversation among librarians in an interpersonal exchange that can enhance our own professional scholarship.

Conversation is communi-tea. We were drawn to the concept of *Grabbing Tea*, as an ode to E Patrick Johnson's *Sweet Tea*, the historiography of African American gay men born and raised in the south, which acknowledges an importance "to employ oral histories as the key methodology," which denotes the insider, private community-centered and hopefully non-appropriating allegiance to a focused queer collection.[8] We were reminded of the work of Sara Ahmed,[9] in that the majority of academic writing can be more of a sense of telling; that, as opposed to a structure of learning informed by hierarchy, our writing can be imbued with a shared experience and mutual respect. We were continually attributing the ethos of traditional feminist publications as foremothers

---

7. Eric Bradley, et al., "Framework for Information Literacy for Higher Education: Frame: Scholarship as Conversation," LibGuide, Private Academic Library Network of Indiana (PALNI), https://libguides.palni.edu/ilframework/scholarship.

8. E. Patrick Johnson, *Sweet Tea: Black Gay Men of the South*, New edition (Chapel Hill: The University of North Carolina Press, 2008): 7

9. Sara Ahmed, "Whose Counting?" *Feminist Theory* 1, no. 1 (April 1, 2000): 97–103, https://doi.org/10.1177/14647000022229083.

for an envisionment of community storytelling in practice.[10] We looked to the works of those whom we admired and realized that our shared appreciation for and absorption of their work was when formatted in conversation—bell hooks in conversation with Cornel West,[11] bell hooks with Stuart Hall,[12] Audre Lorde in conversation with Adrienne Rich,[13] Cheryl Clarke in conversation with Joan Nestle,[14] or Mumia Abu-Jamal in conversation with Marc Lamont Hill.[15] Along with being intellectual giants, these scholars also created a space to invite us in, to allow us to be in conversation with them. LIS scholarship also uses "conversation as scholarship" as a form of critical librarianship.[16]

Conversation is critical action. Applying a queer theoretical frame to the conversation allowed us to break its function down into

---

10. *Sinister Wisdom: A Multicultural Lesbian Literary and Art Journal* exemplifies a longstanding, and accumulative conversation of lesbians and feminists who love them. Julie Enszer, its current series editor, ensures to have each issue reveal the interconnectedness of the bodies of people who form the feminist culture. Sinister Wisdom Issue 103: *Celebrating the Michigan Women's Music Festival* was in direct conversation with trans-activists who protested the space, by offering a deep sharing of the women who have embraced the space, and aimed to reflect on over forty years of accumulated community building, including the creation of a lesbian of color community in its multi-decade-long woman of color tent. Similarly, *Sinister Wisdom 118: Forty-Five Years / A Tribute to the Lesbian Herstory Archives* was a commemorative issue celebrating 45 years of lesbian narrative formation with the practice of self-archiving through community building. This issue highlighted the organization's founding, its existence in 13A-Joan Nestle's apartment, and shared stories of remembrance.

11. bell hooks and Cornel West, *Breaking Bread: Insurgent Black Intellectual Life*, 1st edition (New York: Routledge, 2016).

12. bell hooks, Stuart Hall, and Paul Gilroy, *Uncut Funk: A Contemplative Dialogue*, 1st edition (New York; London: Routledge, 2017).

13. Audre Lorde and Adrienne Rich, "An Interview with Audre Lorde," *Signs: Journal of Women in Culture and Society* 6, no. 4 (1981): 713–36.

14. Sinister Wisdom, "Celebrate Joan Nestle in Conversation with Cheryl Clarke," Lesbian Herstory Archives, November 10, 2020, https://lesbianherstoryarchives.org/calendar/celebration-with-joan-nestle/.

15. Mumia Abu-Jamal and Marc Lamont Hill, *The Classroom and the Cell: Conversations on Black Life in America*, 1st edition (Chicago: Third World Press, 2012).

16. M.T. Accardi, E. Drabinski, and A. Kumbier, "Beginning and Extending the Conversation," *Communications in Information Literacy*, 14, no. 1 (2020): 1–11. https://doi-org.proxy.library.nyu.edu/10.15760/comminfolit.2020.14.1.1.

interlinking parts. What we found as a subtle curation of the *Grabbing Tea* project was the structure of the conversation as a technology that informed our choices at each process point—scheduling conversations, invitations and introductions to co-authors, transcript editing, commissioning of queer copy-editors, and the addition of reflections, to name some core components. Matching queer folks from varying perspectives to engage in a structured conversation took a critical approach.[17] A critical lens to conversations takes into account critical pedagogies,[18] critical race theory,[19] and critical librarianship as a whole. The risk of matching people who could be potentially harmed in a close exchange was at the forefront of our considerations when pairing. We had to consider whether the goal was to pair opposing viewpoints to debate, meeting at points of contention, or whether to match people who may be isolated in this particular part of their professional identities, thereby connecting them with potential comrades. The latter was considered as a way to allow for a looser narrative sharing, without preset inhibitive walls.

Conversations queered. The forty-two conversations were split into two directions: Identity and Libraries—where authors discussed coming out, professionalism, and being queer inside of the space of the library; and Archives and Practice—where authors discussed collections, queering practice, and reclamation narratives. Designed as a two-volume set, each of these texts are in conversation with the other. Both editions

---

17. Sandra Hollingsworth and Mary Dybdahl, "Chapter 6: Talking to Learn: The Critical Role of Conversation in Narrative Inquiry," in *Handbook of Narrative Inquiry: Mapping a Methodology* (Thousand Oaks: SAGE Publications, Inc., 2007), 146–76, https://doi.org/10.4135/9781452226552. Hollingsworth and Dybdahl outline that, in contrast to post-positivist or constructivist epistemological perspectives (two perspectives in which truth would be semi-stable or unstable, respectively), a critical perspective would allow for no stable truths or "temporal understandings situated in history and political relations."

18. Melissa M. Gustafson, "Critical Pedagogy in Libraries: A Unified Approach," *Journal of Critical Library and Information Studies* 1, no. 1 (January 31, 2017), https://doi.org/10.24242/jclis.v1i1.15.

19. Sofia Y. Leung and Jorge R. López-McKnight, eds., *Knowledge Justice: Disrupting Library and Information Studies through Critical Race Theory* (Cambridge, MA: MIT Press, 2021).

of *Grabbing Tea* focus on intersections of the personal, professional, practice, and praxis.

Conversations on Archives and Practice

The queer archive haunts. When it comes to the connection of queer archivists to their collections, wanting to preserve the stories of their own documentation, the "next of kin," or the recognition of ancestral ties, the queer archive is as alive as the community that processes and absorbs its contents.

The queer archival collection has its own legs. To one who is embodied-queer, the archive unleashes the somatic: the felt interconnectedness that we have as subjects and practitioners. In these conversations, the somatic locates us in the archive-as-place.

The queer archive in practice is relational. The conversations uncover what we seek and find in donor contracts, acid free boxes, and finding aids—that within the queer archive is a shared labor that superimposes collections, stories and narratives linking us all to a communal practice.

Grabbing Tea: Queer Conversations in Archives and Practice reveals an inextricable connection to the research, labor, and subjectivities of queer bodies and histories. The conversations in this monograph open us up as readers and community members to the ephemeral, the historical, queer foundings, deep gratitude, collectivity, attribution, our limitations of language, the struggle to remember, and a continual recalling that echoes. The queer archive haunts.

Chapters in Conversation

Brewing Narratives

Perry Brass and Frank Perez take readers back to the New Orleans of the 1980s, paying special attention to the LGBTQ community and the AIDS crisis. In "On New Orleans, and Its LGBTQ Community: A Microcosm" both Brass and Perez have documented this history in prose and print. They discuss the importance of archives for helping to preserve LGBTQ history and how libraries and access to materials documenting LGBTQ experiences were an important part of their own identities.

Megan Paslawski and Meg Metcalf invite readers into the world of a fantastic corpus of queer and feminist thinkers, publications and archival materials. In their chapter, "Towards a Many Gendered Daughters of Bilitis," Paslawski and Metcalf discuss the power and possibilities of historical and literary reclamation and how this gives voice to collections and members of the queer community that have long been silenced. Paslawski and Metcalf invite the Daughters of Bilitis, the first lesbian rights group in the United States, founded in San Francisco in 1955, into the conversation as if the founding group were in the room.

Xena Becker and Donna Langille locate their bodies across various landscapes to think through the ephemeral effect of archival materials. Their conversation, "Ephemeral: Queer Felt Experiences in Archives," engages with their own personal identities as informed by archival spaces. Through their shared reflections in conversation, the two lead us to more questions on the somatic: the felt interconnectedness that we have as queer researchers, practitioners, and bodies when we engage with archives, our communities, and our contents. Readers witness a conversation reflective of the ways that varying embodiments may encounter institutional and community archives in different ways.

Lizeth Zepeda and Liliana C. González discuss latinx identity, desire and sexuality in the archive in their chapter, "Paint Me a Dangerous Woman: A Conversation about tatiana de la tierra's Lesbian Poetics and Librarianship." By centering the work of tatiana de la tierra, a Columbian lesbian poet, Zepeda and Gonzalez map their deep connection to tatiana de la tierra's work and connect readers to more complex themes of sexual erasure, the power of naming, and the problematic role of classification systems.

Bridgett Pride and Chana Pollack take us into their respective workplaces, New York Public Library's Schomburg Center for Research in Black Culture and the Forward, a 124-year-old independent Jewish media organization. In their chapter, "Memory Work: Archival Evidences at The Schomburg and the Forward" we learn how their labor, and the materials they process, intersect with their identities. Pride and Pollack underscore the importance of giving voice to those who have been traditionally silenced.

Sipping Strategies

Gerard Koskovich is interviewed by RL Goldberg in their chapter, "A Responsibility to the Future: Sending Along the Record of LGBTQI Lives." Koskovich shares his knowledge of acquisition and archival processing as a collector, book seller, and historian since the 1980s, and his collecting of queer twentieth-century artifacts from throughout the western world. As a trans studies scholar, Goldberg brings his experience with the use of collections at his own university library to further investigate Koskovich's stamp on LGBTQI archival history. The conversation concludes with a reflective love letter: to each other and to the militancy of archiving.

Jehan L. Roberson and Shannon O'Neill speak on care work, language, memory, slowness, anti-capitalism, and horizontality in their chapter, "Lessons for Archival Practice from Queer Resistance: Care, Intimacy, and Slowness." Inspired by artists and great thinkers, Roberson and O'Neill interrogate issues of hierarchy and power within the profession, along with the ethical concerns that arise when working with queer communities, from acquisition to use, remarking on strategies for undoing, such as messiness, unspooling, untidiness, and even honey.

In their chapter, "Queer Tinge: Adjusting Archival Practice to Meet the Needs of Rural Communities," Emma Curtis and Nicole Martin share with readers archival practices for working with the 2SLGBTQAI+ community. They remind us of the importance of queer spaces, whether physical or liminal, how libraries can be the introduction to these spaces, and how the archive can serve as a place where they can be preserved. They also help shift our thinking from the urban United States context to rural and international archives.

A conversation without borders requires questions of minority-world influences on language, especially from a queer perspective. "(In) Terms of Who We Are: The Homosaurus Board in Conversation," a chapter co-authored by Marika Cifor, Jay L. Colbert, Clair A. Kronk, K.J. Rawson, and Brian M. Watson, interrogates the power, shifts, and implications of the fluidity and culturally based anchoring of queer language. In learning about the history and development of Homosaurus, an international linked data vocabulary of Lesbian, Gay, Bisexual, Transgender, and Queer (LGBTQ) terms, readers will receive an in-depth overview of the implications for cataloging queer vocabularies.

Dr. Danielle Pollock and W. Arthur Maurici also approach the conversation of the catalog. With design thinking in mind, "Preserving Our History, Building Our Futures: Design, Naming, and Queering Library Systems" interrogates non-degreed library staff contributions and queer contributions to library systems. With reclamations of queer history in mind and relying on their own research and experiences, the authors provide select strategies for cishet peoples to avoid design biases, such as misnaming or misgendering.

Steeping in Community

Polly Thistlethwaite and Morgan Gwenwald wanted to add a photo to their chapter, "Representing the Yoni, the Self-naming & Signature Files," because it centers around a photo that Gwenwald took of Thistlethwaite in the HQ stacks decades ago. On that journey, we learn about their relationship as coordinators of the Lesbian Herstory Archives in the 1980s and 1990s, in addition to other early lesbian feminisms. We travel through time in this chapter about a photo-less photo-documentation of the yoni of the lesbian community.

Venturing into the somatic, we then enter the spirit, or the ancestral journey with Zakiya Collier and Steven G. Fullwood in their chapter, "*Are You Family?* Mapping the Genealogy of Black Queer Library Workers." This intergenerational conversation of two archivists, who have managed Schomburg collections, traces a lineage of queer chosen family within the profession, including great practitioners like Hurston or Lorde, whom we would never meet, but have inspired us to our core. We ask ourselves where we stand in this lineage, and who it is that we take with us.

Steven D. Booth and Tracy S. Drake extend the conversation about chosen family in their affirming chapter, "It's a Friendship, It's a Kinship, It's a Relationship." While experiencing these two friends' love for each other, we embark on an extension and a sharing of Black queer archival networks, where community support and the presence of mentors ground success and sustain black archivists in the profession. We also learn the ephemeral value of wearing pins at conferences, especially when they include a black icon holding a rainbow flag.

All social networks are valuable, even if found on social media. Claudia Berger and Claire Fox speak about graduate school, professionalism, and theory and practice in archives, considering what it is to be a library student entering into a field that is, seemingly, open to queerness. In their chapter, "Moments of Complication: Navigating the Profession While Queer," these two new scholars offer each other a roadmap that navigates questions they developed while in library school, including what exactly to do with library Twitter.

In the chapter "Queer Time in Libraries and Archives: Democratizing Personal and Historical Narratives," Julie Adamo and Tanya Pearson discuss both the restrictions and the joy of resisting professionalism in the workplace—a professionalism that they define as being based on white supremacy culture, capitalism, and heteronormativity. Adamo and Pearson address the stress of these restrictions while trying to obtain health, financial security, and the elation of resisting by being openly queer, punk rock, or a combination of both.

M'issa Fleming and Matthew Haugen give readers a behind-the-scenes look at the development, successes, hurdles and future of Que(e)ry. "Que(e)ry Inque(e)ry: Reflections on Ten Years of Fundraising for Queer Archives" highlights the importance for queer spaces in professional spaces, such as the American Library Association (ALA) Annual Conference. Fleming and Haugen describe the thoughtfulness put into creating these spaces and some of the frustrations related to community organizing.

Editors Reflection

This book project brewed somewhere between 2018 and 2019, when we had our meeting of minds. It took us two years to submit a book proposal and hold a virtual information session in June 2020. The Call for Conversations used language from the book proposal:

> The purpose of this book is to produce a volume that re-envisions queer scholarship and queer librarianship. We hope that it serves as a theoretical and methodological guide for placing LGBTQ engagement as central to the LIS field and profession. We argue that libraries and archives have an ethical responsibility to integrate our information access with all communities, especially those that have historically been intentionally siloed or marginal. The application of conversations as a methodology is needed to advance the scholarly landscape as well as connect queer communities to libraries and acknowledge the hidden labor of queer librarians in their engagement practices within instruction, outreach, reference, engagement, preservation, collections, and physical spaces in our libraries and archives.

The Call coincided with COVID-19. The world was experiencing a global pandemic, ripe with social isolation, that locked us into our homes or pushed us back into work when we weren't ready to return. By June 2020, many settled into a COVID reality. During what would normally be a month of celebration, queer folks had to recalibrate our connections to Pride. This was especially significant, since 2019 marked the fifty-year anniversary of Stonewall, a moment memorialized as World Pride that sought to bring the disparities of queer experience across the world to the fore.

In the information session, we invited interested library workers, archivists, cultural workers, students, and community members to contribute ideas—in pairs, groups or individually. While we were hesitant to ask folks to do additional work during a global pandemic, we were simultaneously moved by desire for face-to-face contact, for community connections, and for conversations. Thereby, all conversations and reflections took place between Fall 2020 and Spring 2021. Our desire for the rich quickness and rapid beat of a conversation was coupled with a slow and thoughtful editorial process that cultivated connections built over this multi-year book project journey.

In closing we thank all of our contributors, copy editors, and our amazing editor for being in conversation with us.

Sara: Is there anything else we should reflect on?

Shawn: No, and yes. I mean, we could say so much more—say, about the variety of locations our contributors are from, or the ethics and commodification of Zoom, as two examples.

Sara: Or the relationships built from those who became collaborators due to this project, like those who were colleagues or friends from the start, and what they may have learned from each other since participating.

Shawn: Yes, or we could go into the construction of an index on queer subjectivities and how some of the terms, if read aloud, sound like a spoken word poem.

Sara: Yes, I guess you are right, there is so much more to say.

Shawn: In content and in process. We could do this forever.

Sara: Let's say we save all of that extra for a post-book project journal article.

Shawn: Or blog post.

Sara: Or, we can just continue to talk about it.

Shawn: You mean, save it for another conversation.

Sara: Exactly. Who knows where it will lead us.

Shawn: I'm always here for a conversation with you, Sara.

Sara: Same here, Shawn.

> Shawn(ta) Smith-Cruz and Sara Howard, Editors

Bibliography

Accardi, Maria T., Emily Drabinski, and Alana Kumbier. "Beginning and Extending the Conversation." *Communications in Information Literacy* 14, no. 1 (January 2020): 1–11. https://doi.org/10.15760/comminfolit.2020.14.1.1.

Adams, Kate. "Built Out of Books." *Journal of Homosexuality* 34, no. 3–4 (January 9, 1998): 113–41. https://doi.org/10.1300/J082v34n03_07.

Ahmed, Sara. "Whose Counting?" *Feminist Theory* 1, no. 1 (April 1, 2000): 97–103. https://doi.org/10.1177/14647000022229083.

Bradley, Eric, David Dunham, Sally Neal, Amber Pavlina, and Catherine Pellegrino. "Framework for Information Literacy for Higher Education: Frame: Scholarship as Conversation." LibGuide. Private Academic Library Network of Indiana (PALNI), n.d. https://libguides.palni.edu/ilframework/scholarship.

Collins, Anastasia M. "Language, Power, and Oppression in the LIS Diversity Void." *Library Trends* 67, no. 1 (Summer 2018): 39–51. http://dx.doi.org/10.1353/lib.2018.0024.

"Conversation, n." In *OED Online*. Oxford University Press. Accessed February 21, 2022. http://www.oed.com/view/Entry/40748.

Follett, Mary Parker. *The New State, Group Organization the Solution of Popular Government*. New York etc.: Longmans, Green and co., 1918. https://catalog.hathitrust.org/Record/100764889.

Ford, Emily. "Moving Peer Review Transparency from Process to Praxis." *Insights* 32, no. 1 (October 2, 2019): 27. https://doi.org/10.1629/uksg.480.

———. "Scholarship as an Open Conversation: Utilizing Open Peer Review in Information Literacy Instruction." *In the Library with the Lead Pipe*, April 4, 2018. https://www.inthelibrarywiththeleadpipe.org/2018/open-conversation/.

———. "Tell Me Your Story: Narrative Inquiry in LIS Research." *College & Research Libraries*, March 5, 2020. https://doi.org/10.5860/crl.81.2.235.

Ford, Jeffrey D., and Laurie W. Ford. "The Role of Conversations in Producing Intentional Change in Organizations." *Academy of Management Review* 20, no. 3 (July 1995): 541–70. https://doi.org/10.5465/AMR.1995.9508080330.

Freeburg, Darin, and David Lankes. "Introduction from the Editors of the Special Issue." *Journal of New Librarianship* 4, no. Special (09-23 2019): 293–302. https://doi.org/10.21173/newlibs/7/1.

Godfrey, Paul C. "Postscript: Observations on Conversation as a Theory-Building Methodology." In *Identity in Organizations: Building Theory Through Conversations*, 295–99. Thousand Oaks: SAGE Publications, Inc., 1998. https://doi.org/10.4135/9781452231495.

Gustafson, Melissa M. "Critical Pedagogy in Libraries: A Unified Approach." *Journal of Critical Library and Information Studies* 1, no. 1 (January 31, 2017). https://doi.org/10.24242/jclis.v1i1.15.

Halperin, David M. "The Normalization of Queer Theory." *Journal of Homosexuality* 45, no. 2–4 (2003): 339–43.

Hollingsworth, Sandra, and Mary Dybdahl. "Chapter 6 Talking to Learn: The Critical Role of Conversation in Narrative Inquiry." In *Handbook of Narrative Inquiry: Mapping a Methodology*, 146–76. Thousand Oaks: SAGE Publications, Inc., 2007. https://doi.org/10.4135/9781452226552.

Isaiah Green, Adam. "Queer Theory and Sociology: Locating the Subject and the Self in Sexuality Studies*." *Sociological Theory* 25, no. 1 (2007): 26–45.

Leung, Sofia Y., and Jorge R. López-McKnight, eds. *Knowledge Justice: Disrupting Library and Information Studies through Critical Race Theory*. Cambridge, MA, USA: MIT Press, 2021.

Thomas, Paul, Mary Czerwinksi, Daniel Mcduff, and Nick Craswell. "Theories of Conversation for Conversational IR." *ACM Transactions on Information Systems* 39, no. 4 (August 2021): 39–62. https://doi.org/10.1145/3439869.

Wallace, Susan. "Technology." In *A Dictionary of Education*, edited by Susan Wallace. Oxford University Press, May 21, 2015. http://www.oxfordreference.com/view/10.1093/acref/9780199679393.001.0001/acref-9780199679393-e-1018.

Brewing Narratives

ON NEW ORLEANS, AND ITS LGBTQ COMMUNITY: A MICROCOSM

Perry Brass and Frank Perez

Keywords
AIDS crisis, archives, history, New Orleans

Perry Brass has published 20 books, including poetry, novels, short fiction, science fiction, and advice books (*How to Survive Your Own Gay Life; The Manly Art of Seduction; The Manly Pursuit of Desire and Love*). He has been involved with LGBTQ rights since 1969, shortly after the Stonewall Uprising, co-editing *Come Out!,* the New York Gay Liberation Front's groundbreaking newspaper. In 1972, with two friends, he co-founded the Gay Men's Health Project Clinic, the first clinic specifically for gay men on the East Coast, still thriving as the Callen-Lorde Community Health Service. For more information: www.perrybrass.com.

Frank Perez serves as Executive Director of the LGBT+ Archives Project of Louisiana. He is a columnist for *Ambush Magazine* and *French Quarter Journal* and has authored several books on New Orleans history, including *Political Animal: The Life and Times of Stewart Butler, In Exile* (with Jeffrey Palmquist), *Treasures of the Vieux Carre,* and *Southern Decadence in New Orleans* (with Howard P. Smith). He is also the co-editor of the anthology *My Gay New*

Orleans: 28 Personal Reminiscences on LGBT+ Life in New Orleans. As a licensed tour guide, Perez developed "The Rainbow Fleur de Lis," an interactive walking tour of the French Quarter focusing on New Orleans' rich LGBT+ history. Perez teaches part-time at Loyola University. Learn more at frenchquarterfrank.com

Conversation

Perry Brass: And you live in New Orleans?

Frank Perez: I do. I am sitting in my apartment in the heart of the French Quarter, just a block away from Jackson Square.

Perry: My husband and I lived in New Orleans for three years during the early 80s. It was a wonderful time to be there. There was this amazing interaction among people there. You could make so many friends, and people were so open to friendship.

Frank: Back then, especially, and it's still true today; New Orleans is a really big small town and the queer community is a microcosm of that.

Perry: In those days, it had this gay, organized social life. Because I really was so out … you know, I come from this gay liberation background in New York, I met lots and lots of people. I was actually one of the very first people whom you would call an AIDS buddy in the city. I went to Charity Hospital to visit a friend of mine who was there and who had AIDS. And then in the next bed over was this wonderful man who knew almost no one in New Orleans, and one of my close friends and I became his caretaker and AIDS buddy. And at that point, there really wasn't a lot organized, if anything. So, I'm happy to say I was one of the first AIDS buddies in New Orleans.

Frank: That's really incredible. I mean, it was about the time that you were here that the NO/AIDS Task Force was getting off the ground.

On New Orleans, and Its LGBTQ Community: A Microcosm

Perry: Yes, it was. It was very difficult.

Frank: Sure. And there was just so much ignorance. I remember friends going and having to pick up the trays of food from outside in the hallway because the hospital staff was just so terrified.

And to make a connection to the gay krewes... As the epidemic got worse over the years, throughout the 80s, it really decimated those gay krewes; some of them never came back. We have about ten krewes right now. But in the early 80s, there were probably double that.

Perry: I don't know how many there were. But I was very impressed with the idea that the krewes had a social motive. I mean, they were really a way that you could be gay in New Orleans and have a professional life, and a social life, and a sexual life, and, amazingly, integrate them in a way that you couldn't in most of the rest of the country.

Frank: Well, that's so true. For those who may not be aware, the first gay krew, and the gay krewes in general, date back to the late 50s, early 1960s. So that created something of a social infrastructure, if you will. In most cities, when you study the history of the AIDS crisis, many AIDS services grew out of community centers or vice versa. But we kind of had a head start here in New Orleans because of the Carnival infrastructure.

Perry: I found it very poignant...the Mardi Gras clubs and the way that guys just put their whole heart into it. I was an outsider and also a writer, so I can look at things somewhat differently. And I found it often heart wrenching. You know the thing that's so heartbreaking to me is that so many of the guys that I knew and loved back then are now dead. That's part of the wound that we all share.

Frank: You did some writing while you were here. Did you ever write for any of the gay publications?

Perry: Oh, yes.

Frank: There was *Impact*, as well as *Ambush*.

Perry: I wrote for both of them. I did a lot of freelancing. I was writing plays, wrote poetry, and I also started writing short stories that were published in gay magazines in New York. Short stories that are really more porn.

What have libraries meant to me as a gay person? When I was a young person, I went through hell in high school in Savannah. I graduated in 1964 and I realized that there was something about me that I could not let anybody know about. My high school happened to have a wonderful library run by these two older ladies who stocked it with real adult books—that they couldn't get away with now. When I was about fifteen, I found this book that had a profound influence on me: *The Holy Barbarians* by Lawrence Lipton, a snapshot of the culture of the beatniks. And there was one chapter in it called "Hoods, Junkies and the Illegal Sex," and it said that, among the beatniks, homosexuality was actually esteemed because you couldn't be any more hip and cool and rejected by society than if you were queer. I couldn't even use the word *homosexual*. I was too scared of the word queer because it'd been thrown at me. And here was this thing saying that among the beatniks, homosexuality was not only tolerated, it was actually esteemed.

Frank: I used to be an English teacher, so you triggered a lot of memories for me. In high school, I lived in Baton Rouge, which is like an hour north and much different than New Orleans. I remember we would come down to New Orleans quite often. Even in junior high, I remember seeing...what was it, the pink triangles at that point? Or had they started using the flags? I remember recognizing gay symbols on shop windows and thinking, "Okay, a place where it's safe to be gay." I always bookmarked that in the back of my mind...the need to come back down to New Orleans.

On New Orleans, and Its LGBTQ Community: A Microcosm

I'm currently writing a biography of a local activist named Stewart Butler. He was involved with LAGPAC which was the big gay political organization. I was wondering what memories you might have of political activism when you were in New Orleans, and if you remember Stewart Butler?

Perry: Yes. I did meet him. When we were there, a gay legalization bill was going before the...maybe the city council? I went to the hearing on it, and I wrote about it.

Frank: That's probably where you met Stewart, because I think you're referring to the city council ordinance for New Orleans. They tried in '84. The first time was unsuccessful. They tried again in '86. It finally passed in '91. But Stewart Butler was the only one on all three committees that was working on that.

Perry: While I was in New Orleans, I was writing for a very successful gay newspaper from Long Island called the *Long Island Connection*. So, I started writing pieces about New Orleans in the *Long Island Connection* and wrote a piece on working class gay men in New Orleans. It was fascinating to write at that time because the idea of working class and gay just didn't work...in New York. In New York, the idea is that, if you're gay, you've got to be a professional...an artsy type.

Frank: Or a theater queen or...

Perry: A theater queen, opera queen, Gucci queen...they still had those attitudes. In New Orleans, I met all these guys who worked offshore. I met this guy who was a butcher at Whole Foods...So I wrote this piece on working-class gay men in New Orleans, and I had this idea that I would get George Dureau to give one of his photographs to go with the piece...because I knew Dureau.

Frank: Yes. I knew George.

Perry: He was crazy as ever but very, very charming. I picked out several of his pictures that I thought would be beautiful to go with this piece. And then, after I got back home, he gave me a call. He said, "Perry, I hate to tell you this, but I can't let you use any of my photographs." And I said, "Why?" And he said, "Well, because this piece is going to be in a gay newspaper and most of the men I photograph do not want to be identified as gay...even if they are." So I said, "The fact that this is one of your pictures doesn't mean that they're necessarily gay, because it's just illustrating the story." And he said, "No. I would lose trust from them. And the most important thing in my career is that they trust me." And I said, "You're right."

Frank: Well, times have certainly changed. The city of New Orleans is very queer friendly, gay friendly. And I think part of that has to do with the success and the economic impact of Southern Decadence, which you may remember...

Perry: Oh yes, it was already there...so it's become a big holiday?

Frank: In recent years it's become this five-day extravaganza. My last book was a history of Southern Decadence. It attracts between 250 to 300,000 visitors every Labor Day weekend. Back when you were here in the early 80s, it was all locals and you had to be in the know; but now it's a big event. The economic impact is, like, 350 million dollars. I think we both realize that money doesn't necessarily buy acceptance, but it'll definitely buy a lot of tolerance; so, that's been a big factor in shaping attitudes here.

Perry: I was the co-founder of the Rainbow Book Fair. I think it's the largest LGBT book event in the country. We get as many as 1500 people to that.

Frank: I saw in your biography that you had done some AIDS work. I'm wondering, how has that informed your writing?

On New Orleans, and Its LGBTQ Community: A Microcosm

Perry: It has informed my writing in the fact that I've always believed that being gay was an act of heroism. That is something that a lot of people have a hard time getting their heads around. Although a lot of gay men that I'm close to believe there's a mystical bond among gay men—and I'm one of those people. I believe that too...very much. They believe that there is a heroism to us. And the AIDS crisis—and it was a crisis, it was a horror show—it's hard for people younger than we are to even understand the crisis and the heroism involved.

AIDS did not allow so many queers to hide behind their own self-loathing, their own cynicism, their own rejection of heroism. It did not allow this. They had to either drop the guises that had protected them for so long, including the money guise, the class guises, the racial superiority, ethnic superiority guise: the stuff that was regular currency when I first came out. They had to drop that and take on the mantle of being heroic; that we had to take care of each other, really take care of each other. So, in my work, I've dealt with this idea of the queer hero, the gay hero, and the gay man of action—and of a genuine, warm, rich masculinity. So, the AIDS crisis? It reinforced that with me.

Perry: When I lived in New Orleans, AIDS was really just starting to emerge and, to be honest, I was appalled at the feelings that so many of my friends had about men who had AIDS. Their feeling was, this is never going to happen to me. This is only happening to "them." I remember I was on the way to visit Bob at Charity Hospital, and I met this friend of mine, and I told him I was going to visit this guy who had AIDS. And he said, "Oh, Perry, how can you do that? If I was in a room with somebody who had AIDS, I would throw up." How can anyone feel this way? But, like you said, things changed...they progressed. I mean, this was very early on.

Frank: The challenge for historians is not to get these facts and stories down, but how to communicate them to younger generations who have no clue. A lot of my work with the LGBT+ Archives Project of Louisiana, which is a nonprofit that I lead that Stewart Butler and I co-founded along with a few other folks, is trying to recover all this history that remains in the closet. Fortunately, the AIDS crisis is not so far away or so long ago, that we're still able to get some of those materials.

Perry: One of the things I'm really proud of is a trilogy of plays I wrote called "Here, There and Yonder." Each one deals with a gay environment: the first in New York, the second in Provincetown, the third in New Orleans. Some friends of mine and I did a reading of the trilogy and also did it as a fundraiser for the Stop AIDS Task Force—one of the first fundraisers for the Task Force.

Frank: One thing I do a lot is talking to people who've been around, like yourself, and saying, "Hey, if you've got any material—anything; whether it's video footage, carnival costumes, minutes of board meetings from a political action group; whatever it may be—let's get that to a library, a museum, or an archive." Our organization doesn't operate a repository, but we're a sort of middle entity that reaches out to the community and says, "Get your stuff out of the closet and let's get it to work and be preserved." It's a great gig for me. It's not a paying gig, we're all volunteers, but it informs a lot of my writing, which is all history.

Perry: I think that's so important. I got involved with one of the first big LGBT archives, at Cornell. I was submitting stuff to them a long time ago. In New York, John Hammond decided to start the International Gay and Lesbian Archive; much of my stuff ended up in his archive. I gave him material from the Gay Liberation Front and about my life as an activist. His archive became the nexus for the archive at the New York City Public Library, one of the biggest LGBT archives in the country, except for One Incorporated archive at USC.

Frank: It's important work that a lot of people don't think about.

On New Orleans, and Its LGBTQ Community: A Microcosm

Perry: Now, I just did a piece for the Leslie Lohman magazine called The Archive. Do you know about the Leslie Lohman Museum of Gay and Lesbian Art?

Frank: Yeah, but I haven't visited.

Perry: I just did a piece on a New Orleans artist, J.B. Harter.
When I lived in New Orleans, I was one of the few people I knew—maybe my husband, also—who had never had an incident with the cops. I knew so many people who had an incident, especially around Mardi Gras. Have they gotten any better?

Frank: I'm going to answer that by saying yes and no. Their attitude towards the LGBT+ community has improved, although trans women of color might disagree. Up until the late 80s, maybe early 90s, the police were aggressive in trying to entrap gay men. They don't do that anymore…raids on gay bars are pretty a much thing of the past. But the state Alcohol Tobacco Commission is not so advanced. There was a big incident two years ago. Do you remember the Rawhide or the Phoenix bars, leather bars or backrooms?

Perry: Yes. But what I remember most was a place called Jewel's.

Frank: Jewel's was very notorious, but when Jewel's closed, some of those shenanigans shifted over to Rawhide. A lot of those hijinks came to an end during Southern Decadence two years ago. People got really upset; some of the women were complaining about not being admitted into Rawhide during Southern Decadence, which I can understand. One filed a complaint with the state Alcohol Tobacco Commission, which subsequently launched an investigation and went in with undercover officers and hidden cameras. They found it was like an amateur porn film. They shut down all those activities, so Jewel's and Rawhides are no more.

Perry: Any kind of sexual activity like that is almost banned in New York. If you are a young gay man in New York, this place is about as much fun as a morgue.

Frank: It's been like that for a while up there, right?

Perry: Yes, it has.

Frank: Two years ago, when this big controversy happened, I said, "Look, you weren't supposed to be doing this anyway. You've gotten away with it a lot longer than most people." But they felt like it was an encroachment on their safe spaces and culture; now what we have are a lot of private venues like sex clubs that can't serve alcohol. So, it's not the same.

Perry: New Orleans is the only place where a guy will walk up to the bar and say, "I'll have a triple dry Martini. Can you make that to go?"

Frank: It is a drinking city. People are pretty upset because the bars have been closed.

Perry: Because of COVID?

Frank: Yes. Do you ever get back to the city?

Perry: Not been in a long time. So many of the people I was close to have died. It hurts me to deal with that. Jeff Campbell, who was the ED of the New Orleans Stop AIDS Task Force, was one of my closest friends. I went down several times. I went through this period when, about every three months, I lost someone who was extremely close; it went on for about a year and a half. By the end, I was just absolutely grief stricken.

Frank: People I know had to throw away address books, phone books, but I've been fortunate. I lost one good friend, and I knew a lot of acquaintances.

Well, if you ever do decide to come down. I would love to get better acquainted with you.

Perry: Oh, thank you! I'll keep that in mind. And I will try to send you these things.

Frank: I may reach out to you about Jeff Campbell, because I think I talked about him in my book. I've got a section devoted to the AIDS crisis in those early years and Stewart (Butler)'s involvement. In addition to being a biography, it's really going to be a social history of the gay movement in New Orleans.

Perry: That's so great.

Frank: Been working on it for a while. Just waiting to get to the archives at Tulane.

Perry: That's marvelous. Well, I'd love to read it!

Frank: I'm sure we'll keep in touch. I would very much like to pick your brain more. I do a column every two weeks for Ambush Magazine on local queer history.

Perry: I'd love it!

Frank: Now, what are your thoughts on this *Grabbing Tea* anthology?

Perry: Librarians have made a big difference in my life, so that's why I want to get involved with it.

Frank: The archives project that I work with here, we're a statewide collective, so I have a pretty close relationship with librarians and curators all over the state. And I couldn't do what I do, I couldn't write my history without libraries and archives.

Reflection

Reflection from Perry Brass

This conversation between us, and editing it later, made me revisit how rich and interesting my time in New Orleans was. I was younger and more energetic, but the city was also extremely open to doing so much, as was New Orleans's amazing LGBTQ community. Frank called it a "microcosm" of the city, and I totally agree. New Orleans is a city of endless storytelling and genuinely "romantic" contradictions—at once decadent, restrictive, conservative, and radical. I think that these contradictions came out in our conversation; the problem was just distilling our piece so that the contradictions and their richness, although at times confounding, still remain.

What has always been evident about New Orleans, at least for this writer, is how ingrained and openly invested its queer community is in the city. I knew that when I lived there in the early 1980s as AIDS was emerging in the most predatory way, snapping at the lives of people around me—and, later, as Frank said, regarding Southern Decadence and its impact on the social and economic life of the city; it is even more so now. What I found so seductive about the city is the level of intimacy the community has within it. It's like being queer in New Orleans puts you in a place that is different from being straight, but that does not keep you from engaging with the full history and depth of the city. The Mardi Gras clubs, called "krewes," really bring this out; it's like they have within them a human potential, nurturance, and support missing in most cities until AIDS actually came along and necessitated, even demanded, all of that: in short, that we would take care of ourselves.

On New Orleans, and Its LGBTQ Community: A Microcosm

In many ways, New Orleans is a template for other cities and their queer communities...that is, the multitude of communities that make up the LGBTQ community of any city. Just as in New Orleans you have sub-communities of minority people and their intersectionalities, which we have in New York and other places; in New Orleans you also have another leavening factor: class and its own even more secretive workings within this larger queer community. I spoke about writing a piece on working-class gay men in New Orleans, something I was fairly unconscious of in New York, where class conversations are usually a strict no-no—while money and how it universally works is definitely a big yes-yes. In New Orleans, it became evident to me that class unites people: that there is a shared warmth felt by working-class people that comes from their emotional openness and decency, and I found this missing in other cities I have lived in, especially New York.

The other theme explored in this conversation is the importance of archives, archivists, and librarians as the keepers of truth in difficult times. Growing up in the segregated South, I spent hours in our local library, which was off limits to people of color, and it's hard even to imagine a "gay" book in it. But the rest of the books opened me up to a bigger world than the bigoted one I was in. Librarians were kind of magical people to me: they knew where the right books were and they understood the power of knowledge in a culture where knowledge was often denigrated in favor of the "popular wisdom," which said that people were to be judged by the color of their skin and whom they were attracted to. I can still close my eyes and go back to the library in Savannah, or my high school library: they become part of the secret library of my own life, one every writer has and guards, really, because it's so easy, finally, for these libraries to be locked and closed.

I wish we had been able to speak more about that in our conversation, but you can only talk so much and get so far in this short format.

TOWARDS A MANY GENDERED DAUGHTERS OF BILITIS

Megan Paslawski and Meg Metcalf

Keywords
Archives, cultural consciousness, lesbian, queer, literary reclamation

Megan Paslawski's (she/her) short stories have appeared in *Pembroke Magazine*, *The Texas Review*, *Blue Earth Review*, and elsewhere. Her editorial work with Lost & Found Press includes a collection of Michael Rumaker's letters; Rumaker's memoir *Robert Duncan in San Francisco* (a City Lights/Lost & Found Elsewhere publication co-edited with Ammiel Alcalay); and a forthcoming collection of Lucia Berlin's correspondence. She is an assistant professor of English at Queens College, CUNY.

Meg Metcalf (they/them) is a non-binary lesbian librarian living in Washington, D.C. They work as the Women's, Gender and LGBTQIA+ Studies Librarian at the Library of Congress in Washington, D.C. Meg holds a BA and MA in Women's and Gender Studies and a MLIS from the University of Wisconsin-Milwaukee.

Conversation

Megan Paslawski (She/Her): I have to ask, what's the publication I should be reading?

Meg Metcalf (They/Them): It's hard to say right now. I'm kind of obsessed with *Sisters*, which was the Daughters of Bilitis publication out of San Francisco and was the offshoot of *The Ladder* after *The Ladder* ended. It was really cool because the editor from 1971 to 1972 was Beth Elliot; she was the only trans president of the Daughters of Bilitis, and her artwork is in there. So, that's what I'm kind of obsessed with right now.

Megan: It's that sort of moment that interrupts this narrative we have about the Daughters of Bilitis just being professional-minded or more conservative. You realize that this organization was actually significantly more complex.

Meg: I am so upset, I have to say, about the way that the Daughters of Bilitis have been treated in history. I'm not a trained historian, I'm a librarian, but I feel an obligation to sort of reclaim this history because it's been so generalized. Something that I think is really amazing is that the Daughters of Bilitis were founded half working class and half middle class. I've been doing a ton of research on the working-class founders, because often, class analysis is something that's missing, and I was actually able to track down the Filipino woman whose idea it was to found DOB.

But it just goes to show that no one has gone looking for this before. Or has no one had the institutional access that I've had? Or do we just not care about telling lesbian history as equally as the other types of queer history?

Megan: Some of it just makes me feel really sad; like history has to be blanched out in order for us to feel as if we've created some kind of linear progress.

I was looking over *Robert Duncan in San Francisco*, which is the memoir of this writer named Michael Rumaker I worked with. He wrote it in the 70s about the 50s. The book was actually published for the first time in 2001 and then finally restored to the world around the time of Occupy Wall Street. The book is very explicit that San Francisco was a police state in the 50s, and it had these tremendous psychological effects on Michael Rumaker for his entire life. Only in the 70s did he have the language to describe that feeling of being hunted as a gay man, as someone who was arrested for street solicitation even though he was just having a conversation when he was arrested. The idea of his words being criminalized in that way, I think, profoundly affected him as a writer.

The reason I'm talking about this is because I was thinking about how the book has new context once again. When I was working on this book, it was with someone I was doing jail support with for protesters during Occupy. Then to be re-reading it now, at the tail-end of a Black Lives Matter summer, it feels heavy.

I've dwelled on the heavy part of it, but the fact that Rumaker was able to write this memoir in the 70s and do so in clear, unapologetic language was such a change from the way he was writing in the 50s about himself and his relationships and that felt really vital in some ways and hopeful. The fact that he was able to describe this police experience as traumatic was a big step forward for him because he'd been arrested, taken off the street and put in jail. It was too humiliating. It became this thing that festered because he didn't feel a sense of community that could sustain him through this, but he very clearly had that sense a few decades later.

I was actually wondering...I mean, I'm so fascinated. I want you to tell me everything about the web archive you're working on. What are the communal interactions people have with it?

Meg: It's great because it started out as a desperate need for me, feeling that in addition to starting a zine collection, this is where ephemera is being published online. I need to archive this kind of stuff. That was sort of how it started.

I worry though, too. We talked about this bibliographic encounter, being able to find community through these print resources, and so I've been thinking lately about how we're using social media or state-controlled mechanisms. What is the future going to be of the queer bibliographic experience? What is that queer encounter with community through the print form going to be when we're sort of using corporate, state-sponsored things like Instagram and Facebook? That can all disappear in a second. A lot of the queer history relies on the papers. It does so because these people were well off enough to leave papers. I feel privileged people are still going to be able to write their books, and their resources and their history are going to endure. But how do we ensure that that is happening equally for the community? Especially when there's not equal access to publishing.

Megan: I feel that about how many message boards of the 90s have vanished and have not been recorded, because they were somewhat private spaces.

Meg: I was really surprised by the response and by the way that web archiving can really be a form of outreach because then, not only am I able to save all of these resources that otherwise would never have made their way into my institution, but it becomes this conversation. I'm excited that these things that have been sort of sheltered in community archives are going to be more and more accessible to people. It's a really positive interaction with people who are super excited because it's validating for them to be included in an archive in this way. I think the most marginalized LGBTQ communities have never felt valued by archives, libraries, or institutions of knowledge. And why would they? I mean, they haven't been collected and when these materials have been collected, they haven't been described. It's a mess, and we've got to clean it up.

Megan: So exciting, though. I was thinking, too, that in some ways, the projects that I'm working on can be distilled into something quite small, like a chapbook that maybe offers a kind of connective tissue for thinking about queer history in a less reductive way, a less textbook kind of way. But you are someone who has access to all of it. How do you shape that narrative in a way that makes sense for people who want to start researching or who are interested in your library holdings?

Meg: When I first started, that whole thing totally overwhelmed me. How do you scale the world's largest library for researchers, while also increasingly finding that, surprise, we don't have a cultural consciousness about queer history. It isn't taught in schools, and people do not know who the Daughters of Bilitis are. They do not know what the Mattachine Society is. They may know about Stonewall. When they go to search for Rosalie Bamberger of the Daughters of Bilitis, one article comes up.

So, I started trying to figure out what I could do, how I could use my position to sort of tell a more equal story. Anytime I'm given a chance, I'm focusing on the lesser-known figures and, for me, that's generally the lesbian, trans, gender non-conforming aspects of history. There are historians working on gay male history. There are plenty of books on gay male history. My strategy is to help people find the things that have been obscured or lost. To that end, I built this huge research guide. It's ginormous. What I'm trying to do is compile information and provide a narrative to it, because this information doesn't really exist online; but now I've written a full description of the Daughters of Bilitis on my research guide (guides.loc.gov/lgbtq-studies).

I just think about how a patron came up to me and said something about how they read *Trans Bodies Trans Selves*, which is a book I put on reference, and said "Reading that, I realized I was non-binary," which just rocked my world.

I want every queer kid to be able to access that if they want to. I know how much it meant to me when I discovered that. So there's something to be said for reclaiming these things and making sure they're accessible because it's a way for queer people to resist, not just a depression, but the normalizing effects of these institutions that we find ourselves in.

Megan: That makes intuitive sense to me. I think that, weirdly enough, the archive might do something to intervene against the reductive ways we talk about sexuality online where, if you only have 244 characters, you're going to condense your long and complex statement about the history of police brutality in queer communities, for example, to just #nomore.

I am absolutely fascinated with the way we recognize our queerness and our gender nonconformity in reading. I think that is at the heart of everything I'm interested in and drives a lot of my interest in queer and trans life narrative. I think about someone like Janet Mock, whose book is deeply inflected by the pedagogical autobiography of Audre Lorde, and the way that Lorde becomes this kind of flashpoint in many ways for so many offshoots of self-understanding. We have to make these things available so that people have reference points to understand the complexities of queerness, too. You see it in action with your patrons at the library. Or we see it in the writings of people who have these transformative experiences just through access.

That was my real interest in getting involved with Lost & Found Press because it's doing this kind of literary recovery that means you're focusing on the work of working-class people, women, queer people, and people of color. Or someone like Michael Rumaker, a white gay man whose books never achieved canon status. You start thinking about why that is, and it's almost certainly class-based. He was someone whose working-class background was not particularly mitigated by going to Black Mountain College.

I think that this kind of salvage work that Lost & Found does, like you're doing, gives us a significantly more complex narrative about queerness, and it's just so important. It becomes something that I think becomes difficult institutionally because you have to push back at what are easy ways of classifying things. This is why I was so excited to hear that we were talking together, because I felt a librarian would know how to push back and it seems a lot of your work has been about redressing that.

Meg: I assumed I would be an academic librarian and doing women's studies because I got my master's in library science and women studies at the same time. So, something that struck me as a difference working at the Library of Congress, versus an academic library, is that I started to notice that all of these print resources were not ingested. These are the types of sources that we got sort of by accident or by exchange, but that were not traditionally collected by archives. That's a huge issue because if it's not in the Library of Congress catalog, it's not going to be mimicked around the world, because our catalog records are duplicated. So, a lot of those earlier materials aren't necessarily going to be catalogued in a way that's findable, because nobody knows what they are.

That's also my worry with the transition from print to digital. There's so much focus on the digital right now, and while I would love to digitize all queer history resources, copyright exists. I worry that other people are not going to be finding these resources that we found. They're not going to find their way to the queer community through these print resources if these sources aren't available online, and they're not likely to be digitized. So, if they haven't been ingested into our information ecosystem and they're not going to be digitized, and if they haven't been collected and if nobody does the reclamation work, they're just sort of lost forever. And then I think that's why you see, generation after generation, it's almost like we have to start again.

Megan: I was thinking while you were talking about library access about how old-fashioned much of the work I was doing to produce this chapbook was. I had to travel to the archive. I had to take photos of each page in the archive with my phone. Then, I had to go home. You almost have to have an academic affiliation of some kind to want to do these tedious things.

Meg: What I see, because I work at a library that's kind of an elite institution, is who gets the privilege. If you're not someone who has an institutional affiliation, the ability to go to school, then the chances are that you're not able to travel to an archive. I mean, who can afford to do that? I certainly couldn't afford to do that when I was in school. When I think about the books that we have kids read in schools, those are all government-vetted things, and not just by the State Board of

Education. For example, the CIA and different groups push certain books because of their anti-communist narrative. So, again, queer people aren't encountering themselves. That's not just by accident; that's happening. I think that's very much a result of the way that our institutions of knowledge are controlled by state institutions and state interests. That is why I think it makes sense that these queer history books we're getting are from white gays, because they have a lot easier access to all sorts of resources.

I'm sounding very sexist against men in this interview, so we need to turn that down.

Megan: I don't think so. If you're concerned about the ways in which the canon is received, and you're concerned about access, and you know perfectly well that documents exist out there that disprove or make more complex the contemporary narratives of queer history…. then, how do you do that intervention? Especially now, when the ways that you might do that are shut down? The talks aren't happening.

Meg: The death rattles of capitalism.

Megan: One of the really fascinating things for me to think about is looking at writing from people who hadn't been getting out very much. I was very deeply touched by the way that queer periodicals being mailed back and forth, or poetry being mailed back and forth, was something that managed to nurture this sustaining sense of community when someone was not talking to other queer people in their day-to-day life. I think your queeriodical article index is a profound record of…

Meg: …people subscribing…

Megan: …to each other. Right! I was so excited to see it and I'm so glad that record exists. I was thinking it probably ties into some of the work you're doing on zines, too.

Meg: I feel these types of publications like memoir and bibliography are things that most people are not, like, "Oh yeah, I totally get how that's relevant." There's a lot of talk specifically in the library world about how reference is changing and we don't need a reference desk and all these traditional sources, and bibliography, so who needs them? But I think about my experience of getting to the library and opening up checklist 1960-Barbara-Greer, the self-published bibliography. It's mimeographed. It's aged. And once I'm looking through this list. I'm noticing, "Okay, I've never heard of any of these books before" because, again, these are not the books that are getting ingested into the information ecosystem. So, not only do we need access to the sources, but all that opens it up to a whole other historical realm of sources as well. How do we communicate the value of these tools and these resources? Because not everyone is as excited to talk about bibliography as you are. The eyes glaze over.

Megan: Everyone cares about life, though, right? That sense of community making its way onto the page, the sense that it's just one star in a constellation. This is one life, but this life was part of a movement; was part of a community; had weird affiliations that you probably wouldn't have guessed.

Maybe, in my heart, I'm just really historically gossipy and a bibliography is like a historical or literary scandal sheet. Look at these people who were *publishing* together.

Meg: Yeah, and I feel like it's a type of genealogy that you end up doing or it requires a lot of genealogical kind of digging, and I think about that and the types of resources that that type of research requires and who has those documents that I can find.

Megan: I see students come in who identify as queer in some way, who have very little contact with queer community and also have never really thought about reading to expand their connection to that world. Part of me thinks, why should they have to? But then the vocabulary that they end up with to describe their own experience feels really shallow to me. The terms feel shallow, I think, because they come in a very state-sanctioned way. It's the language of tolerance, and they have sort of built an identity around the hour-long seminar that you get in your eighth-grade wellness class about how it's okay to be gay, but most people aren't.

Meg: Well, what it does is it ends up depoliticizing and decontextualizing what queer identity is. What does it mean to identify as queer and not have a sense of how we came to reclaim that word? Are we understanding it the same way if we don't have the historical context? And then there are all the conversations about butch-femme. I get in trouble all the time for being a non-binary femme. Obviously, these are terms, identity categories in the community that have a history, and I'm very aware of it, but they have certainly evolved and there's also been gender fluidity in the lesbian community forever. But there are some people who are, like, "Well, butch-femme at one point in time meant this," and they're totally erasing everything that happened. Those terms actually evolved. I think that's interesting: *labeling* not just our sexual identities, but our books. You know, all sorts of problems.

Megan: It's interesting you say this about gender fluidity among historical lesbian communities because this has always been a source of sorrow to me: there's something so joyless about the way lesbian history is understood. It's often talked about in the context of a "and now we are more enlightened" sort of standpoint that gay male history doesn't always deal with. But, as you said, gender nonconformity has always been a part of lesbianism. This sense that the community was a fun and nurturing place was also deeply present in some of the accounts that these women write.

Meg: I want to share with people the fact that there is so much fun lesbian history! The Daughter of Bilitis had Halloween parties, chili feeds, and Gab and Java sessions. Something I will say is that the gay historical mainstream narrative has really sort of asserted that white gay men invented gay pride when, in fact, a difference between lesbian organizing and mainstream homophile organizing is that lesbian organizing always worked on this sense of the individual and self-esteem and helping the individual, giving mutual aid, whereas the male-focused Homophile movement was more, "How do we adopt legislative change and, by the way, we're going to push off anyone who messes with our political advocacy." I do think there were more modern forms of activism that were actually happening in the Daughters of Bilitis, and nobody knows about that and I think it's time.

Megan: It is funny that when we're at this moment of crisis during COVID, which has been an ongoing crisis for some people, but suddenly I'm like, yes, the Daughters of Bilitis seem very relevant.

Meg: Yeah, I would love to restart it. I want a lesbian publishing collective. I want to start it. I want to do it.

Megan: Let's do it. Let's just start a collective right here, right now.

Meg: Okay, are we calling it Daughters of Bilitis?

Megan: I'm fine with Daughters of Bilitis 'cause anyone can be a daughter.

Meg: You're right about that. All right, we're starting it now.

Megan: That's a little something that's come out of this, the Tea being grabbed.

Reflection

Meg:

After this conversation I couldn't stop thinking about how loud silences can feel. How do we reclaim our LGBTQIA+ literary and cultural heritage and history when so many resources of our history and culture do not resemble, in form or function, materials that institutional powers have decided and taught others to value? As Audre Lorde asks of us, "What does it mean when the tools of a racist patriarchy are used to examine the fruits of that same patriarchy?"

There is clearly a tension when you realize that these acts of literary and historical recovery and reclamation can and do exist inside of the institutions which would seek to normalize queer lives and bodies. But the assumption that we can't use libraries, universities, or mainstream publishing because of how they've failed in the past is wrong (I think) because it reinforces this idea that they decide what knowledges, what cultures, what identities are deserving of celebration, remembrance and preservation. But our histories don't belong to these institutions and they never did. They belong to us. We must save and tell our stories, but we must also correct the ways in which our stories have been used and told by institutions which seek to normalize or profit off us. The only way to change how this knowledge is collected and contextualized is to push back, from outside and from within. The question that looms largest is, perhaps, how?

In addition to being very serious about fomenting a radical queer publishing revolution, I have some thoughts about how we might interact with the generalized monolith that is queer history commodified by capitalism. You can now buy a beer with Marsha P. Johnson on it, but does that tell you anything about her life and activism? Take that money and give it directly to a BIPOC trans sex worker if you really want to honor Marsha. Let's not pretend capitalism doesn't rely on the suffering and death of the most vulnerable to persist. Let's push back against virtue signaling and remember that revolution is driven by direct action, not by the ability to buy more products.

There is hope and memory in our print cultures. Collective memory can be accessed through these texts and print culture is a portal to history, to remembering. The materials of LGBTQIA+ print culture, like bibliography and memoir, can become tools of good praxis, existing as a sort of queer genealogy when and where no other sources existed. In the end, I think what's most important here is that our existences as LGBTQIA+ folks cannot be denied—now, or in history. We feel the urgency to protect our histories and our futures, and have started to dream of ways that might be possible. Join us!

Megan:
Visiting this conversation again, I'm brought back to the quiet loneliness of a fall spent working from home and waiting for vaccines. Perhaps in response, Meg and I put our faith in queer community—past, existing, and yet-to-be built—as we talked about our motivations for doing our different kinds of archival work. I see how we share a longing for more robust LGBTQ historical narratives based on archival documentation that is accessible, reflective of human complexity and a richly-realized diversity, and resistant to flattening into a linear story of progress at the expense of earlier activists' accomplishments. I also see how, in the true queer spirit, we've tried to answer our own sense of absence by creating resources for the next generation. As a librarian and an editor, we're both immersed in projects of literary recovery that seek to fill the empty places in archives and on bookshelves, and we feel a particular sense of urgency around the documents of people who are lesbians, working class, trans and gender-nonconforming, BIPOC, or otherwise marginalized by the institutions that create our understanding of the historical and literary record. As we see it, this kind of salvage work has multigenerational responsibilities. It respects the lives that history tried to forget by offering a more complete understanding of their existence, and it ensures that new generations are not limited in imagining the future by losing the inspirations of the past. Even as we recognize the cruel and shameful failures that created these absences in the record, an optimism about the transformative power of the literary—or library—encounter with the

queer past bubbles beneath the surface of our conversation. The idea of "people subscribing to each other" describes the zines Meg documents in her library guide, but it also shows us how queer communities were built and can be built better. Every chapbook and every reference guide we compile is an invitation to subscribe more expansively and more communally to people you otherwise may not have known. Think of these people as co-conspirators; they're Daughters of Bilitis with some tips on practicing mutual aid and gay liberationists sharing the language they've found for the psychological torment of living in a police state. There's probably no better advertisement for the importance of making queer historical texts widely—and wildly—available than how quickly Meg and I moved from discussing these figures to plotting our own lesbian publishing collective. If you're reading this and want to start a many-gendered revival of the Daughters of Bilitis, please let us know.

Ephemeral: Queer Felt Experiences in Archives

Xena Becker and Donna Langille

Keywords
Identity in archives, queer representation, institutional vs community archives, affect

Xena Becker (she/her) is a special collections librarian and educator. Her professional interests include accessible engagement with special collections, environmental sustainability in libraries, queer history, and abolition in libraries and archives. She hopes to have a good career of touching old books and talking to people about them. Outside of work, she is passionate about hiking, theater, food systems, and local organizing.

Donna Langille (she/her/they/them) lives and works as an uninvited settler on the unceded, traditional, and ancestral territory of the Syilx Okanagan peoples. She is the Community Engagement and Open Education Librarian, as well as the subject liaison librarian for film studies, theatre, media studies, and the digital humanities at the University of British Columbia Okanagan. Her professional interests include queer history, digital humanities, and open, digital, and public scholarship.

Conversation

Donna Langille (she/her/they/them): What is the unique relationship between queer identities and archives?

Xena Becker (she/her): I think that there are a lot of different answers for that. And I think that's something that I've always thought about as a person who is queer and a person who works in Archives and Special Collections. I remember in another queer conversation, the "Theorizing Queer Temporalities: A Roundtable Discussion," coming across the concept of "historical emotion" put forth by Christopher Nealon, where he describes the way that queer archives create communities across space and time.[1] Nealon would see material from people who were queer in the past that he was researching in the present. They would be writing from all these different places about their own feelings and their own life and wishing for this queer community that could bring them together. But then Nealon was seeing that queer community could be brought together in an archival context that he described as historical emotion, which is seeing the history and desire for queer community laid out in front of you. And then also becoming a part of that queer community as the queer researcher looking at that material. So, I think that's one unique connection between queer people and archives, the way that it builds a community across time, which a lot of queer people seek.

Donna: Nguyen Tan Hoang, another writer from the "Theorizing Queer Temporalities: A Roundtable Discussion," talks about queer experience being transmitted from one generation to another through the past, which I found really interesting.[2] You're looking to these people from the past, not just for representation or to see yourself reflected in them, but also to learn from them. I've always had an interest in preserving

---

1. Dinshaw, Carolyn, et al., "Theorizing Queer Temporalities: A Roundtable Discussion," *GLQ: A Journal of Lesbian and Gay Studies* 13, no. 2 (2007): 179.

2. Dinshaw, "Theorizing Queer Temporalities," 183.

queer history. What makes the relationship between queer identities and archives unique is that, for so long, these identities were contested, ignored, silenced, or oppressed, and there's not a lot of representation in our current cultural heritage institutions of these identities. There is a queer desire for belonging within history because where we tend to go for history—galleries, libraries, museums, archives—our stories are often missing from them.

Xena: That's another reason that relates back to why we use archives to pass on queer history. They are insights to understanding our history. It goes back to not necessarily having a familial connection that exists, because usually the way you learn a history would be because it's passed down through a family, but there isn't always a way to connect with somebody who's able to tell you a story. And so, you go looking for that, and you go to the places where there are paper stories and where there are physical representations of that because you haven't been able to find a person to make that connection with. Because a lot of queer people have trouble, especially when they're younger, finding other queer people or being able to recognize other people who are growing up around them, they then use archives as a way of finding that connection to a past and to a history which they can't necessarily find from a community directly in person around them.

How can we think about queer identities and archives, and what theories or frameworks can we use?

Donna: A book that really resonated with me is Ann Cvekovitch's, *An Archive of Feelings*. Cvetkovitch argues that LGBTQ archives are important because they preserve and produce not only memory, history, and knowledge, but also affect. The queer archive is affective due in part to the traumatic loss of history that we were just describing.[3]

---

3. Ann Cvetkovich, *An Archive of Feelings: Trauma, Sexuality, and Lesbian Public Cultures* (Durham & London: Duke University Press, 2003), 7.

Xena: That's another really good and important one, and they both kind of come at this connection that we see for queer people between this emotional felt sense and then this historical knowledge-based thing. There's definitely this sense of the connection between the known and the felt that exists for how queer people want to experience their history.

Donna: I love that connection you made between the known and the felt. What do you think a queer archive is then?

Xena: A queer archive has queer materials. And then that gets into the question, "What does it mean for an item to be queer?" That goes to the creator of the item, because there are a lot of things that were made by queer people, but that doesn't necessarily mean that that item shows up in an archive and is automatically queer. What is expected to be in an archive? I don't think that anything is expected to be or not be there. It's based a lot on the person—on the creator and their identification.

Donna: What you were saying earlier about the known and the felt—to know that the creator of the item was queer allows for that emotion to happen. I think that's one of the reasons why queer archives are composed of a lot of ephemera because these items are coming from the creators' experiences of being queer. And those queer affective experiences aren't always found in newspapers, books, or official documents—they're found in the more personal, intimate objects.

Xena: I did research on the connection between the word ephemera as a general type of item in archives and the word "ephemeral" relating to queer people. Jose Estéban Muñoz describes queer experience as being very ephemeral because it is this thing that isn't necessarily nameable and capturable.[4] It is something that you can see, but then you can also

---

4. José Esteban Muñoz, "Ephemera as Evidence: Introductory Notes to Queer Acts," *Women & Performance: a journal of feminist theory* 8:2 (1996): 5-16, https://doi.org/10.1080/07407709608571228.

question or deny whether that really happened... Did I know that person was queer or was it just a feeling that I got?

Even the word ephemera has this double meaning that relates to the literal, physical materials and their classification, and also, queer felt experience of interacting with a piece or with each other and asking, what does this tell me? And, what is this about this person and this feeling?

Donna: Yeah, what does this object tell me about this person? In Vancouver, British Columbia, there used to be a gay and lesbian community archive that was located in someone's home, and some of the collections from that archive have recently been digitized.[5] So now, people have the opportunity to look at these records online. What really stood out to me in the items was that they were, for the most part, ephemeral: posters for events, drawings, or zines. What really jumped out to me was seeing the names of places where I had lived: streets, coffeeshops, things like that. And wanting to know more about the people from my community that spent time there.

Xena: Tell me some things you are remembering.

Donna: Well, one thing that really sparked my interest was a poster for a bookmobile called Women on Wheels: Rolling Feminist Library.[6] Three lesbians, I think, who were going to be joining the National Women's March Against Poverty in Canada back in the 90s. But along the way, they were going to drive this van full of queer and feminist books, go to different rural communities within Canada, and allow people to come and take these books. And I remember thinking, like, why have I not

---

5. "BC Gay and Lesbian Archives," City of Vancouver Archives, accessed August 26, 2021, https://searcharchives.vancouver.ca/bc-gay-and-lesbian-archives.

6. "Poster for Watch My Indicator," 1996, Item: 2018-020.0844, Series 3, BC Gay and Lesbian fonds, City of Vancouver Archives, Vancouver, British Columbia, Canada, accessed August 30, 2021; https://searcharchives.vancouver.ca/watch-my-indicator-benefit-reading-for-women-on-wheels-rolling-feminist-library-may-6-96-at-harrys-off-commercial.

heard of this before? It just seems like such a significant moment in the queer history of Vancouver and something I never would have known if I hadn't gone into that archive.

I still have very fond memories of visiting the physical space. The archive used to be cared for by Ron Dutton, an archivist in Vancouver.[7] He took it upon himself and started collecting queer materials and storing them in his house; he had everything in boxes in his bedroom. I was very lucky to be able to go and visit the archive. I walked in and it was his home. He had souvenirs from places that he had traveled and pictures of his partner on the bedside table; and then, you're pulling things out of boxes and laying them on his bed. It was just a very intimate experience but also made me feel incredibly humbled to be able to look through those items in that space.

Xena: That's another aspect that kind of makes a queer archive is really that kind of very personal collecting approach to it. The Lesbian Herstory Archives is known for having also started in somebody's bedroom and having that really personal and homey approach to it.[8]

I'm also wondering whether a queer archive has to be one that's community-run, like the one in British Columbia, or if there's the ability to create a queer archive in an institution that doesn't necessarily have a queer mission. I will say that every archive with queer material that I've encountered has been in college institutional archives and not community-run archives. I am not often a researcher in archival spaces. I pretty much exclusively have been part of them as a worker, either as a page while a student or a graduate assistant, and now as a full-time librarian. Nevertheless, I've often found that I'd either be having these very intimate one-on-one interactions with queer materials in kind of

---

7. "Gay and lesbian archives collection donated to City of Vancouver Archives," Vancouver Is Awesome, accessed August 27, 2021, https://www.vancouverisawesome.com/courier-archive/news/gay-and-lesbian-archives-collection-donated-to-city-of-vancouver-archives-3076316.

8. "Our Herstory," Lesbian Herstory Archives, accessed August 26, 2021, https://lesbianherstoryarchives.org/about/a-brief-history/.

a back-room space, not necessarily in the reading room, or the times when that has happened in the reading room, there was always another person. So, it's been this more communal connected moment where somebody brought out a box for both of us to look at. You could bounce off of another person and have a queer experience in that way. We were both excited about the queer past that we were seeing.

I was doing a research project at the University of North Carolina, Charlotte, and I had this little back corner in the stacks of archival materials. There was one collection from a woman named Sue Henry, who ran a women's bookstore in the 90s in Charlotte that was called Rising Moon Books & Beyond.[9] She had a bulletin board in the bookstore, and she saved things from 1992 to 1995. Because she was a librarian, she saved a lot. When I looked at her collection, I took out those eleven folders from the Hollinger box, and when I opened them, they smelled like incense—it was beautiful. I was able to fully picture the spread tablecloth with the business cards with little incense sticks sitting on it with the bulletin board above it. Even if you have no idea what the bookstore actually looked like (there were no pictures), you could still see and experience it. That was another very felt queer experience that I had in a private space, looking at archival objects; that experience felt very queer to me, even though it happened in an institutional setting.

Donna: So, we've talked a little bit about what queer archives contain, and what makes a queer archive; I'm wondering if maybe we should talk a little bit about the caretakers, the people responsible for a queer archive.

Xena: One aspect of being a caretaker includes factoring in the different ethical considerations that come in, especially about consent. A person who works with queer archives is thinking a little bit more about what the specific ethical and consensual accountings are for queer people

---

9. "Sue Henry Papers," UNC Charlotte Finding Aids, University of North Carolina at Charlotte, accessed August 26, 2021, https://findingaids.uncc.edu/repositories/4/resources/535.

that are different from other communities. It's not necessary to have a knowledge of queer life and experience, but it's definitely really helpful. I can imagine that a queer curator, or somebody who's knowledgeable in the queer community, is going to have a different perspective of a specific item than somebody who doesn't have that awareness.

Donna: I've spoken with some people who feel hesitant to give up a queer collection to an institutional body because there's a lack of trust. With a community archive, there is a stronger chance of the archivists identifying with the material in some way. I'm not saying that they have to, but I think it's much more likely. I'm not sure if that's always the case once it gets put into the hands of an institution. If someone creates a queer project, such as a podcast, film, or exhibit, for me, knowing that that person or archive is queer is much more comforting to me as another queer person; there's a bigger sense of trust there. I think one of the challenges is that a lot of these community archives are not super sustaining and budgets are getting cut, and there's less government support. How can you sustain an archive that's in your bedroom?

Xena: At a certain point, it's not going to be accessible for people to come there and it's not going to necessarily feel welcoming to everybody who does. So, it is also a question of access to make sure that one person doesn't gain too much control over the caretaking of queer materials and queer archives, because that begs the question of whether people are starting to be shut out from that stewardship in any way.

Donna: The material itself of queer archives can also be traumatic. It can be sentimental. There's a lot of emotion in the queer archive. To be someone that's constantly handling that material…

Xena: Ann Cvetkovitch has a quote about security when she's talking about the Lesbian Herstory Archives, which is that they don't have that traditional security setup, but they have twenty-five lesbians who are willing to put their lives on the line for the materials.[10] They have this really strong emotional connection to it, and they really feel for and care for the materials there. But then that also begs the question: should you expect your volunteers at your archive to run into a burning building to save your materials? Or should there be a different kind of stewardship for it that doesn't require people to put so much of themselves into the caretaking for a specific thing?

Donna: Yeah, your point is making me think of Fobazi Ettarh's concept of vocational awe, which can be applied to archive workers, but then also community workers who maybe don't have an MLS or archive training, but are doing it because they believe in the value and importance of the archive.[11] But that's not okay, and it's not sustainable. We need to be putting more pressure on those institutions that do have the funding and the capacity to step up and think of queer materials and queer experiences as worthy of collecting because it makes sense that there's potential distrust. Nobody should have to guard the archives with their lives.

Xena: Yeah, I think that's still a problem, even in institutional archives. But for community archives, because it's so hard won, that's especially something that people think about and worry about and fear.

Donna: Right. Also, that was really a motivation for Ron Dutton; that if he didn't do this, it just wouldn't be recorded, and that's a huge loss.

Xena: We've got to make sure that we do it. Yeah. It's a very emotionally charged thing to think about; it's your family history.

That leads us into this question: What identities do queer archives privilege? We are thinking about that question through the lens of our

---

10. Cvetkovich, *An Archive of Feelings*, 248.

11. Fobazi Ettarh, "Vocational Awe and Librarianship: The Lies We Tell Ourselves," *In the Library with the Lead Pipe* (10 January 2018), https://www.inthelibrarywiththeleadpipe.org/2018/vocational-awe/.

own identities and how we feel connected to queer archival material because of our own queerness.

Donna: It's worth acknowledging that for myself, as a white, queer person, I can talk about the general absence of queer representation in the archives but also recognize that I have privilege and that my identity is reflected in the queer archive; and that is not necessarily the case for people of color, or other queer people with intersecting marginalized or oppressed identities.

Xena: I have a very complicated relationship to many of my words that describe my identity but queerness as a sexuality is the one that I always feel really, really confident in. I'm a queer person. I've had my questions and considerations about gender. I am a white passing person. I'm getting back into my connection to my Jewish heritage. I feel very tangential and at the edge of a lot of my identities—my gender identity, my religious identity, my racial identity. But in my queerness, I feel very centered and I feel very sure. This is my sexuality and I'm very confident and settled in it and it's something that I feel really connected to because of that. I do see myself represented in a lot of ways, because I relate to the things that queer women write about their histories and I see myself reflected in the various parts of my white identity that exists there.

I'm sure that I'm never going to find anybody who's exactly like me, or if there's somebody who does have another identity that I feel a little more tangential to, I really want to feel connected to that person. I get really excited when I see a person who was openly Jewish and queer. That's really exciting. But then I don't always feel the same kind of connection that I do just from somebody who the most important thing to them is just being able to talk about being queer. So I think I do also see myself represented a lot in the way that queer archives are collected and maintained.

My friend Lara talks about being at the center of an identity versus at the edges of it. That is something that I think about now, the ways that

I exist at the center of identities and the ways that I exist at the edge of them, as well as how I can move the center when I do exist there and pull from the edges to make the center a little bit more malleable, too. That's the one thing that I would want to ask queer caretakers and caretakers of queer materials to think about: how close are they to the center and how much can they move the center from where it is right now?

I think that the ability to form communities across time through that historical emotion in the archives—that archive of feelings—is built into that ability to see yourself. A lot of the time, I think: when you can see yourself, you can imagine yourself in those spaces. Or—I'll change that—we can imagine ourselves in those spaces. But there are plenty of people who aren't able to imagine themselves in those spaces and need to seek out other spaces that feel more welcoming.

Donna: Do you ever think of yourself and your own experiences and what you could possibly contribute to a queer archive? Is that a very personal and intimate question?

Xena: It is a little! It reminds me of consented collecting. It feels a little weird to me when people are possessive of paper objects as stand-ins for people, especially if they aren't always getting their consent to collect objects.

I think about it sometimes. I have a lot of personal letters and journals and notebooks, and I want these things to be preserved. If I had enough of a life to be deserving of having personal papers donated to an archive, what things would I want to be publicly shared? I don't think I know what I would donate. I think I haven't made it yet. What about you? That's such a good question. Oh, my gosh.

Donna: I feel very similar in that I have a fear of permanence, so I don't see myself having anything that I would want to contribute to an archive, or that I would want to have preserved or touched or held or felt by anyone else. But I do want to leave something and perhaps it will be my writing and my work. I've included queer studies into everything that I've done up until this point. I will continue to include it in my research. Maybe that's what I'll contribute as a queer person to the archive.

Reflection

In reviewing our conversation, we noticed that our stories of interacting with queer archives emphasize our physical sensations of being in the archive: our felt experiences. For example, Xena recalls the smell of incense while looking at the Sue Henry collection, and Donna remarks on the decor of the Vancouver Gay and Lesbian Archive. Our focus on physically being in and interacting with the archives was particularly interesting to us because the process of conducting and writing this conversation took place during the height of COVID-19 restrictions, when there was minimal possibility of visiting an archive in person. Our anecdotes and analysis focused very little on the queer digital/online experience even though the pandemic highlighted the importance of digitized collections.

We didn't intend to discount digital archives. Access to digital collections has been a huge relief to community members and researchers during the height of COVID-19, thanks to the labour of library and archives workers. Even though we've both had positive experiences and have enjoyed interacting with queer digital archives (e.g., QZAP, events hosted by the Gerber/Hart Library), our interactions with physical archives have, undoubtedly, shaped our memories and had a strong impact on the way that we think about queer history and ourselves as queer people. We obviously feel a visceral connection to our queerness when we visit the archive, but why? And how?

As we reflect on our conversation, we want to move beyond our initial questions around identities and archives and now ask ourselves, how is queer memory and history stored in our bodies? What is the relationship between the (queer) body and the archive? How are specific bodies prioritized and understood as archival objects? These are the questions we intend to explore further in our future work together.

We grounded our conversation using Ann Cvetkovich's theory that queer archives are archives of feeling. Cvetkovich writes, "lesbian and gay history demands a radical archive of emotion in order to document intimacy, sexuality, love, and activism—all areas of experience that are difficult to chronicle through the materials of a traditional archive."[12] Upon further research, we have found other theorists who have raised questions—and offered theories, perspectives, and frameworks—for thinking about the body and queer archives, including Jack Halberstam, James A. Lee, and Marika Cifor.

Realizing the significance of our bodies, we can't help but think back to our last question of what we intend to leave to the archive. If our queerness is felt, experienced, and expressed through and in our bodies, how can we leave that to the archive? For example, will our queer tattoos have a place in the archive? What would that look like? How does an archive of the body differ from Cvetkovich's archive of emotion? With so many available and emerging methods and technologies, the ability to preserve the actual physical parts of us that we could leave to the archive are more possible than ever, but there remains the question of consent and access to our queer stories in whatever form we leave them behind.

Thank you for reading the first item in the Donna Langille and Xena Becker Collection on Queer Scholarship. We hope that one day this essay and all the supporting materials may be found in an archive near you.

Bibliography

City of Vancouver Archives. "BC Gay and Lesbian Archives." Accessed August 26, 2021. https://searcharchives.vancouver.ca/bc-gay-and-lesbian-archives.

Cvetkovich, Ann. *An Archive of Feelings: Trauma, Sexuality, and Lesbian Public Cultures*. Durham & London: Duke University Press, 2003.

---

12. Cvetkovich.

Dinshaw, Carolyn, Lee Edelman, Roderick A. Ferguson, Carla Freccero, Elizabeth Freeman, Judith Halberstam, Annamarie Jagose, Christopher Nealon, and Tan Hoang Nguyen. "Theorizing Queer Temporalities: A Roundtable Discussion." *GLQ: A Journal of Lesbian and Gay Studies* 13, no. 2 (2007): 177-195. muse.jhu.edu/article/215002.

Ettarh, Fobazi. "Vocational Awe and Librarianship: The Lies We Tell Ourselves." *In the Library with the Lead Pipe* (10 January 2018). https://www.inthelibrarywiththeleadpipe.org/2018/vocational-awe/.

Lesbian Herstory Archives. "Our Herstory." Accessed August 26, 2021. https://lesbianherstoryarchives.org/about/a-brief-history/.

Muñoz, José Esteban. "Ephemera as Evidence: Introductory Notes to Queer Acts." *Women & Performance: a journal of feminist theory* 8:2 (1996): 5-16. https://doi.org/10.1080/07407709608571228.

University of North Carolina at Charlotte. "Sue Henry Papers." UNC Charlotte Finding Aids. Accessed August 26, 2021. https://findingaids.uncc.edu/repositories/4/resources/535.

PAINT ME A DANGEROUS WOMAN: A CONVERSATION ABOUT TATIANA DE LA TIERRA'S LESBIAN POETICS AND LIBRARIANSHIP

Lizeth Zepeda and Liliana C. González

Keywords
Lesbian, libraries, naming, poetics, sexuality

Lizeth Zepeda is currently the University Archivist at Loyola Marymount University in Los Angeles, CA. Lizeth holds a Master's of Library and Information Science from the University of Arizona's School of Information and is a Knowledge River Scholar. Her interests include working with traditionally under-documented communities, campus and community outreach, Spanish-language materials, born-digital materials, and Latinx, queer, and LGBT archives.

Liliana C. González is an assistant professor of Gender and Women's Studies at California State University, Northridge. She earned her Ph.D. from the University of Arizona in Latin American literature and culture. Her work is at the intersections of Chicanx, Latinx, and Latin American cultural studies, gender studies, narco studies, and queer theory. .

Conversation

Lizeth Zepeda: This conversation is coming from years of thinking through the impact of tatiana de la tierra[1] and her contribution to librarianship. De la tierra was born in 1961 in Colombia and in 1969 moved to Florida. She received a bilingual MFA in creative writing from the University of Texas, El Paso and an MLIS from SUNY, Buffalo. She moved to California when she became the director of the Inglewood Public library in a working-class Latino and Black neighborhood.

Liliana C. González: Why do you think that it's important to have this conversation?

Lizeth: Although there is scholarship on de la tierra's creative writing and activism within the Latina lesbian community, there hasn't been enough about the link between her work as a Latina lesbian activist, writer, and librarian. She wrote about her body, desire, and other topics related to librarianship. What I admire the most about de la tierra's work is her ability to be her authentic self in all of these spaces. She didn't seem uncomfortable talking about sex and sexuality in her work.

Liliana: When we don't talk about sexuality, we uphold heterosexuality and affirm heteronormativity. When I think of de la tierra's work and how explicit she was about non-normative sexuality, I think about how it disrupts the silences and power of these institutions.

Lizeth: As a queer Latina femme, being sexually explicit is important because the library field, historically, erases our communities. You have to be extra queer, extra femme, and extra brown to make up for that erasure.

---

1. We have written tatiana de la tierra's name in lower case (except if beginning a sentence) in accordance with how de la tierra spelled her name and according to previous specifications. Tatiana de la tierra, "Ode to Unsavory Lesbians," Feminist Studies 43, no. 2 (2017): 489.

Liliana: I'm all about breaking silences. Can you speak about how you came to know her work?

Lizeth: The first time that I heard about tatiana de la tierra was in 2011 while I was an undergrad at CSULB. I was a part of an organization called Conciencia Femenil (ConFem), "Feminist Consciousness," where we organized Chicana Feminisms conferences. We invited tatiana de la tierra to read her work for our event called "Noche de Cultura" (or Culture Night—it sounds better in Spanish.) It was at a coffeehouse in Long Beach, CA. I remember her going on stage barefoot and reading the poem "Paint Me a Dangerous Woman"; it was the first time I heard poetry that was so explicitly about Lesbian desire and about what she wanted to do to women. I was like, damn, I just want to read more.

Liliana: Did you meet her?

Lizeth: Yes, I was a little fangirl. I bought her book and took it with me to Tucson when I moved there for library school. When I found out she was a librarian, you could imagine me with little hearts in my eyes. It confirmed that library school is where I needed to be. I didn't find out she was a librarian until after her passing in 2012.

Liliana: It's amazing that you were able to meet her. It makes me think about Queer women of color icons like Cherríe Moraga, Gloria Anzaldúa, and Audre Lorde who are so formative for many of us. I remember when I saw Cherríe Moraga speak for the first time—it was such an important moment for my identity. Even though I was involved with Queer and Chicanx student organizations, the first time I heard of tatiana de la tierra was through conversations with you, so thank you for introducing me to her work.

I find it fascinating that she was active on various fronts. She writes about the Colombian author, Gustavo Álvarez Gardeazábal. In "A Prisoner of Hope," she talks about his writing and political career as an openly gay man in Colombia. I read his novel *El Divino*, "the Divine

One," and it's about a gay drug trafficker. I was excited to see that she had written about him. She published the piece in 2001, when he was a political prisoner in Colombia. She was bringing awareness to what was going on in Colombia, from US intervention to drug trafficking and guerrillas. De la tierra was interested in maintaining these international networks of solidarity, especially when it came to feminist and LGBT causes in Latin America. I appreciate it as someone who is interested in hemispheric cultural networks and how people of color in the US are connected to international movements.

Lizeth: Yes, she also edited magazines called "Comoción" and "Esto No Tiene Nombre," where she featured authors from Latin America and the US.

Liliana: She would also travel to meet ups with feminists and lesbians in Latin America. The fact that she's also a librarian really brings a twist and shatters stereotypes that people have about Latina librarians, because people don't even think that it's a thing.

Lizeth: I agree, she breaks many stereotypes dealing with Latina lesbians and librarians. One of my favorite ways she does this is by writing creatively in her librarianship and vice versa. She combines things that were seen as separate. In my favorite poem, called "Big Fat Pussy Girl," de la tierra writes about her lover Margarita and how Margarita calls her pussy a papayona, or a big papaya, or a big fat pussy. In this poem, de la tierra writes about her own big fat pussy. She calls it the "World Wide Web of cunts"; the "Disney World of cunts"; the "Sonora Matancera of cunts"; and my favorite, the "Library of Congress of cunts." She addresses the Library of Congress in the same sentence as her pussy, and it just fucks with the system that oppresses queers of color with limiting and offensive language. I think by including the Library of Congress, Disney, and the Sonora Matancera in relation to her cunt, she associates librarianship and Latinidad with the abundance of cunts. What has always been obscured and shamed is now explicit and in your face.

Liliana: As a lover of Latin American music, I love the part about the "Sonora Matancera of cunts." The Sonora Matancera was one of the big bands of Cuba during the pre-Revolution era. People like Celia Cruz and Pérez Prado were a part of it at some point, so it's a big deal. I think it's noteworthy that she mentions all these things as being connected. It's powerful. Speaking of the Library of Congress, wasn't de la tierra a cataloger?

Lizeth: After reading her member spotlight for the ALA GLBT Roundtable newsletter, I found out that she was actually a cataloger at the SUNY Buffalo Library. It's fascinating because de la tierra wanted to break all these barriers, but cataloging has strict rules. She was an advocate for more inclusive subject headings; for example, she discussed other names that Latina lesbians want to be called, like jotas, tortilleras, arepas, etc. De la tierra really advocated to break with tradition and think beyond what the Library of Congress was doing.

Liliana: Yes, de la tierra urges us to think about the power of naming and how language use replicates oppressive structures. That's something that I always tell my students. Language is so important to creating real social change. For example, if we can imagine the centering of sexuality and queerness within libraries and academia in general, I think we can imagine something completely different. Wouldn't it be less white, less heteronormative and homonormative? I think so, just by shifting the language that we use, and that's something that's been happening. You see it with the inclusion of pronouns. We're talking here about libraries and academia, but they are important steps. She really embodied that at a time when the work she was doing was so against the grain. I'm sure that she was rejected in her efforts. She used her own life to make the best case for the importance of making these changes so that queer people could be heard; because the voices were there, but they were being ignored for so long.

Lizeth: I read one of Juana María Rodríguez's pieces where she writes about tatiana de la tierra and introduces her as an archivist. (By the way, she cites tatiana de la tierra, but tatiana also cites Juana María Rodríguez in her work; I think it's awesome that Queer Latina powerhouses are citing each other.) Honestly, I hadn't thought of tatiana de la tierra as an archivist, but she did document the histories of queer people. For example, she wrote an article for a "Serving LGBTIQ Library and Archives Users" anthology where she discusses the "Esto No Tiene Nombre" magazine; she mentions Margarita again and how she helped with the magazine. I remember the quote, "out of all my lovers, Margarita was one of the ones that lasted the longest, she pissed me off and turned me on the most." It's amazing that she wrote about what turned her on in a book that was meant to advocate for LGBT communities within LIS. When it comes to the LGBT community, libraries are like, "You're gay, cool, but don't talk about sex." De la tierra's work teaches us that we could instead say, "I'm going to be in your face about my desire, you're not going to ignore it."

Liliana: When she says, "lasted the longest," is she referring to lasting the longest sexually or as a lover? Or both?

Lizeth: I guess it's up for interpretation. If you're going to be an advocate, you're going to hear about her desires. One of the most important parts of this piece is that she mentions that when Margarita died, she had requested that tatiana de la tierra would get the letters they wrote to each other. Margarita's brother threw away everything that he didn't see as having value, including these letters. This happens so often in queer communities, where family members or archival institutions decide that the queer life of someone should not be documented. This piece was an ode to her relationship with Margarita and a way to recuperate from the erasure of queer love.

Liliana: I'm glad that you bring that up because I also hadn't thought of de la tierra as an archivist, but it makes sense. To have queer of color archives is vital because there aren't many of them. There's the ONE Archive, which is a big archival institution, but the bulk of queer archives are small community archives, as you know through your own work with queer archival projects in Arizona and Tennessee. That's why going to her archive last summer at UCLA, and to the Audre Lorde archive at Spelman College, were incredible experiences—there aren't many collections that document the lives of queer and lesbians of color. My favorite moment at the UCLA archive was finding a program in de la tierra's collection from the Audre Lorde Award, which de la tierra won. Lorde was also a librarian at one point and to be able to see that connection was awesome.

Lizeth: Yes! Fellow librarians, writers, and lesbians! I connected to tatiana de la tierra on a deep level and going to that archive felt like coming full circle. As a Queer Latina lesbian librarian, she inspires the work that I do and reminds me to be my authentic self in everything that I do. Her work has pushed me outside my comfort zone, to be more explicit about my own sexuality in the work that I do. I think that tatiana de la tierra's work continues to challenge what it means to be a queer Latina/x writer and librarian and how to maneuver multiple worlds without compromising one's own identity.

Liliana: I'm so glad that we had this conversation. It's been in the works for a while, and I hope that we can continue these conversations about how her legacy has influenced younger queer latinx generations—within libraries and beyond.

Lizeth: Peace.

Reflection

This conversation emerges from our desire to honor the legacy of tatiana de la tierra and how she daringly approached librarianship. As a Latina lesbian, writer, and librarian, de la tierra fought against the compartmentalization of her life. Her activism was the connective tissue that rendered all of these aspects inextricable from each other. De la tierra's poetics and librarianship expressed that it was not enough to be out as a lesbian; it was also necessary to be explicit about what it means to desire women vis-à-vis the heteronormative environment of libraries.

Being explicit made it impossible for institutions to ignore and pretend she was not a lesbian. Tatiana de la tierra thus broke the silences around sexuality, especially around same-sex desire and queerness. De la tierra's poetic and librarian activism goes against the grain of the intersecting axis of power and domination. Indeed, de la tierra's activism was central towards challenging discriminatory language and fighting for the documentation of lesbian and queer-of-color voices within libraries, archives, and beyond.

De la tierra wanted to transform libraries and archives but also understood the challenges as well as the urgency to create avenues for change within these institutions. Considering that queer people of color (QTPOC) are often under-documented in archives, it's crucial to take up space in terms of the collections themselves and as both archivists and researchers. Libraries and archives have historically restricted access to their collections because, aside from being elitist institutions, their gatekeeping limits the possibility to question collection development criteria. Libraries often pride themselves for being sites of knowledge accessibility, but they simultaneously uphold restrictions that contradict this narrative regarding the cultural capital needed to access and navigate these institutions.

As a librarian, de la tierra possessed the cultural capital to navigate the politics of donating her documents to an archive, something that she writes about in her poem, *Yolanda the Powerful*. In this piece, de la tierra writes about Yolanda Retter-Vargas, a latina lesbian and archivist, at the time at the UCLA Chicano Studies Research Center. In the poem, de la tierra reenacts the conversation that Retter-Vargas and she might have had: "When will they process you, What if they de-lesbianize you, What if they don't care about you like I do.[2]

---

2. tatiana de la tierra, "En Memoria," *Chicana/Latina Studies* 7, no. 1 (2007): 78–83.

The poem embodies how Retter-Vargas and de la tierra understood the threat of being erroneously cataloged or de-lesbianized to fit the heteronormative archive. De la tierra's homage to Retter-Vargas also symbolizes the importance of documenting materials from queer communities precisely because they have been erased from the historical record through established archival practices.

Tatiana de la tierra's lesbian poetics took cues from Black lesbian feminist theorists like Audre Lorde (also a librarian), whose work challenged social and educational institutions. Both Lorde and de la tierra's creative and critical work manifest a politics of resistance—tactics for survival and existence. As Lorde argues in her famous essay, "Poetry is not a luxury," poetry is a necessity for women's existence that gives "name to the nameless so it can be thought."[3] To view poetry as a need is to break with the belief that poetry is for the privileged. Lorde ultimately reclaims poetry for women of color and takes back the power over words, feelings, and voice.

As we mentioned in our conversation, de la tierra was awarded the Audre Lorde Legacy Award to recognize her excellence in lesbian poetry. Yet the connection between the two poets is significantly deeper. De la tierra and Lorde's connection centers around a lesbian poetics, a connection which de la tierra herself notes. For instance, in a Spanish-language interview, "Tatiana de la tierra y el activismo lésbico," she credits Lorde as an influence on her work, noting that, "many of us have an Audre Lorde phase."[4] Both poets recognized the particular impact of naming as a means for action and transformative social change.

De la tierra thus urges us to think about the "power of naming" and how language replicates oppressive structures. More importantly, it eliminates the possibility of not being found by those who need it the most; i.e., minoritized communities. For instance, in "Latina Lesbian Subject Headings: The Power of Naming," de la tierra writes, "[t]

---

3. Audre Lorde, *Sister Outsider: Essays and Speeches*, 1st edition (Trumansburg, NY: Crossing Press, 1984): 37.

4. Our translation from Infogénero, Productora de información de género, *Tatiana de La Tierra y El Activismo Lésbico*, 2010, https://www.youtube.com/watch?v=tKGcLj_wgds.

o not name is to eradicate, to make invisible. It is like banning a book that no one ever knew existed to begin with."[5] For example, and as we discussed in our conversation, de la tierra was explicit in referring to her sexual life (i.e., her poem "Big Fat Pussy Girl") as a way to confront the systemic shortfall of institutions like the Library of Congress (i.e., "Library of Congress of Cunts") and to emphasize the complexity and multifacetedness of language.[6] On a similar note, in the essay "Inside the files of this has no name," de la tierra preserves a love story intentionally weeded out. De la tierra reflects on the devastation she felt when Margarita's brother disposed of the evidence of their love and desire after Margarita's passing. De la tierra reclaims the narrative by exposing and affirming, "Inside the files of this has no name is everlasting Latina lesbian lust, the same lust that Margarita's brother and many others deemed garbage."[7] By writing of her "lust" for Margarita, here and throughout her poetry, she archives their love as meaningful and brings attention to the reality that many QTPOC face when "given" family wants to erase their existence.

Tatiana de la tierra's poetry and librarianship disrupt heteronormative structures and are focal points to reimagine what access and libraries can look like when sexuality is not marginalized or obscured. De la tierra thus continues to be a powerful force for many of us in academia and libraries and reminds us of the importance of centering our experiences as queers of color as the very sites from which to challenge racist heteronormativity.

---

5. tatiana de la tierra, "Latina Lesbian Subject Headings: The Power of Naming," in *Radical Cataloging: Essays at the Front*, ed. K. R. Roberto, Illustrated edition (Jefferson, N.C: McFarland & Company, 2008): 100. http://delatierra.net/?page_id=1037.

6. tatiana de la tierra, "Big Fat Pussy Girl," Blog, delatierra.net, August 12, 2001, http://delatierra.net/?page_id=1037. Originally published: de la tierra, tatiana. "Big Fat Pussy Girl." *Porcupine Love and Other Tales from My Papaya*. Buffalo: Chibcha Press, 2005. Also recorded as: "Big Fat Pussy Girl." *Vagina Dialogues: A Queer Review*. Compact disc recording. Hag Theatre, 2002.

7. tatiana de la tierra, "Inside the Files of This Has No Name," in *Serving LGBTIQ Library and Archives Users: Essays on Outreach, Service, Collections and Access*, ed. Ellen Greenblatt (Jefferson, North Carolina: McFarland, 2010), 162–64.

Bibliography

de la tierra (tatiana) Papers, CSRC.0124. University of California, Los Angeles, Chicano/a Research Center. Los Angeles, California.

GLBTRT Newsletter. "Member Profile: Tatiana de La Tierra." American Library Association, 2007.

Infogénero, Productora de información de género. *Tatiana de La Tierra y El Activismo Lésbico*, 2010. https://www.youtube.com/watch?v=tKGcLj_wgds.

Lorde, Audre. *Sister Outsider: Essays and Speeches*. 1st edition. Trumansburg, NY: Crossing Press, 1984.

tierra, tatiana de la. "Big Fat Pussy Girl." Blog. delatierra.net, August 12, 2001. http://delatierra.net/?page_id=1037.

———. "En Memoria." *Chicana/Latina Studies* 7, no. 1 (2007): 78–83.

———. *For the Hard Ones: A Lesbian Phenomenology / Para Las Duras: Una Fenomenologia Lesbiana*. Bilingual ed. edition. San Diego, CA; Buffalo, NY: Calaca Press, 2002.

———. "Inside the Files of This Has No Name." In *Serving LGBTIQ Library and Archives Users: Essays on Outreach, Service, Collections and Access*, edited by Ellen Greenblatt, 162–64. Jefferson, North Carolina: McFarland, 2010.

———. "Latina Lesbian Subject Headings: The Power of Naming." In *Radical Cataloging: Essays at the Front*, edited by K. R. Roberto, Illustrated edition., 94–102. Jefferson, N.C: McFarland & Company, 2008.

———. "Ode to Unsavory Lesbians." *Feminist Studies* 43, no. 2 (2017): 418–89.

Memory Work: Archival Evidences at the Schomburg and the Forward

Bridgett Kathryn Johnson-Pride and Chana Pollack

Keywords
Collection development, memory, storytelling, Yiddish queer culture, New York City

> **Bridgett Kathryn Johnson-Pride** is the reference librarian for the Manuscripts, Archives, and Rare Books Division and the Art and Artifacts Division of the Schomburg Center for Research in Black Culture, and a Cultural Heritage fellow for Rare Book School. She is an artist and zine maker who enjoys teaching with primary sources and empowering people through storytelling and art.
>
> **Chana Pollack** is the archivist for the Forward, a 124-year-old independent Jewish media organization providing research, translation and production of original Forward archival content for contemporary contexts. Originally a Yiddish newspaper serving the immigrant Jewish community, the Forward was conceived as a socialist daily starting in 1897. The Forward is currently online in both English and Yiddish. In 2021 Pride month, she authored the Forward's first personal essay on its queer archival Yiddish content and its historic silences in their archive and on their pages.

Conversation

Chana Pollack: My spouse lost her wedding ring in the garden. I have to let go. It's not the worst thing in the world, but it was a delightful signifier; it meant a lot, and it has some archival value. The gold for the rings came from their parents, survivors of the Holocaust. Their dad survived and held on to these old gold coins. A last item, ephemera. They lost everything in the war, and he passed this on. So, there's a little bit of that loss.

Professionally, at the Forward,[8] originally a Yiddish language daily and currently the oldest independent Jewish media organization covering Jewish news, opinion, life, and culture since 1897, I'm doing this digital mapping project with Urban Archive,[9] this great historical project in the city on the map of New York, wherein various organizations upload images, creating stories that then get geotagged and mapped onto New York. It's an app as well as web-based. It's free to download. While walking around New York with this app on your phone, when you pass somewhere that appeared in one of our photographs, our archival images will come up on your screen with the related story. This week, they started a promotion called Activism in the Five Boroughs,[10] and we were invited to join along with historical organizations from Brooklyn and Queens, as well as the New York Historical Society.

Bridgett Kathryn Johnson-Pride: That sounds like such a cool project. Storytelling is so important. My partner and I have been traveling between Boston and New York for the past year. Every other week, one of us goes to visit the other. But even though I have been living in the Bronx and working in Harlem, I know the city no better than I did before. I feel like having an app like the Urban Archive would help me learn about the history of the city that I am living and working in. I

---

8. https://forward.com/search/?q=urban+archive.

9. https://www.urbanarchive.org/cities/nyc.

10. https://www.urbanarchive.org/search?q=%23activisminthefiveboroughs

feel like that's a really interesting project to activate folks with the space that they're operating within.

Chana: Yes, just like what you're talking about, a portal opened enabling community members to interact, gathering and uploading images, and creating their own community-based story. It's definitely in the spirit of activism this year to just sort of claim your space and the city.

Bridgett: My fiancé and I live on a college campus in Chestnut Hill. The college was just purchased by Boston College.

Chana: Do you miss the city?

Bridgett: I miss our collections at the Schomburg Center. I drive down every other week-ish to do scanning for our researchers. I was there yesterday, preparing for that fateful day when we finally re-open in some small capacity. And it was so lovely to be in our reading room with these beautiful sculptures and to handle collections that I have grown so accustomed to being around and reading. I miss those aspects of my job. So, being back in the library around things that were joyful and very affirming as a Black woman was revitalizing

Chana: How is it being in New England?

Bridgett: I don't see a lot of people out here, thankfully. (*Laughter*). Grad school was really hard because there were almost no faculty of color, or if there were, they only stuck around for maybe two years. They continue to have a terrible retention rate for faculty of color. So that was not the best experience. But the college that we're living at, the majority of their student body are first-generation and students of color. I think it's 84% students of color, located just outside of Boston.

That was a really affirming choice to make. The institution I was going to call home right after graduate school would allow me to work with young folks, majority Black students who were trying to call academia something that was comfortable for them. When so much of the world around them tells them they're too dumb, or don't have enough money for college, or whatever. To go from there to the Schomburg Center, I'm humbled that I get to affirm Black life every day.

Chana: Beautiful. When I think being told to be grateful for the fact that, despite the horrors of history that have been visited upon Jews, for example, we've been "lucky," even after the Holocaust and events like that, to regain some of our materials and our ephemera. And also, for the practice of gathering and recognizing the importance of preservation. And I know that the African American experience is not that way. The middle passage is just like a horrible cut off; linguistically, familially, from land … So it's a different process. That must be just… I heard you. It was very visual when you talked about just walking into the Schomburg and what it feels like physically to be in that space.

Bridgett: I am so thankful to be at that institution, and that is a really important thing to mention.

The story of the Schomburg Center is that Arturo Schomburg was told that Black people didn't have history. And so he dedicated his life to collecting "vindicating evidences" of Black creativity and intelligence. The Schomburg Center is a place where people can go and be like, yes, we have collected this artwork, or these letters, or these books, or photographs of this group of people who are not in the United States by choice. It is an affirming place for Black people to be. As a queer Black woman, I am trying to affirm that aspect of my identity as well. My personal mini-mission is to teach people how to use archives, and that archives are places for everyone.

Thankfully, COVID has allowed me to have the time to dedicate to other projects, other than just the daily interactions of checking materials out to folks. I get to actually contribute to creating tools for our researchers to use. Since we've been in quarantine, the very first thing I created was a research guide on exploring Black queer studies at the Schomburg Center.

Chana: Beautiful.

Bridgett: In creating this research guide, I learned that the library is struggling to identify collections created by queer folks. Namely, just how we're cataloging this material isn't being done to exhaustion. One of the examples I like to use is when you are looking for materials created by queer folks at the Schomburg center, you would automatically think, "I'm going to do a search for gay African American authors, and users know James Baldwin's going to show up." But if you do that search, he doesn't show up because he hasn't been catalogued that way. So, I'm having conversations with my co-workers to be mindful to not strip people of important parts of their identity. And just keep having this conversation until change happens.

Chana: Right. Wow, very beautiful! That excited me on so many levels to hear. And also, on the one hand, it sounds like it's as simple as adding "gay" to the search term or to the taxonomy. But, on the other hand, it's not. It's also like asking for that to be included and how we consider the art that the person created. Right, like we're searching for "James Baldwin gay," but we're also saying that we're reading him gay. So, I sometimes feel like, more than actually asking for the search term to be included, it's asking for that consideration, and that is what kind of freaks people out. Or like when you said that the institution needs to grow; that's the growth that I'm asking for.

This is just a weird pivot, but I attended one of those diversity and inclusion workshops this week and it was really awkward for me on so many levels. One thing I noticed was that there was a lot about not just assuming that everybody is straight and the things you can say for trans, for queer, for however people identify, and the microaggressions. And it was sort of brought into the conversation, and I realized, to catalog myself in that office, I'm queer! So, I don't know if that's what you're saying, too, that the institution needs to grow. It is kind of curious that we identify, you know, the Schomburg as a progressive, cultivating institution that's accepting of change in society. And not just accepting it, but in part also driving it, making it available for the community by writing about it and by shining a light on injustices. But at the same time, as the conversation was all about queerness and how to treat people who are gay, lesbian, queer, trans and... You know the little industrial videos that they were showing of the bad examples and what could be different. I was like, I'm pretty sure I'm the only queer in the room.

Bridgett: Oh my gosh, yeah. And that's a difficult position to be in. Do you feel like you were ever asked to speak for the community?

Chana: I would say at the beginning, two decades ago, it felt stiffer. And while they were very on their game about being "pro-things," I don't think they would have written what they're writing now and wouldn't have really spent the money or the energy, which at the time was ink; now it's digital, but they wouldn't have given the column space to the topics. I think this is still the issue. We're talking about pivoting. To put energy in this direction and to celebrate the community is still a bit of a pivot. It's not that it's uncomfortable for people, but it's just like, oh, it's this other thing.

If I can search, and thanks to your work, that is part of a general canon, then it's not like I have to do this extra search for gay or lesbian, or I have to do this extra search for trans; it's just included. So that's kind of what I'm feeling. Sometimes they were talking also about just out and out sexism, and then I was like, oh yeah, that happens to me, too; I can relate to that. But then it would pivot back to queer, and I had that thing where I was like...

Bridgett: Which side am I on right now?

Chana: Exactly! Thank you.

Bridgett: Yeah, I experience that so frequently because I'm biracial, I'm bisexual, I am constantly navigating where am I on the continuum. Who is in the room, and how does their presence affect my identity, and how

I am perceived? And it's a weird thing to have to navigate, especially at work. And then, when that also comes into the work you're producing at an institution... I, thankfully, work with several other queer people at the Schomburg, all with different experience and expertise. And it's really wonderful. And then there are conversations with older folks at the Schomburg who are asking me to explain pronouns to them... again.

I remember the first time one of my co-workers asked me to explain pronouns. I was like, "Sure, I can do that. We'll have this conversation. I'm going to send you a couple of resources, and it's going to be great." But then it was a continuous conversation. The first time it was fine. The second time it was fine. But now I'm tired because you are essentially asking me for permission for you to disregard someone's pronouns.

Chana: Right.

Bridgett: It's a weird situation to be in, where a place that's so affirming racially can also kind of be exhausting at other times.

Chana: Yep. Recently there was a discussion about the term "ladies," asking about people's comfort zones with being addressed that way in emails, etc. I realized the irony inherent in their use of the term, but I don't really identify that way and it doesn't feel good for me to be addressed that way, even in jest. I find it tired and sexist. I know I was heard on the issue, and they weren't asking me to explain it. But there was their backstory of how they came to be using the term "ladies." So, that was the issue just coming at me in a different way. It's sort of a very woke choke.

Bridgett: Ooh, I like that.

I remember when I first started being more conscious of what inclusive language looks like. I was trying to embrace gender-neutral language but my professors would cross out works like "folks" and write in the margin "people, she/her, he/him." Do I do what they say for the grade? Do I challenge my professor? How much power do I, as a queer Black woman, have in this conversation with my white cis professor? And where do I sit on that power and privilege spectrum to say, "Well, actually, no. I'm right in this situation, and I need you to adjust."

Chana: So interesting. I think the community has kind of moved forward a little bit. The New York Times is always kind of the decider, right, for the public conversation; but it seems like "they" has become much more acceptable, definitely. And people just asking people's pronouns, it feels like it just happened like a couple of months ago; like with COVID, there's been an advance, right? And I think I'm noticing for myself that "folks" and "y'all" is also coming out of that movement. With COVID, it's just becoming much more rapid change that is needed.

Bridgett: Yeah, I wonder if it's because people have the time and energy to recognize the general unease of the world, and they take time to enjoy self-care and community care. I feel like that's why people were so active in the Black Lives Matter protests: because they decided to take the time to invest in the community. Whereas before, we would have been at work, we would have had a million reasons for why we can't attend a protest. I feel like a silver lining of COVID has been people are checking in with what feels right, being honest with themselves, and asking for respect, space, and acceptance. I do feel like in these past few months, perhaps, we have all come to an awakening, in a sense, that is filled with compassion. And I hope we can hold on to that moving forward.

Chana: Right. Much of my takeaway from the Black Lives Matter movement is along the lines of what you were saying… We used to say in the 80s, "¡No pasarán!" It's like there's no turning back. This is not something that's going to fade. We're saying what we need. We're demanding it. We're putting it into action. And that is kind of "covidien," in a way. Things become clearer in a way, and I think, also, through grief. Like so much death in the community, right? In the African American community. I know in the Hasidic community, there are many horrible deaths. At such a rapid pace… kind of like AIDS. A lot of times in the

LGBTQ community, whatever advances we've made have been built upon the horrible death that happened. It shifted power, like in the ACT UP movement. A lot of tremendous change occurred that we're still looking at. And, of course, the 60s too, all the different power movements that came out of that. So, it's like there has been this shift, you know...which is in a way, a silver lining.

Bridgett: But at a high cost. We have been through a group trauma over the past eleven months. And I mean, it's been a global trauma of folks losing people opportunities, major events, and milestones. Everything just kind of hit pause—and it's hard. I'm exhausted.

Chana: Right. You know, one thing I worked on at the very beginning of the pandemic... I had to look at 1918 and how our paper, which was speaking at that time, for sure, to the majority community of immigrants that had recently arrived. Who, yes, while they may have heard of cholera and other pandemics in their time and primarily in Eastern Europe before they immigrated to America, were here in a land where they hardly understood the language. They were dependent on a Yiddish press and on community support just to be able to navigate layers of authority, directives, and fines. In 1918, if you didn't wear a mask, they fined you five bucks, which was a fortune. And the directives... just like us, they were changing every day. And the amount of people dying, and they all lived in crowded spaces, and they couldn't leave for the Upstate or rural spaces. They couldn't get out of the city. And so, resilience. A lot of art was created at the time, like short stories and stuff that were just like in the moment. For example: November 6, 1918, Yiddish writer Yente Serdatsky, published a short story[11] in our paper about what the scene was like in the pharmacy when she was standing in line, and the person behind her was coughing up a storm, and the pharmacist was terrified to help. It's exactly the same story. So, like, when we don't have the option

---

11. Yente Serdatsky, "From the Forverts Archives, Influenza 1918: Scenes from a Jewish Drug Store," The Forward, March 24, 2020, https://forward.com/news/442317/from-the-forverts-archives-influenza-1918-scenes-from-a-jewish-drug-store/.

to actually act out, you know, like you're saying, to make community, we can rely on art, culture, and digital media. Like, Passover was one of the first holidays for us when it started, and it was, like, all about the Zoom, you know, the get togethers—called a Seder—to celebrate the festival. At this point… we all have fatigue. It's not so exciting to have Zoom Thanksgiving.

I guess I'm thinking that this is not the first time it's happened. We know how to do it. But how do we how? Do we self-care? And how do we connect?

Our archive always tries to add, you know, LGBT, African American, any kind of outside of that universe of taxonomies to broaden and be most inclusive for searches.

Finally, finally, in my years of doing this type of cataloguing, and archiving, and processing this collection of photographs for this newspaper, the Forward Newspaper,[12] which will soon be 125 years old, I came across a photo where I went, here are my people! Clear as the light of day for me.

Bridgett: Oh, it is! (*Laughter*).

Chana: Thank you for affirming that. So, when I added his story on the digital mapping project, writing about this individual as, for me, signifying. He [David Carey] was a Yiddish theater actor. There are no other out gay Yiddish theater actors that I know of, in as much as he can be considered out. There may be some that we suppose were, but this was clear for all intents and purposes. So, I said he identified as gay and functioned as one of the assumed first known out gay Yiddish actors.[13] I was determined to get that photo of him on that map, to preserve [David Carey's] memory and the queer nature of the story. I love it, but it's also somewhat fraught. I don't want to prejudge somebody.

---

12. https://forward.com/yiddish/.

13. Forward, The, "David Carey, Star of the Yiddish Stage | Urban Archive," in Urban Archive, June 4, 2020, https://www.urbanarchive.org/stories/BUZscDF7z2d.

I wonder what you say about it because it's a very interesting fine line where I'm naming it, and I feel like that's my right as the archivist doing the research. I have my citations of why, but at a certain point, I got some feedback from his brother who is still alive and who is also queer.

[Henry Carrey][14] called me on it and was like, "Let me tell you about my brother." And so, he relayed to me a painful anecdote about how, yes, this individual, David Carey, participated in certain activities within the gay community. For example, he would go to synagogue services at the new, in those days—like in the 70s and 80s—the newly formed LGBTQ Synagogue in New York. So that was one way that we knew that he identified. And he had male intimate romantic partners. To his much older Yiddish theater cronies, though, his acting world, his artistic community, he would call these men that he loved his "roommates." That's a choice for a lot of queer people. I'm not here to judge.

Anecdotal evidence relays that he was just so charming. You know, I want to say he resembled a sprite: a delightful, energetic, hardworking, hard driving character. He charmed the older community of actors so much, even hosting salons for them at his house. His brother, who is also gay, remembered going over there this one time and observing this moment where David called out Henry for being queer, making some kind of derogatory comment that abandoned Henry as the queer one and David, of course, was still closeting himself in front of this community of Yiddish theatre folks.

So, Henry affirmed that his brother David was in and out of the closet. I totally get it. I adjusted the language, to say that he was, for the time and place, as out as possible for a Yiddish actor. And we built the story to memorialize him and all the beautiful things he did in his tragically short life. And when there was a partner, there was room to talk about a partnership. And the family never hid the fact that he died of AIDS. In the Yiddish theatre community, in our newspaper's archives, he was not memorialized that way. Here is one of the Yiddish

---

14. Yiddish Lives, "Henry Carrey on The History of Yiddish Song," Blog, Yiddish Lives (blog), accessed July 3, 2022, https://yiddishlives.org/henry-carrey-yiddish-song/.

community who died of AIDS, who was of you, who did so much for you, and yet, we never we hadn't for example, memorialized him on World AIDS Day. So, for me, this also opened the door to activate that because there are more people I know like that. I have less of an ability to actually call it as openly as I can, but because here I had a whole story from a family member, we could. And I had activities that I could track that were out gay activities, like that synagogue membership or whatever, and his different partners, and that he died of AIDS. He was an active, vibrant, talented Jewish gay man. He had a busy love life. There were witnesses to that. So, I wanted to share this because that also led me to wanting to talk to you—somebody who also just created a critical research guide.

Bridgett: I thank you for sharing that with me, this is fantastic! I really appreciate your story about calling him out, and like me, perhaps, outing him in a sense, even though this picture very much tells us he is out, but she knows that's our reading of it.

Something I struggled with when I was creating my lib guide was that we have a list of our collections that we organized by subject heading. And so, one of the local subject headings we use is queer studies, which is used for collections that study queerness. However, collections created by people who happened to be members of the LGBT community would not show up under the subject heading if they were not discussing queerness in their papers. So again, an example is James Baldwin or Lorraine Hansberry. Their papers do not discuss their lifestyle, and so they would not be included here. And so, I really wrestled with, if I create my own list for this research guide, that does the work of identifying all of the collections created by members of the LGBTQ community. And I decided not to. Because if I don't have the evidence at the Schomburg Center to say, "This is why I am including this person in this guide," then what do I have to stand on?

I was up against a deadline, trying to get it published in June. The year before, NYPL down at the 42nd Street library had this huge exhibit on

Stonewall 50, but the majority of the exhibit talked about white folks and excluded many stories of Black folks.

This guide is important because it shows people how to use our tools to find queer Black people; but more importantly, it shows their absence from our collections. I think this is in part because we hide that aspect of their identities. I don't think it's intentional, I just think it wasn't a priority to the folks who were processing these collections.

I've made it my personal mission to just take any chance I have to mention the fact that our cataloging practice is not inclusive of the LGBT community. That's my soapbox. I've had faculty contact me to teach class sessions about how to find queer folks in our collections. And I have to bring up my guide, explain what the guide includes, and then explain what it doesn't include. And it's so frustrating because our users want this information, but I don't feel empowered to make that list on my own. And that's really weird for me. I hope that there is a day soon in the future when we can face this head on.

Chana: It feels like the same process as taking anybody who's written out of history. It's really important what you're doing. Thank you.

Reflection

Dear Bridgett,

Our official conversation took place via zoom, as do so many in these days of pandemic connectivity. And it's all making me reflect on archival correspondence methodologies, you know? Simply put, what if, instead of a digital conversation, we'd had to "talk" via letter writing? What if the urgent thoughts I felt coming on while talking to you had to be conveyed slowly, like dripping tea?

So, here's tea dripped, rather than spilled. And it feels so very long ago that we had that conversation about taxonomies, and pronoun preferences in the workplace, and how to respect history; all the while desperately determined to move it forward. If I leave a question of how I'd like to be addressed at the office ignored—how will inaccuracies in the chronicles of our time and our peoples ever truly be uncovered? These, too, are connected over time and over digital space.

Dear Chana,

Thank you for your letter. It has put me at ease to speak with a colleague who shares similar concerns about our institutions and the ways that we move within them. A year is a long time to reflect on our conversation. In the reflection process, I worry that too much vulnerability may have been shared because I felt that I was speaking to a friend. In moments I forgot that others would read out words. However, I want to be brave and share our words so that others can also be brave.

I was married this year, and speak highly of you to my wife. I never realized that so many couples are faced with living apart. I also shared the story of your lost wedding band, and we both felt the pull of the loss of ancestral treasure and family we had to turn our backs on in order to remain true to our commitments to each other.

Dear Bridgett,

Thank you for your letter that arrived recently, offering joy and wisdom of the ages. And congratulations on your wedding! It's so uplifting to learn of loving commitments despite the current plague and grief. My issue of M's lost wedding ring isn't as pressing as it was in my last letter, so I hope I didn't worry you. To think back in time of how LGBTQ's expressed loving vows to each other, to community without archival or research guides; such crazy olden days! Stories make everything possible, I'm certain of that. And you shared yours and listened to mine and we spilled some zoom tea. Talk soon again, I'm sure.

Dear Chana,

I like the notion that archives can be the collection of objects that we leave behind to tell the stories that we can no longer speak. Through objects, papers, clothing, photographs and more, archives allow our stories to be heard, read, and understood across time. I am heartened that so many LGBTQ+ archives and memory projects are being funded, created, and celebrated so that members of our community can be documented for the future. Thank you for sharing your stories with me, and I look forward to many more conversations to come.

Dear Bridgett,

Since receiving your last letter, I've had the joy of being invited by my organization to write an essay[15] that just about summarizes all we've been discussing! Out loud and proud, we announced to readers that we've not recognized enough LGBTQ in our archives. Phew. Sad. So necessary to account for the lack before moving forward with recovering the lost ones. This letter is short because I'm desperate to share the exciting news with you and to thank you for being a partner in this type of historical reparative project. Cheers!

Dear Chana,

Congratulations on this exciting project! While it is disappointing that it has taken so long, I share your joy that the wait for such a public recognition is now over. I know that this project is safe in your careful and thoughtful hands. Similarly, I was able to engage in a project with my amazing colleague Zakiya Collier to write a blog post highlighting LGBTQ+ individuals in our collections. The Fight Continues: Schomburg Archival Collections to Explore for Pride Month[16] paid tribute to the NYC 2021 Pride theme, reflecting on the "multitude of battles we've been fighting as a country and as a city." Furthermore, Zakiya completed the #Schomburg Syllabus,[17] which includes a section on LGBTQ+ materials that people should be aware of and study.

---

15. Chana Pollack, "We're Here, We're Queer, We're Yiddish: LGBTQ Stories, and Silences, in the Forward Archives," Blog, *The Forward* (blog), June 21, 2021, https://forward.com/archive/471747/pride-lgbtq-jewish-yiddish-history-forward-archives/.

16. Bridgett Pride, "The Fight Continues: Schomburg Archival Collections to Explore for Pride Month," Blog, *The New York Public Library* (blog), May 26, 2021, https://www.nypl.org/blog/2021/06/01/fight-continues-schomburg-archives-pride-month.

17. Zakiya Collier and New York Public Library, "#SchomburgSyllabus," Website, #SchomburgSyllabus, accessed July 3, 2022, https://www.nypl.org/schomburgsyllabus.

I am thrilled that there are so many new projects entering the world that celebrate our community!

Dear Bridgett,

Your last letter was such a thrill! And how busy you've been! I can't imagine you've had time for a tea break, so know that I do appreciate your constancy with our trying to grab some. Since my last letter, I had what I thought was a setback of sorts in that the subject of my first LGBTQ archival recovery, the Yiddish actor I wrote about, David Carey—well, I was determined to shine the light of out Yiddish gay actor on him and his brother, Henry; a fellow queer had some difficulty with what I'd written. And so, I went ahead and amended the tale somewhat. I understand David was more closeted than I originally knew. Oy. And yet, I cannot let this story go. The more people read my post about him, the more anecdotes and interest in him seems to emerge. The digital capacity to grab and then spill tea seems endless. I wonder and keep wondering, what do you think?

Dear Chana,

Oh my, I understand this struggle so deeply. As we have previously discussed, we want to share stories and celebrate our community, but it is not our intention to cause harm. What right do we have to "out" the elders of our community who have passed on, perhaps still closeted? I would do as Mr. Schomburg would do and present the "vindicating evidence" of David Carey's life. We can use what we know of him, and present the facts. The evidence. We can share his moments of pride and shame. These are what make him and tell his story.

I hope that this helps you find the balance that you need to move forward. I look forward to learning how this story unfolds. Until next time, do take care.

Bibliography

Collier, Zakiya and New York Public Library. "#SchomburgSyllabus." Website. https://www.nypl.org/schomburgsyllabus.

Forward, The. "David Carey, Star of the Yiddish Stage | Urban Archive." In *Urban Archive*, June 4, 2020. https://www.urbanarchive.org/stories/BUZscDF7z2d.

Pollack, Chana. "We're Here, We're Queer, We're Yiddish: LGBTQ Stories, and Silences, in the Forward Archives." *The Forward* (blog), June 21, 2021. https://forward.com/archive/471747/pride-lgbtq-jewish-yiddish-history-forward-archives/.

Pride, Bridgett. "The Fight Continues: Schomburg Archival Collections to Explore for Pride Month." *The New York Public Library* (blog), May 26, 2021. https://www.nypl.org/blog/2021/06/01/fight-continues-schomburg-archives-pride-month.

Serdatsky, Yente. "From the Forverts Archives, Influenza 1918: Scenes from a Jewish Drug Store." *The Forward*, March 24, 2020. https://forward.com/news/442317/from-the-forverts-archives-influenza-1918-scenes-from-a-jewish-drug-store/.

Yiddish Lives. "Henry Carrey on The History of Yiddish Song." *Yiddish Lives* (blog). https://yiddishlives.org/henry-carrey-yiddish-song/.

Sipping Strategies

A RESPONSIBILITY TO THE FUTURE: SENDING ALONG THE RECORD OF LGBTQI LIVES

RL Goldberg and Gerard Koskovich

Keywords
Archives, cisheteronormative historiography, historical imagination

> **RL Goldberg** is a Junior Fellow at the Dartmouth Society of Fellows. Their work has appeared, or is forthcoming from, *TSQ*, *The Paris Review*, the *Los Angeles Review of Books*, and *ASAP/J*.

> **Gerard Koskovich** is a book dealer and public historian who divides his time between San Francisco and Paris. He has been active in the movement to create LGBTQ archives and museums for four decades, has curated numerous exhibitions, and has presented and published widely in English and French.

Conversation

RL Goldberg: So, I wanted to ask about your own archival practice: How would you describe it? How has your archival practice changed over the years?

Gerard Koskovich: I guess my first question is to ask what you mean by archival practice.

RLG: I'm really interested in talking about university archives in this discussion. So, I know Princeton University has acquired a ton from you—how do you determine the contours, the shape, of what becomes an archive at a university? I know, to some degree, that librarians are making selections, but it's within a list that you've provided.

GK: Yes—they select from what they're offered, so I've already shaped the selection in some ways. But I'd actually go back further and say that my earliest interactions with university archives were when I was a young graduate student at Stanford in 1981. I worked on an initiative that we called the Stanford Gay and Lesbian Archives project, which was a voluntary project of undergraduate and graduate students to try to locate documentary evidence of the history of LGBTQI people at Stanford. At the time, the university archives had a single folder with about thirty documents—newsletters and so on—and when I left my graduate program, they had about thirty-five linear *feet* of archival material.

    I started out the project by talking with the university archivist about what kinds of materials would be useful and how we might organize them and make them available. But it also was an act of faith on their part that somebody would want to use this material someday, thinking that historical questions might arise from this body of material if we could only locate it in some way. And I think that early experience conditioned my practice, first as a collector and then as a dealer. As a collector, I began very actively looking for every last stray bit of paper that might give me a window into the LGBTQI past and searching in places that are not conventional ones for doing research: garage sales and thrift stores; estate sales; recycling bins, quite literally; and talking to every last older queer person I could come across, saying, "That box of old paper in the garage, under your bed, in the closet—hey, can I have a look at that?"

RLG: Tell me more about how that early experience with developing an LGBTQI archive at Stanford shaped your later work as a dealer.

A Responsibility to the Future:
Sending Along the Record of LGBTQI Lives

GK: Pretty early on, I realized that, in fact, although we were invisible in university collections, there was material that existed. So that's been an engaged part of my practice as a dealer but also an extension of my work in the movement, having been involved as a queer activist since the late 1970s, early 1980s. It was a kind of library activism to tempt libraries into acquiring these sorts of materials. University libraries that want a Marcel Proust first edition already have one, and they generally don't want to pay the prices for the kinds of things that are fought over by collectors looking for fetish objects. University libraries are looking for material that will have intense research value, and that has pointed me further towards what was really one of my first loves anyway, which was personal papers; ephemera; near-print materials; print publications that are so obscure, have such small runs and such erratic distribution, that if you find a copy, it may be the only copy that's left. Well, it just so happens that LGBTQI+ material very often falls exactly into that category. Until the recent past, we scarcely had the resources to generate print material, scarcely had the resources to distribute it. We had very few resources to preserve and maintain our own materials—and particularly when you start looking at intersectional identities, the more people find themselves in a situation of race, class, gender that marginalizes them, the further and further they are from economic power.

Despite those obstacles, when we look into history, there are LGBTQI people who have recognized that having a past and leaving a record is crucial, and they invest immensely in what tiny resources they have in preserving those materials. One of the great collections at the GLBT Historical Society—the Bois Burk collection[1]—is from a man who was the son of the first president of San Francisco State University. He was a teen in the early 1920s, and he was such an unruly, irrepressible queer that he just kept falling further and further down the social and economic ladder, what with arrests in tearoom raids and being too obviously

---

1. "Bois Burk Papers," Finding Aid, Collection Number: 1989-07 (San Francisco, California: GLBT Historical Society), https://oac.cdlib.org/findaid/ark:/13030/c8bv7h6s/.

queer to hold a job. He ended up living the last couple decades of his life in a single-room-occupancy hotel, the walls of which were covered with photographs of his life and his queer circle—literally a collage, like wallpaper. And he kept a half dozen bankers boxes of his personal papers and records, in which he obsessively preserved every little news clipping mentioning queers back to the 1920s; every letter that he had received; a handwritten list of everybody he ever slept with, where he picked them up, how many times he slept with them, et cetera.

As for obscure print material, for example, the Bois Burk Papers include a broken run of a publication called *Hobby Directory* from the late 1940s–early 1950s. We have the only known copies at the GLBT Historical Society. It's ostensibly a contact magazine for men to get in touch with other men to share carpentry tools or tips on building model airplanes or model railroads and so on. But many of the personal ads say things like, "My hobbies are flower arranging, collecting seashells, sunbathing. I collect photographs of body builders. I would like to meet other men in my area ages 18 to 25 who also have these interests." Hmmm.

Both: **laugh**

GK: The copies that Bois Burk kept are marked up with his notes, and if he contacted the person, what came out of the interaction. He preserved his copies like a sacred text.

RLG: What factors do you think prompted Burk and similarly marginalized LGBTQI people to safeguard such apparently inconsequential documentation?

GK: Precisely because they were pushed to the edges of society, some LGBTQI people from at least the 19th century onward seem to have thought, "I'm going to hold onto these materials at all costs. This is proof that we existed, that we belong in time, that our lives have value, that we are actors in history." Another collection at the GLBT Historical

Society is the Jiro Onuma Papers,[2] the personal papers of a gay working-class Japanese immigrant who arrived in San Francisco in 1920. Same thing—throughout his life, he kept documents, including when he was sent to the internment camps where the United States forcibly detained Japanese nationals and Japanese Americans during World War II. People who were deported to the camps were dispossessed of all their belongs except what they could fit in a small suitcase—yet Jiro Onuma held onto material documenting his life as a gay man, including an album of body-builder photos from a mail-order physical culture course. If we identify such material and move it to a place where it will be preserved for the long term, then used by researchers, and be the basis for producing historical knowledge—that's the dream right there.

RLG: In terms of research, what do you imagine the possibilities are for using these texts that we don't have many facts about?

GK: To me, that's part of the excitement. For example, one of the items the Princeton University Library acquired from my stock is an album of photos from a transgender woman who evidently was a sex worker in Paris, circa 1990. If we look at what we might think of as a cisheteronormative historiography, we don't necessarily know how to interact with materials of this sort. We're forced back on our own resources and what I call our "historical imagination," not that we will simply make up what happened in the past, but that we have to think much more creatively about how to interrogate these materials—how, with what we know about them and the past, we might cause them to start to speak in some way. To all appearances, the photos in the Paris album are all personal snapshots, so they represent ways that this person viewed herself and saw her own social circle. How can we see not only each individual image as an act of representation, but the gathering of

---

2. "Jiro Onuma Papers," Finding Aid, Collection Number: 2000-27 (San Francisco, California: GLBT Historical Society), https://oac.cdlib.org/findaid/ark:/13030/c8kd24vj/. [Editor's note: Digital images of the Jiro Onuma Papers can be found at the GLBT Historical Society website: https://www.glbthistory.org/jiro-onuma-papers.]

those images as forming a larger narrative or representation? Once we get good at that, we could take our thinking back to a cisheteronormative family album and start interrogating it in a more sophisticated way. Because there's so many conventional family albums available, people haven't been forced to actually look that closely; there's such a tidal wave of cisheteronormative family albums that it might not seem important to ask, "How exactly did grandma choose this group of photos?" It turns out, beginning to do this interrogation is quite intriguing and tells us about social and cultural practices that are distinctive to LGBTQI people, but also are *appropriated* by LGBTQI people. By analyzing the outcomes of that act of appropriation, we may also make what we have appropriated itself more clearly visible and comprehensible.

RLG: So, we were talking about the historical imagination; that, whatever place we're in, whatever site we're starting from, we can read into these objects, these texts. I imagine, too, there's a question here about when we invite these texts to speak in some way; it matters where we're coming from. So how do you imagine a collection at a university library—an elite, private university—shapes the way researchers are engaging and gaining access into this historical imagination?

GK: That is an excellent question. I suspect it's the case that you come with a certain privilege of interrogation and an expectation that sources will, of course, be available to you. I worry about how fragile, how scarce, how amazing it is that these materials that are there might not be visible; that the context from which they emerged—of struggle, of longing, of scarcity, of violence, of trauma—might not be as evident. As part of training young scholars to use materials like this in universities, it would be great to prompt them to ask, "Where did this come from? How was this produced? What are the obstacles that it went through before it got here?" In short, if we could pull away the veil that placement in an elite library can inexorably produce, that might help students and scholars look at these materials in a slightly different way.

RLG: Do you think that slightly different way, that different perspective, happens at something like the GLBT Historical Society?

GK: Definitely. There are distinct differences between community-based LGBTQI archives and major institutional research libraries and archives. The first is, if you go to one of the community-based archives, virtually everybody running it is a member of what anthropologists would call the source community. Most of them are doing the work out of an intense love and out of a kind of militancy. Even at a place like the Historical Society where there's salaried staff, they aren't getting paid the way people are getting paid at Harvard or Yale. Those trained professionals likely could get a job where they would earn more; part of what they're getting paid at the community-based archives is the opportunity to experience and to act on this intense love and engagement with a cause.

Another difference is, you have this immensely dynamic conversation going on between large groups of practically lost, incredibly scarce, fragmentary, complex, sometimes difficult to understand materials, and you can leap from one point to another across collections in a much richer way. As a result, you can begin to see the materials in a clearer way that you can't necessarily do at a major university library because they don't have enough collections like this. The Bois Burk Papers again offer an example: No library ever thought keeping the *Hobby Directory* was worthwhile, at any time. Even as queer archivists, we might at first glance say, "Well, it appears to be something about model railroading and carpentry." Yet it turns out to be one of the most cited publications in the holdings of the GLBT Historical Society. It has been an incredibly rich resource, yet to mainstream culture, it looked like recycling. And even to queer culture, at first blush, we couldn't see what the point of it was, but we kept it because Bois Burk kept it, and we thought, if he kept it, it must have had a queer meaning to him.

RLG: What does this tell us about the conventions that long guided the collections practices of traditional research libraries and archives?

GK: All those professional standards of what matters for libraries and of which materials have so-called patrimonial value—all those principles and practices were created in the first place to serve the interests of cisheteronormative, imperialist culture. Each and every one of them must be open to question and to being set aside at every moment in our practice as community-based archivists. And the result is that you create a critically self-interrogating archive that leads to the production of different forms of historical knowledge. Let's just say, I'm always hesitant about relying entirely on institutions of the state to preserve and reconstitute the memory of LGBTQI people. That's kind of like giving the executioner the power to decide whether to keep you on life support.

RLG: *laughs*

GK: I'm exaggerating a little, of course, but part of the job of hegemonic institutions of knowledge for the last three hundred years has been to erase us. I don't think they're going to just suddenly know how to not do that and do something that's the exact opposite. The institutional structures aren't there. Now, fortunately, because of the emergence of critical librarianship, feminism, race and ethnic studies, postcolonial studies, queer studies, and trans studies, librarians and archivists at some of the leading universities bring a quite different practice to their work. They're really strongly looking for ways to open bridges between community archival practices and the weight of traditions within their profession, and the weight of organizational and budget priorities within their institutions, to find some ways to actually queer the systems of knowledge production within their libraries. That's been really exciting to see.

RLG: Do LGBTQI community-based archives and traditional research collections such as university libraries work at cross-purposes? Are they competing at this point or complementing one another or simply not even in the same universe?

GK: One of the things I've written about in terms of community-based archives is that the ones that work well, much like the concept of being queer or the concept of being trans, read their work as a strategy, not as an expression of a fixed identity. They are working to enact a practice, not to reify an institution, and, therefore, the process is open to constant self-questioning. Not merely open to it—it *requires* constant self-questioning. So, the archival practice doesn't become conventionally professionalized, cemented, fossilized. It remains a very dynamic, open practice that invites constant critique. It's harder to do that in the setting of major institutions, where the weight of expectations is different. As a result, it's useful to have parallel tracks with richly evolved community institutions, which we make sure have the resources to continue to exist, and major traditional institutions alongside also collecting in these areas. To have those things running side by side also opens productive possibilities of dialogue and critique between the two of them.

RLG: Maybe just to circle back for a moment to this question of fetish objects, are there objects or texts that you discovered that helped you to articulate this understanding of history?

GK: Yes. Certainly, knowing Allan Bérubé in the 1980s, following his work and reading it, helped me to start to see particularly the class issue, which is present in the way that people think about their queerness, the way they position other people's queer or trans or gender positions, and that there's such a profound class structuring of those things. And, similarly, George Chauncey's *Gay New York* was one of the things that helped me understand the historical shift in links between sexual orientation and gender identify: from wolves and fairies, to trans and sissies, to the gay-straight binary.[3] Later, I benefited from reading the work of trans historians such as Susan Stryker, and queer historians of color such as Amy Sueyoshi, both of whom I've had the honor of working with at

---

3. George Chauncey, *Gay New York: Gender, Urban Culture, and the Making of the Gay Male World, 1890-1940*, 4/19/95 edition (New York: Basic Books, 1995).

the GLBT Historical Society. All of them are among the historians who helped me start thinking about how what I had seen as individual fragments of the past could be understood as operations of a system—a cultural, political, economic, historically-connected system of sexual identity, sexual subjectivity, gender identity, and forms of desire.

RLG: One of the projects where you bring together your practices as a collector, a dealer and a historian is your research on the history of LGBTQI history in the United States. What does that work suggest about the ways independent scholars and public historians bring alternative materials and alternative approaches to the production of queer historical and cultural knowledge?

GK: In doing the work on the history of LGBTQI history as a cultural practice in the United States from the late 19th century to the late 20th century, I saw the desire for history and an urge to engage in the production and diffusion and use of queer historical knowledge, but excluded from the setting of the academy—it was an alternative history, a counter history. And some of the best and most interesting LGBTQI history is still being produced in that way, in part because the lack of resources produces ingenuity. The resources that are always available to LGBTQI historians are passion and love and agency and the desire to claim a place in time and in our contemporary society. In my work on the history of queer history in the U.S., the questions I've asked and the materials I've used come out of forty years of obsessively filtering through random pieces of paper and random books and periodicals in libraries and used bookstores and garage sales and junk stores in the U.S. and in Europe, out of my love for this material. After years and years of reviewing all those documents, I began to say, "Oh, you know, I see something going on here."

And that's where we circle back to the intense value of collectors and the handful of radical LGBTQI dealers that exist in the entire world. We are out there like blue whales filtering millions of tons of krill across a career, only to come back with the five little bits of krill that are going to astound you. And then those materials are acquired by a library, where they can be used by a researcher—who may not have the possibility, the resources, or the time to engage in that process of filtering through the vast amount of potential material and beginning to spot the exceptional finds on the very edges of cultural expression in the most marginalized, random places. But it occasionally turns out that something was happening on those edges that gradually moved more towards the center of our culture—and we're going to find the traces of that movement way off in little bits and pieces that were never kept by anybody except a few obsessed LGBTQI collectors. The transgender movement is one great example of this process.

RLG: I love this metaphor of the blue whale. And I'm thinking, too, how fascinated I am by the different frequencies that this handful of collectors must be attuned to, both to what else the handful of y'all are doing but also to what possibilities the archive offers us. And thinking back for a moment to this question of counter history, I'm reminded of a student I have this semester who wrote a response about reading the first trans memoir they ever read early in their college career, and their response was, "I'm not the only transsexual in the world anymore." It was just so poignant and beautiful, and I'm thinking about the possibilities of not only counter histories, but counterfactuals. So, my last question for you is: What archives do you want to see in the world? What queer archives do you want to see in the world?

GK: I'm not terribly interested in classic hero history, the major cultural contributors. Those are people who, in some ways, refine and distill into a clearer form a process that other people are creating in little daily acts and in lifelong struggles. Great art and important culture emerge from that ferment and that cauldron, and I'm more interested in actually looking in the cooking pot instead of seeing the meal that was finished and served up by the Nobel-Prize-winning whoever. I want to go back and look at how the materials came together and how people were accidentally poisoned or found out, "Oh, that one tastes good."

And then how do they decide what matters? What are they going to hold onto? I've been lucky as a community archivist, as a collector, as a dealer, to help settle the estates of numerous LGBTQI elders since the early 1980s. Of course, it's a touching moment and a moment of grief if you knew the person well, but you also get to see what's there once they're gone. What did they keep? What objects, documents, photographs? There's this physical performance of a life in people's personal spaces and personal papers: they create their own portrait, even if unintentionally, by what they leave behind. And of course, given my practice, the thing I most want to buy at an estate sale is something they'll practically pay me to take. Why, *yes*, I want those four boxes of business records, papers and photo albums and journals that were of no interest to anyone else at the sale.

So, the archives I dream of the most are like that little album of transgender sex worker snapshots. When I saw that, I said, "Holy Grail." This is what we're looking for. I can't imagine how this kind of object survives. I know that they must have existed, but they never find their way from the disruptions of life or from the finality of death into the hands of scholars. Instead, such materials often go to the recycling. They don't have any value in the eyes of most people. That little album was meaningful as a souvenir to the person who owned it, and when they're gone, it becomes valueless—unless a collector or dealer happens along who recognizes that it has invaluable stories to tell.

That's one reason I love doing work on trans archives and gender-nonconforming materials, because it turns out there's a vastly rich history there that hasn't been gathered. For instance, a French book from 1952 that I bought at a vintage paper fair in Paris—*Carole, l'androgyne* by the pseudonymous Peter Habenson—turns out to be a previously unnoticed porn novel about an intersex person.[4] It's one of only two recorded copies; the other is in the Bibliothèque Nationale de France. And it's positive: the intersex character is the protagonist in the novel. Her body

---

4. Peter Habenson, *Carole l'androgyne* (Yorkshire: n.pub, 1952).

is taken as the norm for her. And her sexual partners, discovering how her body differs from their expectations, are briefly baffled and then say, "Oh, well, this is cool." How come no one's ever heard of this extraordinary text? How can it have previously left no trace? *That's* what I'm looking for. So, it isn't always ephemera or manuscript material; even a published book from the 1950s can be a surprisingly scarce and as-yet unspotted source for LGBTQI history.

RLG: Have you read the essay by Katherine Schultz—it was printed in *The New Yorker* in 2017— "When Things Go Missing"?[5]

GK: I don't think I have.

RLG: It's a really pretty essay. I think about the last line a lot; it's about loss, and sort of the movement of missingness from objects like keys of one's father. The last line is, "We are here to keep watch, not to keep."[6] I really like that, and I think that the only place that seems inaccurate to me is when thinking about the archive, in which we are here both to keep watch and to keep. It sounds like you're describing this ethics of both witnessing and preservation.

GK: Yes. I scout, observe, and acquire LGBTQI materials as a witness, but I'm also engaged in a cultural, militant act of saying, "I want the future to know about this and to know things about it that I can't even yet know." And so that is keeping watch—keeping watch over the dead because, in many ways, they have many more things to tell us. And keeping watch over ourselves! We have a responsibility to the future to leave a trace, to send along the record of our own LGBTQI lives and our own queer world, as well.

---

5. Kathryn Schulz, "When Things Go Missing," *The New Yorker*, February 5, 2017, http://www.newyorker.com/magazine/2017/02/13/when-things-go-missing.

6. Ibid.

Reflection

To the Queer Archivist Who Knew Me Well Before We Met

We've never met in person and yet you know some of the most private details of my life: what I look for in the archive; the texts that excite me; the pitch I'm tuned to, like a little radio, buzzing as I search for histories of queer and trans life.

I remember the first time I looked for queerness in the archive; I found myself holding a handwritten letter that Joe Brainard wrote to Ted Berrigan. I was so nervous that I'd crease a page, my hands shook. *Unbelievable*, I thought, to be touching these same pages Brainard wrote, to feel the soft indentations his writing left on the page, to feel where his hand must have so gently pressed down onto paper across the queer temporalities of our lives. Since that day in the archives, I've been obsessed—I don't know that I can call it anything else—with queer archives. To go into the archive is to experience a past that is not my own, that exceeds me, but that forged the conditions of possibility for my life. On a grander level, it is, as well, to proffer new—at least to those of us digging in the archive—ways to live in the future. Less grandly, though no less importantly, to spend time in the queer archive is to unknow. I unknow everything I thought I knew about queer and trans life; I unknow what queer means as an identity; I unknow the structures of the archive, the kinds of promises it holds out, and the modes of engagement it enables. In the archive, I am forever a student; in the archive, I am interpellated by the dual etymologies of the term archive: *Arkē*, signifying both *commandment* and *commencement*.

But before I found Brainard's letter, there was you, a graduate student at Stanford, a volunteer archivist growing the collection on the history of LGBTQ people at Stanford from a single folder with some thirty documents to *thirty-five linear feet* of archival material. *An act of faith* for you and your co-archivists. How could you have known whether there would be people—scholars, researchers, teachers, curious learners—in the future who might use that material someday? Laboring to collect the material remains of historical lives, to save and preserve them in hopes that in some unknown future someone else will seek them out, open to learning something they could not have imagined—it is an act of faith.

It's an act of faith, it's an act of love, and it's an act of militancy. Archives don't exist independent of the institutions that keep them. You've done trailblazing work in both community archives and university archives. Most of my own research has happened at university archives. Engaging with queer texts in a university archive—especially universities like Harvard, and Princeton, and Cornell, and Yale—is vexing. Sitting in the comfortable, well-lit, pristine reading rooms, I'm far removed from the lives I read about and attempt to reconstruct: formerly incarcerated drag queens in San Quentin; trans sex workers in New York; hack writers trying to string paychecks together by writing queer sleaze in Times Square. *Try to remember, I remind myself, that these lives were not lived on the manicured university campus. Try to remember the context for these lives—and how these texts ended up at Harvard, at Princeton.* The archive, especially the elite university archive, registers this paradox: against all odds these materials have made it to these neat, climate-controlled, safe, ordered, exclusive shelves. This is not, of course, always, or even often, the condition of their production, their distribution, their precarious material lives. What struggle, what scarcity, what silent routes brought them here? How do I incite them to speak to me in some way from within a context they were never meant to speak from? How do I best listen to these texts and let them guide me, fighting my perhaps baser impulse to make them speak?

You build archives out of love: out of love for a cause, and love for histories. That's clear to me when we speak. What also becomes clear, over the course of our conversation: how important you've been to my own archival practice, how you shaped it decades before I knew you. More accurately: when I think of any encounter I've had in the archive, it's hard, now, not to imagine you there, facilitating that encounter, as if introducing me to an old friend of yours. Joe Brainard. Star Distributors. Pauli Murray. Finocchio's. When we speak, it is easy to be swept up in the love you have for these stories and to remember the importance of sharing them, of opening archives to communities and students and queers who aren't yet alive, who haven't yet learned the meanings of queer. And you remind me, too, how, like any practice, like any discipline, there is a militancy involved. In fact, you frame your investment in this work as militancy. This surprises me: the archive is one space that feels so denuded of politics: so quiet you can hear pages turn and nothing else; all of us in the reading room work at our own desks, tiny monastic cells, scribes laboring with the most intense of efforts not to crease a page or leave a file in disarray.

But *militancy*, you're right: fighting against time, fighting against the institutional forces that erased, erase, and would erase trans and queer archives. Not engaged in warfare but engaged otherwise: in uncovering and discovering those lives we cannot name, cannot share, cannot inhabit, but must remember and learn from. To militate for them—this is the promise of the queer archives you've built.

Bibliography

"Bois Burk Papers." Finding Aid. Collection Number: 1989-07. San Francisco, California: GLBT Historical Society. https://oac.cdlib.org/findaid/ark:/13030/c8bv7h6s/admin/#prefercite.

Chauncey, George. *Gay New York: Gender, Urban Culture, and the Making of the Gay Male World, 1890-1940*. 4/19/95 edition. New York: Basic Books, 1995.

Habenson, Peter. *Carole l'androgyne*. Yorkshire: n.pub, 1952.

"Jiro Onuma Papers." Finding Aid. Collection Number: 2000-27. San Francisco, California: GLBT Historical Society. https://oac.cdlib.org/findaid/ark:/13030/c8kd24vj/.

Schulz, Kathryn. "When Things Go Missing." *The New Yorker*, February 5, 2017. http://www.newyorker.com/magazine/2017/02/13/when-things-go-missing.

Lessons for Archival Practice from Queer Resistance: Care, Intimacy, and Slowness

Jehan L Roberson and Shannon O'Neill

Keywords
Care work, language, memory, slowness, anti-capitalism, horizontality

Jehan L. Roberson is a writer, educator, and text-based artist. She has worked in archives and cultural sites such as the Hemispheric Institute of Performance and Politics, the National Civil Rights Museum and the Center for Southern Folklore. Jehan is a PhD student in the department of Literatures in English at Cornell University, and her writing has been published in *Public Books*, *Women & Performance*, and *Apogee*, among others.

Shannon O'Neill is the Curator for the Tamiment-Wagner Collections at NYU Special Collections, a department within NYU Libraries. She joined NYU in August of 2019. Prior to NYU, she worked at the Barnard College Archives and Special Collections as its Director, and the Los Angeles Public Library and Atlantic City Free Public Library. She is currently a graduate student in NYU's Archives and Public History program, working towards a master's in public history.

Conversation

Jehan Roberson: I'm excited to be here with you and to have yet another amazing and inspiring conversation. I always feel like I walk away from our conversations so energized.

Shannon O'Neill: When we get off a call with one another, I want to spend the rest of the day journaling.

JR: I guess I should say that I'm currently a PhD student in Cornell's Literatures in English department where I'm continuing to theorize and work in archives. But we met when I was the Collections Specialist for the Hemispheric Institute Digital Video Library (HIDVL),[7] where I managed a digital repository of performance practices in the Americas. HIDVL is a post-custodial repository of performance, as well as scholarship and activism about/around performance, such as social acts, demonstrations, teach-ins, and performance art in the Americas.

So within this framework, I found it really powerful to think of how to make archival processes as accessible and horizontal as possible. And this is in line with our shared dedication to thinking critically and carefully about access, and to doing the least amount of harm possible.

SO: To introduce myself, I'm the curator for the Tamiment-Wagner collections, a repository within NYU Special Collections, which documents social movements, political and radical left politics, labor, and histories of immigration and migration.

I keep thinking about the first meeting we had together. In that conversation we talked about how we bring our full selves and our politics to our work. We started asking: how do we do justice to, and with, an archive such as Hemi's—an archive that documents people, ways of being, and ways of thinking that have been systemically stigmatized

---

7. Hemispheric Institute, Hemispheric Institute Digital Video Library, accessed June 12, 2021, https://hemisphericinstitute.org/en/hidvl.html.

and erased—within an institution that is complicit in those harms? We asked: what does care work look like in archives—particularly when we're working in institutions that have enacted violence on communities?

JR: You said something in one of our conversations about Saidiya Hartman's quote, "care is the antidote to violence."[8] Could you elaborate on that?

SO: This idea that care is an antidote to violence offers us a way to disrupt institutional harm. Care is a liberatory tactic for shaping another world, freeing us of the harmful structures of the world we currently inhabit. If care is a way to counteract archival violence, we can conceive of care as a form of resistance.

JR: For me, the creation of the Collections Specialist position was great because it was a recognition that subject specialty was needed. I nonetheless felt really uncomfortable when I initially stepped into the role, because I didn't want to presume any sort of ultimate authority over people's materials. What became a really organic and beautiful part of that work was having regular conversations with the artists about their needs around the materials, what they needed to feel safe, and to feel as though their works were being accurately represented and contextualized within the archive. A huge benefit of this model was that we could establish a horizontality where artists were offered the opportunity to co-write intellectual descriptions. There are some who didn't have the capacity, but for others it was a major compelling factor in working with us. They wanted to make sure there was attention to the process of stewardship.

SO: What you're saying brings to the fore that archival work has been figured as transactional, but what it should be is relational. I like that you

---

8. Saidiya Hartman, "In the Wake: A Salon in Honor of Christina Sharpe," Barnard Center for Research on Women, Barnard College, New York, NY, February 2, 2017.

use the word conversation. Conversation, when it is authentic, involves active, deep listening. What I value about your work is that you work relationally. You ask your community partners: "What are your needs? How do we support your needs?"

In conversation, listening is a mode of relationality. Listening is not a passive activity; it's not merely receiving someone else's words. It's about holding and making space. In this way, it is a form of care work. Care work is central to queer embodiment and queer politics. Something that I learned from queer community is that there is power in our mutual care and interdependence. No institution is going to save us. No government is going to save us. We have to take care of one another. This approach is a foundation for the work of the HIDVL.

JR: For sure. I think it's both a queer principle and approach, and also for the queer folks who entrusted their materials to us. Care is a foundational understanding that grounds the work we do and the communities we try to support through archival work.

SO: Community needs change over time. We've talked about how archival relationships are bureaucratically formalized by an institution through paperwork and how institutions describe and name communities with metadata that is often built upon harmful descriptive practices.

JR: That's totally true. What you said about the needs changing is a really important point and I think it's an institutional difficulty we've both encountered. There's a necessary reflexivity that needs to be built into the archival process. I've had to push for it in different ways: a name change or a pronoun change. Sometimes there are people who are fine with multiple names appearing in searches for their work, but for others that's really violent.

There have also been moments where especially provocative performances create issues for the artists, like when they're job searching. Multiple artists have said, "I can't have that show up when someone Googles me. I need that taken down." I think, in a more traditional setting, removing items from the archive wouldn't always have been possible. That's part of that linear transactional model—once you turn materials over to the archive or the institution, you cease to have control. But I think part of what the ethos is that we're discussing is a sense of community responsibility. It's caring for people and their needs. It would be counterintuitive to all of our principles to ignore or not value the people whose works comprise our collections.

SO: It's an intimate conversation. Someone is trusting you with their life, saying, "This is my name, and this is how I want and need to be identified and represented." This makes me think about our conversation around archival intimacies and how queerness is also about intimacy and closeness. I feel this especially now. Our lives have been drastically changed by this pandemic. The world doesn't want us to be able to rely on one another or to have that immediacy with one another; when we can be intimate, or very real, with one another, we build power together.

JR: Yah!

SO: Being queer has made me so much more ready to be intimate. It's interesting to see the way that gets translated into my work.

JR: I agree. I think especially because I came out as queer while I was working at Hemi, my queerness bore a lot of additional intimacy and aligned with so much of the work I was doing. And so many of the artists who are represented in the collection are queer. The intimacy fostered there was so important to me, and being able to stand tall within my newly articulated queerness.

SO: Yeah, that's so profound! I came out while working at Barnard. Something cracked open inside me in a beautiful way. It changed how I approach my work. When I applied for the job at NYU, I talked about representation, positionality, myself as a white queer woman, and what that would mean in the role of curator. It was the first time that I had ever identified myself in a job interview as a queer person, and it felt empowering to say that aloud.

JR: So powerful! You're reminding me of that feeling of naming yourself and having that act affirmed. I think you're also articulating the inherently vulnerable position that naming puts us in. It undoes a sort of hierarchy or depersonalization of the "I am a representative of the institution" model and reminds everyone that there's a human here who is also sharing and giving of themselves in this work.

I have a recent, tender memory of when some queer Brazilian artists were in residence at Hemi and my boss, who is also gay, suggested we go to Stonewall. From there we did an impromptu walking tour of queer history in the Village. It was just so amazing, and a beautiful moment of community building. I think part of what's articulated in all of this is a necessary slowness and a necessary investment in building community. It's that investment and everything that blossoms from it that's so magical and transformative.

SO: Let's discuss slowness as a form of queer resistance.[9] In *Emergent Strategy: Shaping Change, Changing Worlds*, adrienne maree brown writes that a tenet of emergent strategy is moving at the speed of trust—trust is not something that is a given.[10] It's earned. When I think of slowness, the first thing that comes to my mind is honey.[11] Slowness is a refusal of capitalist constructs of time. Under capitalism our time has become another form of exchange; we are told to think about our time as a

---

9. Kemi Adeyemi, "The Practice of Slowness: Black Queer Women and the Right to the City," *The Journal of Lesbian and Gay Studies* 25, no 4 (2019): 545–567. For more on slowness in archival work see the work of Kimberly Christen and Jane Anderson in "Toward Slow Archives," *Archival Science* 19 (2019): 87–116 and the work of Chaitra Powell in "This [Black] Woman's Work: Exploring Archival Projects That Embrace the Identity of the Memory Worker," *KULA: Knowledge Creation, Dissemination, and Preservation Studies* 2, no 1 (2018):5.

10. adrienne maree brown, *Emergent Strategy: Shaping Change, Changing Worlds*, (Chico, CA: AK Press, 2017), 42.

11. In this evocation of honey, the authors paused to discuss the work of author, poet, and performance artist Karen Finley in her 2001 piece, "Shut Up and Love Me."

form of currency. I'm suspicious of speed and urgency. They're almost always a byproduct of white supremacy and capitalism, which are two extreme forms of violence that academic institutions enact.

JR: I think slowness is also deeply queer. I also think it's cultural and racialized in certain ways. There are queer and also queer-of-color temporalities, in addition to diasporic temporalities. Which is to say, it's important to try not to impose a US-centric/capitalist construct of time on the work we're doing and, whenever possible, just allow things to develop.

For me, this also means pushing back on those top-down demands for results. I don't want to prioritize a product or end result over everything else, because everything doesn't have to move towards a certain end.

SO: Institutions expect that there's a terminal point or a product rather than something that is ongoing and generative. When I think of a relationship with a predefined endpoint, as opposed to a relationship that doesn't operate on a fixed timeline, I think about the difference between a book that can be closed rather than a story that can unspool. Institutions are fearful of "unspooling" or "messiness." We've talked about queerness as messiness and the importance of this. Resisting tidiness is a means to push against the fixedness of archival work.

JR: Yes! I often think of "resisting tidiness" as a concept informing both methodology and theory, especially around how we can try to create anticolonial archives. I remember us previously talking about that Katie Rawson and Trevor Muñoz article, "Against Cleaning," and extending their argument to the debates around the term "queer." It's not a universally accepted identification marker for everyone who might fall under that umbrella. And that's okay! It leads to some tense and uncomfortable conversations, but I think part of that is also resisting fixedness, and pushing back against a sort of tidiness that discourages being able to sit with, and in, discomfort. It's the need for the reflexiveness that we were talking about earlier.

We've seen this year how institutions have all of a sudden rushed to have Black Lives Matter posts everywhere. I've been (kind of) shocked to see institutions that are actively profiting from violence against Black people post a hashtag and do nothing to address their actual practices—hiring practices, salary discrepancies—that might actually support and foster Black life.

I think that's part of what Rawson and Muñoz talk about, like, let's not wash everything away and get rid of these problematic histories; let's dive into the messiness. And hopefully we can emerge from that with greater understanding.

SO: I'm also thinking about the ways that queerness resists categorization. Queerness doesn't want to be put in a box, and the image that an archives often conjures is literally "things in boxes."

Reflecting on your point about institutional responses to Black Lives Matter, the hollowness of those responses is irresponsible because it's not tied to any real change. Care work and queer resistance both have accountability at their centers. An institution won't hold itself accountable; we, through our work, have to push for that.

JR: I completely agree. I think part of that push-back looks like not prioritizing quantity and amassing things, that sort of consumer-capitalist model of how institutions further themselves.

Part of what I'm thinking about with accountability is that doing less increases your capacity to be accountable, because you are more available to the people that you're partnering with.

I was just talking about this in relation to novelty in one of my classes. It's a very neoliberal Western, white supremacist construct that novelty is always what's needed, and one of the most important factors in being able to lay claim to something is being the first, or at the forefront of the new. In that class we were reading José Muñoz's *Cruising Utopia*, an amazing work by a queer ancestor who, in the introduction, explicitly says utopia is not a new concept, and I'm not claiming that it is.[12]

It made me think of how the desire for novelty often leads to a lot of erasure and violence. Audre Lorde says this, too—there are no new ideas, just new ways of articulating old ideas. If institutions were to divest from that model, then archival practices would no longer mirror capitalist, imperialist spread. We can talk about this especially within universities. The "global university," I think, is a phrase we're both familiar with. One remedy is to be a lot less diffuse and to seek much more depth, which I think is a concept in *Emergent Strategy*.

SO: "The small is all," right?[13]

JR: Yeah!

SO: "Newness" troubles me because it presumes that people, places, and geographies haven't always been there all along.[14] It's a colonial attitude. Similarly, institutional insistence upon ownership is troubling, especially if we consider that archives are very much alive, that they are someone's life. That an institution says it can lay claim over someone's life is a violent assertion.

JR: Right, and I think that also guides the ways in which archives and institutions try to ascribe meaning and value within archives, as opposed to communal, creator, or donor standards of what's meaningful and what needs to be included.

---

12. José Esteban Muñoz, *Cruising Utopia: The Then and There of Queer Futurity*, (New York: NYU Press, 2009).

13. brown, *Emergent Strategy*, 41.

14. Yusef Omowale, "We Already Are," *Medium*, September 3, 2018, https://medium.com/community-archives/we-already-are-52438b863e31.

That search for newness and "cornering the market" guides how the archive is framed and how value is described in institutional frameworks. And for whom. Because it's never for the people who are actually creating the work. It's for some other audience that usually replicates all of the systems of white supremacy and capitalism that we know.

SO: Reflecting on the capitalist impulses in our profession, the terms we use, like "acquisition," are often economic in nature. I've been playing with other phrasing. For example, in place of "acquisition," I've been trying out "transfer of materials." I hope that what it communicates is that the power or choice rests in the creator, or the donor. This is in opposition to the term "acquisition," which implies taking or buying, where the power or the action rests on the part of the institution. I'm still wrestling with the correct language to use. It's not quite right just yet, but I'm thinking about the impact of my words, and I am attempting to refuse transactional language.

JR: Yeah, that makes sense. That's an ongoing practice, thinking through the vocabulary we have and issues of language. Naming, and what you're talking about—not using transactional language—makes a big difference in how we can approach archival practices.

This topic makes me think about the HIDVL process. Once I was working on a collection, I would collect the artists' materials and then I would do some unofficial cataloging for the official cataloger to finalize. Cataloging was the bulk of my work, and that resulted in many detailed conversations where I had to push for a lot of localized terms. The language that is available is so troubling, in part because we are still reliant on the Library of Congress for subject headings, which we know is a deeply problematic relationship. There's a real need for new languages, from micro to macro, or from the transfer of materials to generating the descriptions.

SO: On the topic of language, we talked before about the tension that institutions produce around requiring formal agreements with donors and creators. Deeds of gift or letters of agreement are legal documents. They're contracts that express a difference in power. This is a relationship we need to unpack as archivists, especially when we are working with communities. The act of codifying a relationship through these documents is often about protecting the institution. Can we infuse care into these practices? I'm not entirely sure. One practice we can make more routine is ensuring that letters of agreement are documents of mutual creation, inviting the signer to inscribe their needs and to make revisions to the language that is used. Archivists should position themselves as advocates for donors or creators and ensure that their needs are met and can be upheld by the institution. I am still grappling with this issue. I understand the necessity of having a record of how materials have moved through space and time, and yet I feel a lot of resistance to the ways in which deeds are about institutional control. A second approach is to take up post-custodial models[15] where individuals or communities retain power over their materials and then they share with an institution what they want the institution to access.

JR: Yeah, absolutely. My archive experience has primarily been with community archives, in the sense that the community informed how they were run.

I think part of what I appreciated, and what I hope is possible within post-custodial models, is a de-centering of permanence. This gets into what you were just talking about with institutions: on the one hand, there's the baseline necessity of "this is what has been agreed upon by all parties." That, I'm fine with. But I think there are other instances where permanence and the issue of liability factor in, which is so much of what the institution is wary of. This goes back to what you were

---

15. T-Kay Sangwand, "Decolonizing Archival Practice and Diversifying the Historical Record Through Post-Custodial Human Rights Archiving," talk delivered at Digital Humanities Forum 2015: Peripheries, Barriers & Hierarchies, University of Kansas, September 25th, 2015: https://idrh.ku.edu/dhforum2015. See also: T-Kay Sangwand, "Preservation Is Political: Enacting Contributive Justice and Decolonizing Transnational Archival Collaborations," *KULA: Knowledge Creation, Dissemination, and Preservation Studies* 2, no 1 (2018): 10.

saying about accountability. How does permanence stand counter to accountability to the people and the communities we're working with?

I'm getting at permanence because so much of the issue of liability is to be infallible and because sometimes, accountability means things need to be dissolved. People may need to resign. Permanence can become really pernicious and it just presumes that institutions need to exist in perpetuity. This is part of the resistance to fixedness because the institution could exist in some other iteration that looks wildly different from how it looks right now.

For me, the issue of liability brings up issues of accountability, and what true accountability requires.

SO: Liability is a way for the institution to position itself as infallible. I see liability as something different from accountability. Pushing institutions towards accountability throws them into a state of existential crisis. Institutions don't want to be self-reflective. This spurning of self-reflection is a way of eliding or deflecting accountability. There's something about queerness that invites self-reflection. It makes me want to be accountable to the world that I'm moving through.

JR: I completely agree. When institutions so fervently resist the work of reflexiveness, it just begs the question of why. Obviously, there are ways to take up even just a couple of the things that we've been discussing here, but I think it runs counter to White supremacist, capitalist logic.

I'm thinking about institutional entanglements with queerness in part because academia is unique—there are a lot of queerdos running around here. The pull of educational spaces in particular, and places in which we are exposed to writings and resources and histories that are otherwise intentionally kept away from us and away from non-academic spaces; it's not coincidental that a lot of us gravitate towards these spaces. I think educational institutions have a particular responsibility because so many of us queer folks and other vulnerable populations gravitate towards these spaces; because this is where we're able to access more information and to learn about ourselves and to be able to fully articulate those selves.

SO: One way I attempt to address my complicity of working for a "global," imperialist institution is by understanding that part of my role is to make sure institutional resources are redistributed. I feel a responsibility to extract what I can from the institution. A form of institutional extraction is pushing for slowness. The institution sees my time as its time. I get paid for a certain number of hours to work here, so using those hours to move in relation with communities is important to me as one small form of queer resistance. We can invite others to join us in this. Our reclamation of time then becomes a communal act.

JR: Right. For better or worse, so much of the lesson this year has been is that so much more is possible than what we thought. 2020 has been a year of massive devastation in so many ways but, also, slowness has been central. It's not always easy. What slowness continues to require is to really stay in touch with myself and stay honest with myself about my capacities.

I feel like that has been coming up a lot for me within archival and memory work, but also within all of the different types of intimacies and spaces we hold. I'm meditating a lot on what slowness looks like, professionally and in my relationships. With slowness comes a tenderness. I think it was because you introduced me to the term memory workers. I love it so much! There's something that's so much more tender about memory work than terms like archive or repository.

SO: In spite of all of the critiques that we've made, I'm leaving our conversation thinking about the ways in which we found one another through our workspace. It's important to find those spaces of tenderness or friendship or intimacies. It's another way of countering the harm of an institution.

Reflection

Shannon Reflection:
We recorded our conversation in September 2020 following a long summer of protest and pandemic. That summer, Jehan and I met virtually several times, having not seen one another in person since we shifted to remote employment the previous spring. Occasionally, we spoke about the forthcoming *Grabbing Tea* project, but mostly we offered support and kinship. Although we prepared a loose outline to guide ourselves while recording, we allowed our thoughts to unfold and expand in real time. When we reconvened in May 2021 to begin edits on our piece, we decided to read our words aloud to one another. It felt funny at first, to be transported in time by way of phrases I had pronounced seven months earlier while conversing with Jehan through a screen. Going back in time is perhaps the last thing I want these days, but this reenactment did not relay the anxieties, grief, or fears of the previous months. It was sweet to time travel with Jehan, to have the chance to relive the unfolding of our friendship, and to reflect on everything I learned with and from her in the last year. It felt vulnerable, reading through my "umms" and the points where I lacked clarity. At the same time, I felt safe doing so with Jehan. Our side-by-side reading spoke to our process, our collaboration, and our shared queer identities: it was open, horizontal, mutual. And joyful. More than once, we cackled. What did I mean when I said that in September? It didn't matter; we would figure it out together. Perhaps this is what drew us both to the project in the first place: *Grabbing Tea*, as a site and space of dialogue, is about the undoing of hierarchies.

In our conversation, we focus quite a bit on language and the act of listening. Both are important to the ways being queer shows up in our roles as archivists. Though archives, or perhaps because archives, are built upon the foundations of capitalist, carceral, white supremacist, hetero-patriarchy, they invite queer defiance. Archives demand rigidity, transaction, compliance. Queerness, as we discuss in our piece, rejects categorization. Queer is abundance.[16] Queer is interdependence. Queer is refusal.[17] Queer is messy. Queer is entangled.[18] Queer stretches and bends. Queer flows and unravels. Queer is the cultivation of pleasure.[19] Queer is world building. Queer is capacious and generous. In these ways, Queer is resistance. Centuries of Queer resistance have demonstrated the power of care work, closeness, and intentionality. Queer resistance centers these as values, practices, and tools for survival, and Jehan and I discuss how these queer strategies of care, intimacy, and slowness can be adopted in archives. Through refusing the order or demands of the archive as they currently operate, through practicing a relational modality of queer resistance, we can constitute a more liberatory archival practice.

Jehan Reflection:
I'm so thankful for this opportunity to reflect on our methodologies, to be able to remind readers and also ourselves that there are people attached to the preservation and production of memory. I'm just as intrigued by the materiality of archives as I am by how archive practitioners come to the work. And across queer materials, queer praxis, and queer practitioners, healing echoes as our most powerful driving force and methodology. For me, queer healing is Black liberation, and Black liberation is queer healing. To be a memory worker in this sense is to attend to the traces of those histories in the present, and to affirm Black and queer living.

---

16. Anjali Arondekar, "Abundance: On Sexuality and Historiography," paper presented at Stanford Humanities Center Feminist and Queer Colloquium, February 3, 2020.

17. Tourmaline, "Refusal, Resistance, Existence: Trans Feminisms, Always Already," Institute for Diversity in the Arts, Black Community Services Center, Stanford University, YouTube video, https://www.youtube.com/watch?v=jRk1CeV_Vio. See also: Heather Love, "Queer Critique, Queer Refusal," *Radical Philosophy Review* 16, no. 2 (2019): 443-457.

18. Tourmaline and Sasha Wortzel, Interview, Artforum, video, 00:05:53, accessed June 10, 2021, https://www.artforum.com/interviews/reina-gossett-and-sasha-wortzel-talk-about-their-film-happy-birthday-marsha-74735.

19. adrienne maree brown, *Pleasure Activism: The Politics of Feeling Good* (Chico, CA: AK Press, 2019).

One of the most beautiful experiences of revisiting this conversation has been meditating on the repeatedly emphasized need for new languages/articulations. After the year we've all experienced, and the losses we've all endured, the urgency with which our culture is moving towards liberatory learning is truly a summons for us as memory workers to help reveal the past's imprint on the present.

In so many ways, these new articulations expanding our ways of knowing and being have been decidedly queer undertakings. I believe this is integral to how we come to express ourselves, how we continuously strive for queer living outside of the normative roles prescribed to our bodies and our desires. I think of this as recognition, as trace knowledge of what Ashon Crawley terms "the irreducibility of otherwise possibilities."[20]

So much of this I've learned from witnessing, which often looks like me standing agape and in awe of my colleague and dear friend Shannon. Learning from and being in dialogue with her has so deeply informed my understanding of what archives and archivists can do. Shannon has helped me recognize how profoundly I have been shaped by the archive, and she's inspired me to write towards illuminating the importance of memory work, a term I didn't know before we began conspiring together.

I think of my initial trepidation around entering the archive as both a practitioner and a theorist, not yet realizing that to be a practitioner is to theorize, and to theorize is to practice. As queer folks, I see and feel this dynamic in the ways that we articulate ourselves, in how we enact strategies of care, not as abstract strivings but as guiding principles for fostering queer community. Shannon and I had no idea what would occur in the world when we first set out to participate in this project, and yet the multiple pandemics have made it clear how memory work is at once evergreen and incredibly timely. Inherent to the field are the tasks we addressed in our conversation—the questioning, the critique, and the necessity of intimacy and vulnerability. It's as liberating as it is

---

20. Ashon Crawley, *A Blackpentecostal Breath: The Aesthetics of Possibility* (New York: Fordham University Press, 2016), 32.

unnerving to lean into these "otherwise possibilities" in the archive; still, the feelings of pride, joy, kinship, and hope that this archival document offers me form that most transcendent experience of seeing and being seen. It's a recognition that's distinctively queer, distinctively archival, and absolutely possible.

Bibliography

Adeyemi, Kemi. "The Practice of Slowness: Black Queer Women and the Right to the City." *The Journal of Lesbian and Gay Studies* 25, no 4 (2019): 545–567.

Arondekar, Anjali. "Abundance: On Sexuality and Historiography." Paper presented at Stanford Humanities Center Feminist and Queer Colloquium. February 3, 2020.

brown, adrienne maree. *Emergent Strategy: Shaping Change, Changing Worlds*. Chico, CA: AK Press, 2017

brown, adrienne maree. *Pleasure Activism: The Politics of Feeling Good*. Chico, CA: AK Press, 2019.

Christen, Kimberley and Jane Anderson. "Toward Slow Archives." *Archival Science* 19 (2019): 87–116.

Crawley, Ashon. *A Blackpentecostal Breath: The Aesthetics of Possibility*. New York: Fordham University Press, 2016.

Finley, Karen. "Shut Up and Love Me." May, 2001. Performance Art. *Performance Space* 122, New York, NY.

Hartman, Saidiya. "In the Wake: A Salon in Honor of Christina Sharpe." Barnard Center for Research on Women, Barnard College, New York, NY, February 2, 2017.

Hemispheric Institute. Hemispheric Institute Digital Video Library. Accessed June 12, 2021. https://hemisphericinstitute.org/en/hidvl.html.

Love, Heather. "Queer Critique, Queer Refusal." *Radical Philosophy Review*. 16, no. 2 (2019): 443-457.

Muñoz, José Esteban. *Cruising Utopia: The Then and There of Queer Futurity*. New York: NYU Press, 2009.

Omowale, Yusef. "We Already Are." *Medium*. September 3, 2018. https://medium.com/community-archives/we-already-are-52438b863e31.

Powell, Chaitra, Holly Smith, Shanee' Murrain, and Skyla Hearn. "This [Black] Woman's Work: Exploring Archival Projects That Embrace the Identity of the Memory Worker." KULA: Knowledge Creation, Dissemination, and Preservation Studies, 2, no 1 (2018): 5.

Rawson, Katie and Trevor Muñoz. "Against Cleaning." Curating Menus, July 7, 2016, http://www.curatingmenus.org/articles/against-cleaning/.

Sangwand, T-Kay. "Decolonizing Archival Practice and Diversifying the Historical Record Through Post-Custodial Human Rights Archiving." Talk delivered at Digital Humanities Forum 2015: Peripheries, Barriers & Hierarchies, University of Kansas. September 25th, 2015. https://idrh.ku.edu/dhforum2015.

Sangwand, T-Kay. "Preservation Is Political: Enacting Contributive Justice and Decolonizing Transnational Archival Collaborations." *KULA: Knowledge Creation, Dissemination, and Preservation Studies*. 2, no 1 (2018): 10.

Tourmaline. "Refusal, Resistance, Existence: Trans Feminisms, Always Already." Institute for Diversity in the Arts, Black Community Services Center, Stanford University. YouTube video. https://www.youtube.com/watch?v=jRk1CeV_Vio.

Tourmaline and Sasha Wortzel. Interview. *Artforum*. Video, 00:05:53. Accessed June 10, 2021. https://www.artforum.com/interviews/reina-gossett-and-sasha-wortzel-talk-about-their-film-happy-birthday-marsha-74735.

Queer Tinge: Adjusting Archival Practice to Meet the Needs of Rural Communities

Emma Curtis and Nicole Martin

Keywords
2SLGBTQAI+, reclamation narratives, rural activism, community

Emma Curtis (she/her) is a queer femme immigrant of English ancestry. She is a project-based archivist, librarian, and cultural heritage professional with fifteen years of experience, and most at home within community-led archives, libraries, and centres of cultural heritage. Her Master of Library Science she received from Queens College, CUNY, and Bachelor of Fine Arts from Concordia University. Emma is grateful for the opportunities to have worked with and learnt from the Lesbian Herstory Archives, Taller Boricua (Puerto Rican Workshop), Simpcw First Nation in Simpcw traditional territory and others who have and continue to work in service to the reclamation of essential histories for past, current, and future generations. Her professional interests include community-based research practice(s), intercultural communication, creativity and creative practice within information service and workplace culture, and reclaiming queer femme narratives.

Nicole Martin is the associate director of media archives at Human Rights Watch and established the organization's first digital archive. Nicole formerly taught digital preservation at New York University, and worked as the archivist at Democracy Now! They are the creator of the digital preservation resource website twobitpreservation.com.

Conversation

Emma Curtis: I wanted to first acknowledge that I'm speaking from the traditional, ancestral, and unceded lands of the Musqueam, Squamish, and Tsleil-Waututh Nations in a place now known as Vancouver, British Columbia.[1]

Nicole Martin: This is a very joyful project and a pretty horrific time, and I'm curious to see how it shakes out.

Emma: It is a troubling but deeply observational time we are living through. I think about the resilience of 2SLGBTQAI plus, non-binary and gender-diverse people, especially during this time as we're cultivating our internal strengths for lots of different purposes. The consciousness raising ignited by the Black Lives Matter movement in the U.S. and Canada also raised the level of public awareness to the Indigenous lives that have been lost and taken here in British Columbia across urban and rural contexts. In the last couple of years, calls for action from the Missing and Murdered Indigenous Women and Girls movement,[2]

---

1. "The Nation Today," Squamish Nation, last accessed June 24, 2022, https://www.squamish.net/about-our-nation/; "Musqueam's Story," Musqueam: A Living Culture, last accessed May 26, 2021, https://www.musqueam.bc.ca/our-story/; "Our Story," Tsleil-Waututh Nation, last accessed May 26, 2021, https://twnation.ca/our-story/.

2. University of Winnipeg, Two-Spirited People of Manitoba, Inc., and Queer & Trans People of Colour (QTPOC), Winnipeg, "Findings of C2C: Two Spirit & Queer/Trans People of Colour. Calls to Action 2019, https://www.uwinnipeg.ca/c2c/docs/c2c_calls-to-action_final.pdf; "C2C: Two Spirit and Queer People of Colour Call to Conversation with LGBT and Allies," University of Winnipeg Archives, last modified February 19, 2019, https://www.youtube.com/playlist?list=PL6dBiXABaCmYYMuwEH6tNFSrw3xIL98nT; Uzoma Chioma, dione haynes, Myra Laramee, Albert McLeod and Raven Heavy Runner, "History, Origins, and Resurgence," (Panel session held at the C2C: Two Spirit & Queer/Trans People of Colour: A Call to Conversation

including the National Inquiry into Missing and Murdered Indigenous Women and Girls (2019)[3] and the Truth and Reconciliation Commission (2015),[4] have highlighted the potential to change how information and cultural heritage professionals respond to the needs of the broader spectrum of 2SLGBTQAI plus, non-binary, and gender diverse people and communities in rural and urban Canada.

Nicole: How does that impact our work on a day-to-day basis?

Emma: In archives, libraries, and centers of cultural heritage, we're being asked to serve the diverse publics present within the society in which we operate. The queer, trans, non-binary, gender-diverse, and Two-Spirit spectrum is expansive and diverse. By providing more access to knowledge and information resources, and public facing services that provide for that diversity, we're very much in the process of really acknowledging what that entails. How do we authentically conduct this work?

Nicole: Thinking about issues that affect 2SLGBTQAI+ people as well as other communities, but specifically queer people, like issues of

---

with LGBT Allies conference held at the University of Winnipeg, Winnipeg, Manitoba, October 20-22, 2017). Within the 2017 conference proceedings, some C2C participants criticized the manner in which Two-Spirited and Indigenous LGBTQAI+ people were included within the National Inquiry into Missing and Murdered Indigenous Women and Girls Inquiry. Records from this conference are now housed at the University of Winnipeg Archives (see Fonds 17.026 and Fonds 18.006).

3. National Inquiry into Missing and Murdered Indigenous Women and Girls, 2019, "Reclaiming Power and Place: The Final Report of the National Inquiry into Missing and Murdered Indigenous Women and Girls. Volume 1a,": 214-218. The report notes the challenges of the term Two-Spirit, even as an umbrella term used for activism and organizing, in that it "...does not necessarily reflect the diversity of ...all Indigenous 2SLGBTQQIA people [and] perpetuates the erasure of other gender identities and sexual orientations."

4. Truth and Reconciliation Commission of Canada, 2015, Truth and Reconciliation Commission of Canada: Calls to Action, https://nctr.ca/records/reports/#trc-reports; Canadian Federation of Libraries Associations, 2017, *CLFA-FACB Truth and Reconciliation Committee Report and Recommendations*, http://cfla-fcab.ca/wp-content/uploads/2017/04/Truth-and-Reconciliation-Committee-Report-and-Recommendations.pdf.

displacement, disappearance, homelessness, and violence. Violence certainly isn't unique to our community, but homelessness and the concept of home really emerge as a strong theme for us.

Emma: In a smaller community, you get to experience the realities and challenges of how information networks operate, including accessibility issues. In the North Thompson Valley, for example, which is located within Secwépemc Nation territories,[5] the power would go out if there were strong weather conditions. Multiple communities in that area would be without power and Internet access. Recently, the Greyhound bus system was drastically reduced and then completely shut down in Canada.[6] These situations affect personal and community safety, particularly for 2SLGBTQAI+ people. Challenges can include how 2SLGBTQAI+ access resources in archives, libraries, and centers of cultural heritage, and how that changes the experience of creating and accessing a safe space (or spaces) to learn about yourself, your identity, and your community (or communities).

Nicole: One of the interesting things you bring out are themes of isolation. Whether that's physical access or networking issues (that I'm sure are more extreme now than ever because we're not able to gather in public spaces), this distance impacts how folks are living and what the pandemic is like for them. Libraries and archives have been a place where folks can gather to manage isolation. I'm curious about your experience working in rural communities where an inherent isolation and distance is built into daily life. How might this relate to libraries, archives, and information exchange in rural areas? How does this impact how we gather or make queer community?

---

5. "Secwepemctsín," First People's Map of B.C., last accessed May 24, 2021, https://maps.fpcc.ca/languages/secwepemctsín.

6. Ian Austen, "When the Bus No Longer Rolls into Town," New York Times, May 14, 2021, https://www.nytimes.com/2021/05/14/world/canada/Greyhound-ends-Canada-service.html.

Emma: As a rural newcomer to the Thompson-Nicola and North Thompson region, I was curious about how people were meeting up and connecting. I had the opportunity to know some local gay and lesbian residents and organizers, and they brought my attention to the history of services for the community. A crisis line, which wasn't specifically LGBT, provided services relating to safety, health, and wellness, as well as social support.[7] Local groups, including some that have been active since the 1980s, included the Thompson Area Gays (TAG), and later on the Gay and Lesbian Association of Kamloops (GALA) and the Gay and Lesbian Association of Northern BC (GALA North).[8] When some of the legacies shared in these oral histories didn't map to the 2SLG-BTQAI+ presence in the present day, the BC Gay and Lesbian Archives [9] was very useful in fleshing out some of these survival narratives, that history of creating community. It is the story of a grassroots initiative that sought donations from the *Kamloops GALA News* readership to acquire "gay and lesbian" books in local libraries.[10] Or the transmission

---

7. Robert Jones (retired cultural professional – Western Canada Theatre, Kamloops Art Gallery), in conversation with the author, June 2014; Robert Jones (retired cultural professional – Western Canada Theatre, Kamloops Art Gallery), in conversation with the author, June 2020.

8. "Gay and Lesbian Association of Kamloops," on Gay and Lesbian Association of Kamloops' official website, accessed May 17, 2014, https://www.gaykamloops.ca/.
As of April 24, 2018, the organization's website was discontinued and a new web presence (http://galakamloops.weebly.com/) was created; *TAG [Thompson Area Gays] News*, June 1981, Periodicals, Fonds AM1675 BC Gay and Lesbian Archives, City of Vancouver Archives; *Kamloops GALA News*, February 1994, Periodicals, Fonds AM1675 BC Gay and Lesbian Archives, City of Vancouver Archives; *GALA North [Gay and Lesbian Association of Northern BC] News*, August 1994, Periodicals, Fonds AM1675 BC Gay and Lesbian Archives, City of Vancouver Archives.

9. Danielle Cooper, "Personal Touches, Public Legacies: An Ethnography of LGBT Libraries and Archives," (PhD diss., York University, 2016), 9, 12, 21, 44, 47, 52, 52-53, 67, https://yorkspace.library.yorku.ca/xmlui/handle/10315/33440; Ron Dutton (archivist, BC Gay and Lesbian Archives), in conversation with the author, Summer 2015; Jana Grazley, "BC Gay and Lesbian Archives donated to the City of Vancouver Archives!" *AuthentiCity*, May 30, 2018, https://www.vancouverarchives.ca/2018/05/30/bc-gay-and-lesbian-archives-donated-to-the-city-of-vancouver-archives/.

10. *Kamloops GALA News*, February 1994, Periodicals, Fonds AM1675 BC Gay and Lesbian Archives, City of Vancouver Archives. (See page 9 for "Money and the Book Project"); *Kamloops GALA News*, March 1994, Periodicals, Fonds AM1675 BC Gay and Lesbian Archives, City of Vancouver Archives (see page 1 for "Library books Project: February Update").

of advertisements for gay and lesbian and gay and lesbian allied groups serving different neighboring regions (i.e., Shuswap, Okanagan, Northern BC) or specific communities (i.e., First Nations and women's groups).[11] Those stories and others made me think about our collections and what stories are held within them.

Nicole: I read a book review recently about an archive in Guatemala where citizens were disappeared by the government and secret police records associated with those disappearances were made public.[12] Archivists invited members of the community, specifically families of the disappeared, to take these "cold" bureaucratic records and allow family members to review them, add information, and fill in the lines of what happened as best they could. That's an inspiring example of how archives can be repurposed or reclaimed by members of the community. This reminds me of a larger question of how we adjust archival practice so that it matches the needs of communities, instead of the needs of institutions. Archives often aren't used just as repositories for information, but as sites of legitimacy. Top-down imposition of archival practice doesn't serve ordinary people. Have you seen examples in your work of how archival practice has been adjusted to serve people in a way that matches their needs?

Emma: It has been interesting to watch the growing awareness in our professions. Just in the last five years, guidance and lessons from

---

11. *GALA North [Gay and Lesbian Association of Northern BC] News*, August 1994, Periodicals, Fonds AM1675 BC Gay and Lesbian Archives, City of Vancouver Archives. Content from Healing Our Spirit BC, First Nations AIDS Society, and local Friendship Centers is reproduced in the GALA North News issue of August 1994 and can be found on page 10. Both GALA and GALA North newsletters reflect information-sharing with sister gay and lesbian organizations in their regions and across the neighbouring regions, such as the Okanagan and Kootenays (i.e., West Kootenay Gay and Lesbian Society) in the case of GALA.

12. Cora Currier, "A Vast Archive Exposed the Secret History of Kidnapping and Assassination in Guatemala. Now It's Under Threat," *The Intercept*, June 8, 2019, https://theintercept.com/2019/06/08/guatemala-historical-archive-national-police-jimmy-morales/. [Editor's addition]

community-based approaches or partnerships with communities representing Black, Indigenous, 2SLGBTQAI+ and communities of colour are being shared, and perhaps shifting the normative standard archival practices.[13] If we value our relationships with our users, the idea of doing no more harm should resonate.[14] We have users from across different generations and across the 2SLGBTQAI+ spectrum who use specific terms to describe themselves, the social norms, and contracts that they have had to navigate living their lives in an often heteronormative society, and a hostile one in many instances. There should be an investment in the tools and resources that allow you to meet the community's needs with integrity.

---

13. Raphael Costa, Emanuel da Silva, Gilberto Fernandes, Susana Miranda and Anna St. Onge, "Archiving 'From Below': Preserving, Problematizing and Democratizing the Collective Memory of Portuguese Canadians – the Portuguese Canadian History Project," in *Identity Palimpsests: Archiving Ethnicity in the U.S. and Canada*, eds. Dominique Daniel and Amalia Levi (Sacramento, CA: Litwin Books, 2014), 87-100; Nicholas Matte, Elspeth Brown, Al Stanton-Hagan & Jade Pichette, "Activating the Archives: Making Trans*/+Histories Accessible at the Canadian Lesbian and Gay Archives," (Presentation at the Moving Trans History Forward conference of the Transgender Archives at the University of Victoria, Victoria, B.C., March 2016); Rachel Bickel and Sarah Dupont, "Indigitization," *KULA: Knowledge Creation, Dissemination, and Preservation Studies* 2 no. 1 (2018): 11. https://doi.org/10.5334/kula.56; Celeste Brewer, "Processing LGBTQ Collections Then and Now," *Archival Outlook* (May/June 2018): 4-5; Society of American Archivists, "SAA Council Endorsement of Protocols for Native American Archival Materials," accessed August, 2018, https://www2.archivists.org/statements/saa-council-endorsement-of-protocols-for-native-american-archival-materials; Elvia Arroyo-Ramirez and Jasmine Jones, "Applying Radical Empathy Framework in Archival Practice" (PowerPoint presentation given for a workshop of the Society of California Archivists, Sacramento, CA, September 2018); Faith Charlton, Kelly Bolding, Betts Coup, Jennifer Garcon, Cate Peebles, "Implementing Inclusive (Re)Description at Predominately White Institutions" (Papers presented at the Virtual Joint Annual Meeting of the Council of State Archivists and the Society of American Archivists, August 2020); "Two-Spirit Archives," University of Winnipeg, accessed June 1, 2021, https://archives.uwinnipeg.ca/our-collections/two-spirit-archives.html. Elder Albert McLeod has been continually raising awareness of the rising resurgence in the reclamation of place and position by Two-Spirit individuals and activists and whose collection material began the formation of the Two-Spirit Archives at the University of Winnipeg.

14. Elvia Arroyo-Ramirez and Jasmine Jones, "Applying Radical Empathy Framework in Archival Practice," PowerPoint presentation given for a workshop of the Society of California Archivists, Sacramento, CA, September 2018

Nicole: One objective is to highlight historically important collections, whether that's about queer community, rural community, or any community that has a shared experience, and to think about who most values those collections. Does an institution value their collections in the way that a community might?

Emma: I observe that dialog, discussion, and partnerships are vitally important to be able to work together in determining solutions to these issues. The University of Victoria and the Transgender Archives have been providing a conference every couple of years on Vancouver Island that has become an important forum for transgender scholarship and broader 2SLGBTQAI+ contexts—academic scholarship, community activism, and community in general.[15] It is an important space where people can share their knowledge, then bring it back to their communities and pass it on.

Nicole: It's interesting to think about partnerships. Maybe mapping partnerships that have worked well, finding positive examples, and trying to troubleshoot it from a systems perspective—and see how that partnership works. Community drive and interaction can inform archival practice. How can that be replicated elsewhere for folks who undertake partnerships in archives working more closely with the community?

Emma: Recently, the Council on Library and Information Resources have been enquiring on how to ensure more equitable institution/community partnerships after reviewing the popular grant program,

---

15. Jeffery McNeil-Seymour and Kennedy Healey, "Unsettling LGBTQ Complicity in Pride Celebrations: A Performance of Authentic Settler Allyship from the Frontlines of Two-Spirit and Gender Non-Binary Resistance in Secwepemcul'ecw at Kamloops BC's Inaugural Downtown Pride Parade," (Presentation presented at the 2018 Moving Trans History Forward conference of the Transgender Archives, Victoria, B.C., March 2018). The presentation shared lessons learnt about building relationships between the settler LGBT community and Tk'emlúps te Secwépemc as a result of organizing annual Pride events with the intension of inclusivity in Kamloops.

Digitizing Hidden Collections.[16] That brings me back to your previous questions. How does information gathering impact people in rural areas? How are queer collections from home different from queer collections one might encounter elsewhere?

Nicole: I'm reminded of the local punk scene in my hometown, how queer it was and what that meant to us. I think about all the flyers and records and audio cassette tapes that my friends collected and how powerful it would be for our community to see those objects in an archive. Art, social movements and activism are present everywhere and help folks identify each other. The queer folks in my town had similar interests, sensibilities, and these themes in our lives brought us together.

Emma: In a rural context, navigating social connection is an interdisciplinary effort. What was important about getting to know the 2SLGBTQAI+ infrastructure that existed in the Thompson-Nicola and North Thompson region at the time was really to get out there and participate. Take people up on their invitations to attend a queer fundraiser for 2SLGBTQAI+ homeless youth, join in on longstanding traditions like an annual Take Back the Night anti-violence march, or go to community dances held at a Legion or curling club, which may not appear as the most 2SLGBTQAI+-friendly spaces.[17] These spaces had multiple purposes. There's a 2005 article by Lesley Marple, "The Loss

---

16 Kathlin Smith, "More Equitable Partnerships in Grant Funding," *CLIR News*, February 21, 2019, https://www.clir.org/2019/02/more-equitable-partnerships-in-grant-funding/.

17. Adele Cameron (Simpcw First Nation Band Administration, Simpcw First Nation), in conversation with the author, June 2014; Name Redacted (First Nations Education Council Administrator, FNEC and School District No. 73 -Kamloops/Thompson) and Name Redacted (Coordinator of the Sexual Assault Counselling Centre, Kamloops), in conversation with the author, Fall 2012; "Take Back the Night Foundation. "Take Back the Night Foundation." Accessed June 1, 2021. https://takebackthenight.org/; "My Safe Space," Safe Spaces – Interior Community Services, accessed Feb 14, 2015, http://safespaces.info/my-safe-space.
As of August 8, 2017, the youth program's "Safe Spaces" website was discontinued, and a new web presence was created assessable at https://www.interiorcommunityservices.bc.ca/programs/youth/safe-spaces.

of the Rural in Queer" and in it she described this as a "queer tinge."[18] Instead of 2SLGBTQAI+ spaces you have spaces that you can infuse queer tinges into because maybe you're competing for the same space. It's important to know those dynamics, to be able to respond, serve and act in an appropriate way for that particular rural context.

Nicole: That's actually really heartening to think about just following your motivation and letting things unfold to see what's around in your rural communities. I feel like the way things come out of the woodwork and in rural areas can be an interesting reveal. I really miss that connection that comes from in-person interaction that's unexpected and spontaneous. Libraries, archives, and centres of cultural heritage are some of these venues, and this reminds me of how we might leverage those spaces.

Emma: There is a such need to reduce the barriers to make that accessibility happen because of the deep value of learning more from each other about the vast spectrum of 2SLGBTQAI+ lives that exist. There's so much value in working and learning together.

Reflection

Libraries, archives, and centres of cultural heritage can serve as hubs of information, community, and connection, especially in rural arenas where these networks are less visibly available or present than in urban centres. The isolation possible in rural life is only exacerbated for 2SLGBTQAI+ people, making archives, libraries, and centres of cultural heritage potential sources of relief from seclusion and possible places of comfort, collaboration, and refuge.

 The landscape of 2SLGBTQAI plus, non-binary, and gender diverse archival practice, librarianship, and cultural heritage work is continually

---

18. Lesley Marple, "The Loss of the Rural in Queer," *Canadian Women's Studies* 24, no. 2-3 (2005): 72, 74; File F1510 - Rural life, Subject Files, Fonds AM1675 BC Gay and Lesbian Archives, City of Vancouver Archives.

evolving, built upon the shoulders of our predecessors, and yet we are reminded—in our growing consciousness of a deeply expansive spectrum of experience—the work still ahead of us, particularly in rural contexts. There are also lessons within the rural experience(s) we can and should learn from. Two-Spirit, gay, lesbian, bisexual, queer, trans, non-binary and gender-diverse erasure in our institutional, organizational and community histories is a reality and an ever-present risk without investment, dedicated action, and care.

Our *Grabbing Tea* conversation explores these themes, particularly covering experiences working with and learning from Two Spirt, gay, lesbian, trans, queer, non-binary, and gender diverse communities in British Columbia, to consider potential solutions on how we adjust archive, library, heritage, and information practice to build community-centred relations and partnerships into our day-to-day roles, responsibilities, and provision of public services to better meet the needs of 2SLGBTQAI plus, non-binary, and gender-diverse individuals and communities across rural contexts.

Bibliography

Austen, Ian. "When the Bus No Longer Rolls into Town." *New York Times*. May 14, 2021. https://www.nytimes.com/2021/05/14/world/canada/Greyhound-ends-Canada-service.html.

Black Lives Matter Canada. "Black Lives Matter." Accessed June 1, 2020. https://www.blacklivesmatter.ca/.

City of Vancouver Archives. "Fonds AM1675 BC Gay and Lesbian Archives." City of Vancouver Archives. Accessed May 1, 2020. https://searcharchives.vancouver.ca/bc-gay-and-lesbian-archives.

Currier, Cora. "A Vast Archive Exposed the Secret History of Kidnapping and Assassination in Guatemala. Now It's Under Threat." *The Intercept*, June 8, 2019. https://theintercept.

com/2019/06/08/guatemala-historical-archive-national-police-jimmy-morales/.

Gay and Lesbian Association of Kamloops. "Gay and Lesbian Association of Kamloops." Accessed on May 17, 2014. https://www.gaykamloops.ca/ (site discontinued).

Marple, Lesley. "The Loss of the Rural in Queer." *Canadian Women's Studies* 24, no. 2-3 (2005): 71-74.

"Moving Trans History Forward 2018," Transgender Archives, University of Victoria, last modified on February 20, 2017, https://youtu.be/y2H2wpeOsUs.

National Inquiry into Missing and Murdered Indigenous Women and Girls. *Reclaiming Power and Place: The Final Report of the National Inquiry into Missing and Murdered Indigenous Women and Girls. Volume 1a.* Accessed on October 22, 2020. https://www.mmiwg-ffada.ca/wp-content/uploads/2019/06/Final_Report_Vol_1a-1.pdf.

Royer, A. "Warming Up Records: Archives, Memory, Power and Index of the Disappeared." *InterActions: UCLA Journal of Education and Information Studies* 6, no.1 (2010). Accessed on June 13, 2021. http://dx.doi.org/10.5070/D461000669.

Smith, Kathlin. "More Equitable Partnerships in Grant Funding." *CLIR News*, February 21, 2019. https://www.clir.org/2019/02/more-equitable-partnerships-in-grant-funding/.

Truth and Reconciliation Commission of Canada. *Truth and Reconciliation Commission of Canada: Calls to Action.* Winnipeg: Truth and Reconciliation Commission of Canada, 2015. Accessed on May 5, 2021. https://nctr.ca/records/reports/#trc-reports.

University of Winnipeg, Two-Spirited People of Manitoba Inc. and QTPOC Winnipeg. *Findings of C2C: Two Spirit & Queer/Trans People of Colour. Calls to Action 2019.* Accessed on June, 2021. https://www.uwinnipeg.ca/c2c/.

Weld, Kristen. *Paper Cadavers: The Archives of Dictatorship in Guatemala.* Durham, NC: Duke University Press:, 2014

(In) Terms of Who We Are: The Homosaurus Board in Conversation

Marika Cifor, Jay L. Colbert, Clair A. Kronk, K.J. Rawson, and B.M. Watson

Keywords
Cataloguing, vocabularies

Marika Cifor, PhD, (she/her) is Assistant Professor in the Information School and adjunct Assistant Professor in Gender, Women and Sexuality Studies at the University of Washington. She is the author of *Viral Cultures: Activist Archiving in the Age of AIDS* (Minnesota, 2022) and over twenty-five articles on archives, affect, and the intersections of gender and sexuality with information technologies. Cifor has served on the Homosaurus Editorial Board since 2016.

Jay L. Colbert is the Metadata & Discovery Strategy Librarian at the University of New Hampshire. He holds a MSLIS from the University of Illinois at Urbana-Champaign, where he completed a thesis on patron-driven subject access and queer-controlled vocabulary via a critical framework of queer theory and semiotics. His subsequent publications build on this research. Jay haunts New England with his bearded dragon Coop and his tuxedo cat King

Arthur, constantly bugging them by dancing around his house being a shameless opera queen.

Clair A. Kronk (she/her) is a postdoctoral biomedical informatics researcher at the University of Cincinnati School of Medicine. She is the creator of the first LGBTQIA+-specific controlled vocabulary for usage in health care, the Gender, Sex, and Sexual Orientation (GSSO) ontology. She also serves on the Health Level 7 (HL7) and Systematized Nomenclature of Medicine (SNOMED) committees considering equitable representation of sexual orientation and gender identity (SOGI)-related data.

K.J. Rawson (he/him) is an Associate Professor of English and Women's, Gender, and Sexuality Studies at Northeastern University. He is also the founder and director of the Digital Transgender Archive, an award-winning online repository of trans-related historical materials, and he is the chair of the editorial board of the Homosaurus. His work is at the intersections of the Digital Humanities and Rhetoric, LGBTQ+, and Feminist Studies.

B.M. Watson (they/m) Watson (@brimwats) is a PhD. student at the University of British Columbia's iSchool focusing on queer nomenclature, histories of information, and equitable cataloging in GLAMS (galleries, archives, libraries, museums, and special collections). They are the Director of HistSex.com, a free and open access resource for the history of sexuality and serve on the editorial board of Homosaurus, an international linked data vocabulary for queer terminology. Additionally, Watson serves as the Archivist-Historian of the Consensual Non-Monogamies Committee of the American Psychological Association.

Editor's Note: This conversation references The Homosaurus, https://homosaurus.org/, an international linked data vocabulary of Lesbian, Gay, Bisexual, Transgender, and Queer (LGBTQ) terms.

Conversation

B.M. Watson (bri; they/m): To start us off, I wanted to read a couple of quotes from an amazing literature review that Homosaurus Editorial Board member Chloe Noland put together discussing some of the older conversations in queer cataloging:

> The literature concerning efforts to develop inclusive and valuable dynamic vocabulary for LGBTQ material reveals an active and radical history... It starts with the ALA task force for gay liberation formed in 1971, where they're really trying to go after this idea of sexual inversion social pathologies and this is where LC, library Congress, got the topic headings from earlier psychological literature which, as we also probably know is not that very queer friendly also. Sandy Berman really comes as a focus of attention. And there's also this long running to be in these queer vocabularies about how we want to if we're either going to essentialize or call out, or what the right way is really is to describe these minority groups. You can argue for universalization saying everybody's queer, or you can argue for a minoritization being like, well, these are the minorities.

One of the foundational voices that had a big influence on this vocabulary was Ellen Greenblatt. She argues for the use of distinguishing vocabulary using umbrella terms, such as gays, to apply to all material.[1] Others, like Ben Christensen, argued really vehemently against using gay as an umbrella term and argued instead for using terminology like lesbian or transsexual.[2] So while it's true that these naming preferences of one group over the other often happens at the expensive of another, many minority voices have been captured by this process of queer boundary

---

1. Ellen Greenblatt, "Homosexuality: The Evolution of a Concept in the Library of Congress Subject Headings," in *Gay and Lesbian Library Service*, ed. Cal Gough and Ellen Greenblatt (Jefferson, NC: McFarland & Company, 1990); Ellen Greenblatt, "The Treatment of LGBTIQ Concepts in the Library of Congress Subject Headings," in *Serving LGBTIQ Library and Archives Users: Essays on Outreach, Service, Collections and Access*, ed. Ellen Greenblatt (Jefferson, NC: McFarland & Company, Inc., Publishers, 2011), 212–28.

2. "Minoritization vs. Universalization: Lesbianism and Male Homosexuality in LCSH and LCC," *Knowledge Organization* 35, no. 4 (2008): 229–38, https://doi.org/10/ggcjs6.

defining and development of vocabulary. Folksonomies is really the more modern example of this with *LibraryThing* or *Archive Our Own* or Melissa Adler who has talked probably most broadly about this.[3] But when a cataloger is trying to decide what a book is or even as queer individual is trying to decide who they are, what they are, there's this question about what the aboutness of something is. It's the aboutness of establishing this framework for queer vocabularies that has been a really tricky thing because of the nature of queer.

So I'm going to read the last paragraph here:

> Serving as both a solution to these levels of ambiguity into the destructured content of tagging and cultural folksonomies, the development of authorized thesauri is a tool used by libraries and scholars to contextualize these collections.[4]

But there is still this long-term history of thesauri becoming victims of their own success: either embraced by cultural heritage institutions and removed from a community, or they're used for a while then ignored. So we could really think of Homosaurus as a culmination of this long history of vocabularies. K.J., do you want to talk a little bit about the history of Homosaurus and your impressions?

K.J. Rawson (he/him/his): I'm happy to do that. I learned about Homosaurus in 2015 when I launched the Digital Transgender Archive (DTA). In doing so, I sought out a vocabulary that would do a better job of

---

3. Melissa A. Adler, Jeffrey T. Huber, and A. Tyler Nix, "Stigmatizing Disability: Library Classifications and the Marking and Marginalization of Books about People with Disabilities," *The Library Quarterly* 87, no. 2 (April 2017): 117–35, https://doi.org/10/gft4b3; Melissa A. Adler, "The Case for Taxonomic Reparations," *Knowledge Organization* 43, no. 8 (2016): 630–40, https://doi.org/10/gft38p; Melissa A. Adler, "Transcending Library Catalogs: A Comparative Study of Controlled Terms in Library of Congress Subject Headings and User-Generated Tags in LibraryThing for Transgender Books," *Journal of Web Librarianship* 3, no. 4 (November 23, 2009): 309–31, https://doi.org/10/fvxmwg; Melissa A. Adler and Lindsey M. Harper, "Race and Ethnicity in Classification Systems: Teaching Knowledge Organization from a Social Justice Perspective," *Library Trends* 67, no. 1 (2018): 52–73, https://doi.org/10/gfw9tz.

4. Brian M. Watson, Chloe Noland, and Amber Billey, "The Homosaurus," *Catalogue and Index*, no. 202 (March 2021): 44–47.

allowing us to describe LGBTQ+ resources. In our case, particularly trans resources, because I just wasn't finding the terms that I needed in order to make these materials more accessible online. So I came across the Homosaurus and I reached out to Jack van der Wel. From him, I learned that the original Homosaurus was created by IHLIA LGBT Heritage, a cultural resource center based in Amsterdam. They developed the Homosaurus as both a Dutch and English gay and lesbian thesaurus in the 1980s, and it was meant to be a standalone vocabulary to describe their materials. Over time, more concepts were added, but this original version we refer to as version zero and it is the ground that we have continued to build upon. It became apparent pretty early on that it would be quite useful to other LGBTQ+ archives to be able to use this and apply it.

After the DTA started using the Homosaurus in 2015, I began some conversations with Jack about what it might mean to really revive this vocabulary and transform it into a linked data vocabulary. Since he was enthusiastic, we established the editorial board, which is still going strong, meeting monthly since 2016. In that process, we developed the second version, version two, which is what's currently available now and which is what we put all of our love and efforts into continuing to work on. In this conversation we have people who've joined at various points in the process. So I might ask Marika to jump in first since you're one of our members who's been on the board for the longest.

Marika Cifor (she/her/hers): Sure. Thinking back, I don't think I had come across the Homosaurus before K.J. put out a call looking for board members, for folks who were interested in collaborating on updating and making the Homosaurus and giving it its next life. And for me, seeing K.J.'s proposal and being familiar with some of K.J.'s work on queer and trans archives—I was really excited about the possibilities.

For creating a vocabulary that specifically would serve LGBT archives, because my own academic research has been significantly focused in that space, and though I'm not a cataloger by training I know enough about cataloging to know the real limits of standard vocabularies like

Library of Congress, which becomes the scapegoat. But it's often what we use to make resources successful and what, in turn, I teach students who are training to be librarians and archivists. As we're talking about finding aids, they're also thinking about how you create MARC records that will pair for those. We are also really keenly aware of the limitations of those. And so I was excited to become part of a project that might allow us to make some of these materials more accessible and to just capture a better sense of what the queer world of archival knowledge might look like. It's been a really exciting and rewarding process to be part of the long, slow labor of this long, fun process. It's pushed my understanding of what the boundaries of LGBT knowledge might be in really interesting and exciting ways.

bri: I, ironically, was introduced to the Homosaurus by Marika. I was in library school at the time and learning about linked data vocabularies, and I was really excited about the concept of linked data. For better or worse, I always tend to jump right into something without even looking to see other work that might be being done. So I was like, "well, I guess I'll just make a queer vocabulary just...by myself. Luckily, Marika came to our very next class and introduced this thing called the Homosaurus, and I was taken with it immediately.

While I do love to drag LCSH, it is still such an important and longstanding system. Like any monolith, LCSH gets into a lot of trouble because it is an antiquated thing that requires constant maintenance. In some ways, queer vocabularies can be more nimble, and it gets to the diversity of different languages and like the fact that Homosaurus can now be used in MARC and can be used in any library catalog that depends on MARC; that is really exciting. I think Clair can speak a little bit to the longer history of queer vocabularies.

Clair Kronk (she/her/hers): My introduction to the Homosaurus was a little different in that I had seen how the pathologization of queer people had changed and shifted in medical care, especially in psychiatry and psychology over the past 150 or so years. You have the DSM [*Diagnostic* *and Statistical Manual of Mental Disorders*], and the International Classification of Diseases (ICD), and the different ways those conceptualizations are still being utilized. I was looking at a system last week and saw an electronic health record where they were using "gender issues" as an umbrella term. It was being used for trans-related stuff. It was being used for sexual assault-related resources. It was being used to indicate a preference for a female clinician or male nurse and all that was just stuffed into "gender issues." And so I ended up constructing an ontology: The Gender, Sex and Sexual Orientation (GSSO) ontology.[5] [...] I was presenting about that ontology and trying to get community-based organizing into that. And so of course you contact the GLBT Historical Society because, you know, who doesn't do that at some point in their careers as a queer person, and they sent me on a mailing list hunt, and somebody on the mailing list asked, "Have you heard of the Homosaurus?" I was like, no, because I'm not a librarian or archivist by trade, I'm an informaticist. And so as soon as I started looking into it, I was like "Oh my gosh, it's becoming a link data vocabulary," and "Oh my gosh, is part of the most important to archive to me personally," and in my professional experience, the Digital Transgender Archive (DTA) is being run off of that. I was like, you know, I have to meet the celebrity K.J. Rawson [*laughs*].

The conversations led me to bringing the medical perspective to the board. And so, a lot of the issues with medicine right now is you have the Open Biological and Biomedical Ontologies (OBO) Foundry, and they don't really talk to anybody else. So you have the Medical Subject Headings (MeSH), which you would think because, okay that's a government-related thing, it's going to talk to the Library of Congress subject headings (LCSH). They usually don't. And so you end up with things like "lesbianism" still being a term in PubMed. Instead of, you know, a more modernized heading. Or the fact that "transsexualism" is still in there, or that "intersex" was just added like six months ago to

---

5. Kronk, Clair and Judith Dexheimer. "Development of the Gender, Sex, and Sexual Orientation Ontology: Evaluation and Workflow," *Journal of the American Medical Informatics Association* 27, no. 7 (2020): 1110-5, http://doi.org/10.1093/jamia/ocaa061.

MeSH and it was still DSD up until 2020; so there's a lot of work to be done in that space.

Activists are so far ahead of this side of things and I'm so lucky to be a part of this, the Homosaurus, and you know, every so often, it's like the discussion between meetings that asks, do we use the colloquial term here? How do you decide what term goes in, right, because obviously we're all coming to the board with our own biases that we have to acknowledge as well. And I think at that point, you know, of trying to inspire more diversity and integration in the board and consulting and getting more opinions. I think it's something that we've all been working towards in one way or another. So now, I do want to pass it over to Jay who's been adding an entirely different section and perspective to the Homosaurus.

Jay Colbert (he/him): I just joined in June. So I've only been on for a couple months, but I've been aware of it since I was in grad school in 2015, before it was in its current form. I knew when I went to grad school to become a librarian that I wanted to work on subject vocabularies and especially with the whole radical cataloguing realm. That's why I wanted to be a librarian. While in school I had to do posters, and I wanted to do mine on LGBT people, resources, and cataloging; and I thought, surely there's some sort of vocabulary out there that is for queer things, or surely someone's done a study on the language that people actually use. I found out about IHLIA and I Interlibrary-loaned their archival-controlled vocabulary, physically, to look at it. I was in grad school the same time that K.R. Roberto was at University of Illinois working on his Ph.D. with Kathryn La Barre, and that's how I found out about the Word document of the Homosaurus—because I was given access to it. But I didn't know that this type of work was going to start happening. I graduated in 2017, so I think it apparently had just started up. That's how I became familiar with it: "There's this Homosaurus Word document that lives on K.R. Roberto's laptop that he gives to the grad students who are interested."

(In) Terms of Who We Are:
The Homosaurus Board in Conversation

The vocabulary that I'm working on adding now is about fandom and fanfiction. This is an area that is starting to get more academic attention. And I think when people think of fandom and fanfiction, they think it's a bunch of 14-year-olds or straight girls or horny wine moms who are writing slash fiction, when there's really this very rich queer history with fan fiction. But it needs to have vocabulary to talk about it. I thought it'd be interesting if we also incorporated that history into the Homosaurus. Instead of just terms about identity, also activity and culture and ephemera and the more pop culture stuff.

K.J.: I want to credit our other active board members, Amber Billey, Janaya Kizzie, Chloe Nolan, and Jack van der Wel. We also have a few board members who are no longer working on the board, and I want to pay particular tribute to Walter "Cat" Walker who worked on the board for many years until he passed recently. We are still continuing to work on some of the initiatives that he started and his legacy certainly lives on in the Homosaurus. Orla Egan and Alice Galvinhill left their stamp on the project as well. Beyond the individual people, I think the takeaway is that this is a community effort. And even though we released version two, we have not stopped working on the vocabulary. In fact, I think it has inspired us to work harder.

Marika: K.J.'s point there is really apt. Part of what's interesting about this project, as someone who's spent a few years working on it, is the process we've engaged in. That process has truly been a conversation: where people bring their different expertise, their questions, and we have meetings that look, actually, a lot like this conversation. We work on terms and concepts and what one can do within the constraints of something that is hierarchical. And it's been a process of working through terms, one by one, for years. Out of that, I have learned so much about LGBT domains and spaces. It has also exposed the places where we as a board have a lot of knowledge and the places where we as a board do not. For me, it's part of what's beautiful and queer about this project. It honors everyone's individual expertise and opinions and thoughts and queer experiences.

K.J.: This is a good place for us to step back, though, and try to answer the question, "What is the broad political project of the Homosaurus?"

Clair: I mean, of all of us, you're the most senior member K.J.!

K.J.: Which is precisely why I should not answer the question!

bri: Well, I think Jay's comment partially answered that. While fanfiction is stereotyped as being for moms and teenagers, it also tells this long history of queer people who could not imagine themselves existing in any other way—so they had to create these spaces, insert themselves into it, and try to develop their own vocabulary for the indefinable. Speaking for myself, I will admit to "discovering myself existing" in fanfiction when I was younger (to quote from Marika's article).[6] Another example might be Alison Bechdel's comic, where the most poignant moment to me is when the main character is going through the card catalog and she finds the subject heading "lesbian"—it's like that.[7]

Clair: Homosaurus services and its eventual uses are so intertwined with the confusion of what queerness is and what queerness means and how queerness has extremely different meanings to different people. And some people construct it as a political identity. Some people construct it as a very innate and born Identity—a born this way structure, or structure socialization within a broader queer community. I tend to think of the Homosaurus as a community-driven project and therefore connected to community queerness and queerness as community. And so that it can only function if it speaks to that community at large.

---

6. Michelle Caswell, Marika Cifor, and Mario H. Ramirez, "'To Suddenly Discover Yourself Existing': Uncovering the Impact of Community Archives," *The American Archivist* 79, no. 1 (June 2016): 56–81, https://doi.org/10/gfc3hf.

7. Alison Bechdel, *Fun Home: A Family Tragicomic*, 2015.

(In) Terms of Who We Are:
The Homosaurus Board in Conversation

Marika: I think at the root of it, the Homosaurus is about queerness, but it's also about making queer knowledge and experiences—whether contemporary or historical—more accessible to people in our communities, and people beyond them, in ways that reflect how we talk about ourselves and have talked about ourselves as queer people, broadly defined, over time—and whether we even use that word.

K.J.: It's such a political venture. So it's not just that we have developed this resource that can improve the accessibility of LGBTQ+ resources, but we are also implementing a queer practice of language use and circulation that is speaking back to more of a top down model. And we are building something that does a better job of describing ourselves, describing our materials, describing our communities, and really trying to continually push against the inaccuracies, the reframing, and the speaking for us that so often happens within cultural institutions. That being said, I think one of our continued focuses is thinking about intersectionality and thinking about the ways that LGBTQ+ interacts with various identities within the vocabulary.

Marika: Bringing together the work that had been done and the Digital Transgender Archive and the really rich vocabulary of trans knowledge that you all had created there and bringing that into the Homosaurus means that some parts of the vocabulary are more built out, or are more developed than others. Bringing in work from the DTA dramatically enriched the trans and gender-based content in the vocabulary, but it is far from a finished process. But we've always had certain limits in terms of who we are.

Though the project began in Europe, most of us who worked on it are in the United States. Most of us are English speakers and it reflects a very Western tradition of knowledge-making and vocabularies. It reflects things about the identities of the people who've been involved in it, both the people who were involved in its creation, and also the people who have been involved in more recent versions. There are real limits as a result, not only in geography, but in our professional experiences, our personal experiences, and most importantly the gaps left by who's not been in the room as part of those conversations and where that means our knowledge is limited and constrained. It's important to acknowledge our limits, and I think we've tried to address some of these—but there's a long way to go.

bri: One of the future vocabulary revisions that I would like to propose might be changing from 'people with disabilities' to 'disabled people.' Generally the Homosaurus tries to favor "people first" language, but speaking for myself as a disabled person, people in the queer Crip community see that people-first phrasing as oppressive, and tend to prefer "disabled person" or "crip person." Intersectionality and the different identities that people bring to this work is really important. Linked data allows these linkings and intersectionalities.

Jay: One thing that I think is special about this project in this vocabulary, but also still one of its limitations is that, yes, it is a queer vocabulary and queer people are making it, but there's still the problem of we—this small group of people—we're the ones who get to decide at the end of the day what those terms are. And because we are "within the community," we might have a better sense, than, you know, someone at the Library of Congress looking at a book and saying, "This is the term because of literary warrant" and, "I saw someone on my Twitter get mad at this term, so I gotta fix it." But at the end of the day, we are still trying to speak for a "community." What is that community? Can there be a community that broad? There are still going to be disagreements over the terms that we pick and especially because of the limitations of who is in the group, the lack of non-"American Western" voices and people of color, we're still reinforcing and upholding some of the very things that we're fighting against by creating this vocabulary, just because of the nature of making vocabularies. So it's a fun tension there sometimes.

Clair: The culturally specific gender identity[8] section is an interesting section because it begs to question: does it fall under the broadest definition of queerness? Probably in a sociological sense, but if you were to sit down individual people belonging to those communities and ask, Are you queer? Do you identify as queer? It's honestly up in the air on what they would think of that. And a lot of times we end up having to add, to the best of our ability, a scope note indicating that that is the term that's used in this particular community, and we base it on a particular resource or resources. But it needs to be a living document. And there are always going to be new evolutions of queerness, that have definitely happened during all of our lifetimes, when the terminology has shifted greatly.

You have these conceptualizations where, [...] especially with Native American and First Nations peoples; there's so much gender role diversity that has been documented, at least archaeologically, for almost 6000 years. How do you put that under Two-Spirit? Two-Spirit is a conceptualization that was formed as an umbrella term in the 1990s. In the same way, how do you put all of trans-ness from the last 2000 years under "trans" as an umbrella term; and you know it's difficult to make these decisions from a cataloguing perspective, like you want to make sure these terms are findable and oftentimes people are connecting these terms, but yeah, there are always going to be these disagreements, and ultimately, in my opinion, I think these disagreements are good. I think they're healthy. I think that's how we make better vocabularies—by listening and really hearing when people are representing themselves.

K.J.: One of the ways that we've done that is to add in terminology that we imagine there have not yet been use cases for, but we're still putting it in anyway because we want there to be space for those things. It's a

---

8. Note that this heading has been removed in favor of "Non-Euro-American Gender and Sexual Identities" as of 1 July 2021.

bit more of a theoretical argument, but if you don't have the language to describe it, then you're not going to see it as you're trying to process materials and make those materials available. So, we have things like transgender Buddhists and transgender Afro-Canadians, and there are all kinds of categories that, if you looked at usage, you might not find many instances, but at the same time, we are making arguments that these communities and these individuals and these practices exist. So therefore, we need to be able to have the terminology to describe them. But given everything that everyone has already said about the limitations of our own knowledge, and our own constitution as a board, and the overwhelming whiteness of our group, I think it is important to never lose sight of. We're putting it out there, wanting and expecting and hoping for critique, and we are also thinking about ways to continue to improve and expand, not just who's on our board, but who gets to contribute to the vocabulary.

Jay: I'm sure we've all read Queering the Catalog by Emily Drabinski,[9] but there's also this great article called Dewey Deracialized[10] that talks about the history of changing the term used for Black Americans and the Dewey Decimal System. With critiques of the Homosaurus, it makes me think about this legacy of when we do change terms and as our language shifts, and consider the politics of correctness, like what Drabinski talks about, do we have to be correct and hide our mistakes? Or how do we present evolution and changing of this as a living document while honoring that we do mess up and make mistakes.

---

9. Emily Drabinski, "Queering the Catalog: Queer Theory and the Politics of Correction," *The Library Quarterly* 83, no. 2 (April 2013): 94–111, https://doi.org/10/f4rjgb.drab.

10. Jonathan Furner, "Dewey Deracialized: A Critical Race-Theoretic Perspective," *KNOWLEDGE ORGANIZATION* 34, no. 3 (2007): 144–68, https://doi.org/10/gfrgjg.de.

K.J.: And just a quick side note, we have an over representation of trans folks on our board, yet some of the trans terms are some of the weakest in the vocabulary right now.

Marika: And I think some of the comments you all have been making makes me think further about the fundamental challenge of deciding what is in and out of scope. What is LGBTQ knowledge? What falls into the scope of that? Sometimes I think we've made interesting theoretical decisions, and sometimes we've made practical decisions about what else has been done well by others. If there are already great vocabularies in a space, why are we trying to replicate work that is strong and already exists. But the question of deciding where LGBTQ begins and ends is by no means simple, even if we just use those words. I think that's been a continual conversation throughout this process of what does it even mean to try to scope our project at all?

bri: I have been reaching out to other classifications vocabularies to identify some of the weak places, and even in the case of QZAP [the Queer Zine Archive Project],[11] they're not interested in a hierarchical vocabulary. At least we're aware of each other and we can connect where we can work together when we can. Another example is me trying to work in the Lavender Library fiction classification and plugging into other libraries that do this work.

Clair: To be queer is to have disagreements. When you come out and when you arrive in the queer community, you are very beholden to the standards of the time and the place where you enter. And I think a lot of times, a lot of us hold on to that terminology because it's almost sacred to our own constructed worlds. I think for that reason, it's really important to consider historical terminology, various types of contemporary terminology, the differences between connotations of words

---

11. https://www.qzap.org/.

and their usage in different countries, and the importance of the scope notes. And considering, hey, is this term a slur? Has it been reclaimed? Has it been reclaimed partially in some places? Because I have been to conferences where I have used the term 'queer' and have had older LGBTQ people come up to me and say, 'That's not okay. You can't put that in a research document or you can't discuss that at a podium.'

My experience of the terminology is very different from theirs, and I don't want to necessarily say that either of our conceptions are wrong. And so, I think the Homosaurus does a really good job balancing the acknowledgement that this historical terminology exists and it's important to our current conceptualizations. You know, you couldn't have LGBTQ without sexual inversion.

K.J.: Clair's example of sexual inversion is interesting. Here's a historical term, and we want to put it in that framework, and a scope note is a perfect place to do that and keep querying that term. But then, at the same time, when it's used in practice, the scope note will often become completely detached from it. And so, it loses the richness that we're hoping to instill within that. A lot of what we try to accomplish is a separation between the materials themselves and the people that they're trying to represent. We're not trying to develop the vocabulary to always describe the people. But recognizing that the vocabulary is used to describe resources, which then represent or describe or are about people. And so, there are multiple layers there that I think are so important to keep instilling and keep educating about because again, the importance of vocabularies for queer communities and naming is critical. It's life defining. Our role as information professionals is not to use language to hoist on to other people. It's instead to help make materials discoverable. And in an ideal situation, to allow those materials to express and to represent the people who are represented in those materials so that it's a space where they're able to speak for themselves. And we're just trying to facilitate access to that space.

(In) Terms of Who We Are: The Homosaurus Board in Conversation

Jay: I think a lot of the discourse that is happening with Library of Congress subject headings is this sort of tension between what the materials are describing and the fact that it's just people who aren't librarians that are seeing the terms. The whole thing about the "Illegal aliens" subject heading is, yes, we all as a profession agree that should not be the term anymore and that's one of the only cases where it was actually the people it applied to who brought that change. But people forget that the Library of Congress is actually not our National Library. It is the library for Congress. And a Congress person actually vetoed that down and said "No" because technically, the literary warrant for that term is government and legal language. What is the scope of the vocabulary? It's sort of a chicken and the egg. What comes first, the things that shape the vocabulary or the vocabulary that shapes the way that people talk about it? I don't know if one is more correct than the other.

Marika: I think we also have some advantages, though, in the practical sense, in how archival description works in comparison to most bibliographic description, like LCSH. The norm in archives is to use as many subject headings as possible, because the assumption is that you're describing unique resources and that multiple headings will make those resources more discoverable. And so I think there are some advantages to how this vocabulary actually will be used. There's not going to be the same pressure, because archivists won't have to narrow it down to three terms. You can have both historical and contemporary terms living alongside one another, and it's not perfect, but I hope that it allows the use of the Homosaurus, to reflect some of the richness of things that are reflected in spaces like the scope notes, and things that users might not see, but to see historical and contemporary terms living alongside one another. I think there are some advantages in the traditions of archival cataloging and how it works.

K.J.: We could talk about future directions too. I know that one of the limitations that we're aware of is that it's an English-based vocabulary.

We have the capacity on the back end to include equivalencies in other languages, and I know that one of our board members, Jack, is working on a Dutch translation, and we've caught wind that some other folks are working on translating the Homosaurus source into other languages. For me, that, of course, invokes broader questions of colonialism and naming. If we're starting with an English-language vocabulary, we cannot just translate from English to other languages, but we also have to think about how these other languages will shift the Homosaurus. Will it cause us to rethink, not just particular terms, but structures; and how can we continue to be nimble and not hold on too tightly to entrenched ways of conceptualizing particular relationships within the vocabulary, along with particular terms?

Clair: The idea that we're moving into a linked data vocabulary, specifically, is that we can utilize a lot of the resources that other linked data vocabularies have provided. And I just got into this recently with Wikidata because they have a bunch of different levels of translateability between terms with direct translation and terms in which there exists no word in X language [...]. For example, I've definitely come into contact with a lot of people trying to translate transgender terminology into Arabic where there is almost no terminology for it, except for extremely offensive words that confabulate identities a lot of the time. And so, you're forced to come up with new words, and whether those words are a byproduct of colonization, the answer is almost always, yes. You want to provide as much as you can for as many people as you can, while also being considerate of those persons' needs.

bri: My idea about how others could use the Homosaurus was partially shaped by Brian Dobreski, who argues that we should augment description by using multiple vocabularies "side by side."[12] We should

---

12. Brian Dobreski, Jian Qin, and Melissa Resnick, "Depicting Historical Persons and Identities: A Faceted Approach," *KNOWLEDGE ORGANIZATION* 47, no. 8 (2020): 668–79, https://doi.org/10.5771/0943-7444-2020-8-668; Brian Dobreski, Jian Qin, and Melissa Resnick, "Side by Side: The Use of Multiple Subject Languages in Capturing Shifting Contexts around Historical Collections," *NASKO* 7 (2019): 16–26.

use the LCSH term, the Homosaurus term, and others—add in as many vocabularies as possible because that captures different angles of the item. Obviously, there's a way to be cautious about that; for example, describing indigenous material in LCSH is a pretty awful experience, but maybe in the future, a brand-new linked data vocabulary could be used to push back against the LCSH term. I think that it's an act of power to redescribe things in an empowering way. I know the Lesbian Herstory Archives and the Sexual Minority Archives in Massachusetts do this in an analog way.

Clair: Does the vocabulary contain words or does it contain concepts? Or does it try to leverage both of those things and do its very best; and if somebody is searching for "transgender women," they probably are also searching for "transsexual," as in "male-to-female transsexuals"? I like that the Homosaurus includes a lot of historical terminology because a lot of search-based mechanisms that I've been trying to push through my work are based on the terminology mapping backwards, or mapping forwards as best as possible and saying, if I'm set on searching "transgender," I also want to search all the way back and get sexual invert results, even though some of those might refer to gay people and lesbians today. I want to include that just in case, so I don't miss trans history, whatever that broadly means.

K.J.: Well, one of the interesting things to think about for this project is how we actually get feedback, and the mechanism for tracing usage. We get some direct emails and some people who reach out to the project directly, but we don't get as much as I would like. One of our perpetual challenges is thinking about that feedback loop and the mechanisms and tracking usage. In thinking about moving forward, we have aspirations to create some training documents, or some videos, or resources we can share, so that the vocabulary becomes more welcoming to new users. We're also trying to publish about it more and more.

Marika: And our hope is that people will continue to point out places where terms are inadequate or problematic, or where something should be there but isn't; because there are always going to be gaps and problems and things that should be addressed and some of those get lost, and in the larger work we do, we need folks who are using it to talk about the challenges or opportunities they're finding and implementing, or gaps they find as they use it.

Clair: I do think, honestly, that the Homosaurus has been an amazing part of my career, and I really hope to continue here for as long as K.J. will let me!

K.J.: And I don't have that power. This is not a hierarchy!
Clair: Beautiful, beautiful, but yeah, the connections I've made through the Homosaurus and its usage within my research and within the other archives that I've spoken to, and I know that Bri has spoken to other archives as well, which has been wonderful and that everybody on the board has been incredible. This led to this opportunity here today to speak to everyone about the Homosaurus, which is phenomenal. I almost want to call the Homosaurus 'perfect, but flawed.'

Marika: We've been so concerned about addressing things that fall outside of normativity that we sometimes forget core concepts. We realized recently that we have many nuanced terms about types of relationship models, but that we don't have 'husband' or 'wife' as terms in the vocabulary, right? So while we've been concerned about representing the breadth of queerness, the relationships between people, and the queer kinds of family, sometimes we forget mainstream terms as well. There's something very central to those words "husband" and "wife" to LGBT activism; there has been this fight for access to marriage and to be able to use these terms, but in the Homosaurus those terms are on the marginal ends of queer understanding.

(In) Terms of Who We Are:
The Homosaurus Board in Conversation

Clair: To be fair, within LGBTQ+ as a construct, there are hundreds of thousands of potential terms and we are a small group of people. So, I think K.J. would agree, you know: getting users' feedback and ideas for potential additions are always great to hear.

Jay: Yeah, because of the topic of our vocabulary, it's a topic that is antithetical to being limited and controlled. So it makes it this uphill battle. It forces us to question what it means to be a controlled vocabulary and a thesaurus. Yeah, like you said, while we decided that this term was the one that you'll use to describe this, others will disagree. We have to accept that whatever we do is going to make some people mad. I think it's just an interesting position to be in, the subject of queerness being a thing that refuses to be controlled.

bri: We're not the queer vocabulary police.

Marika: Sandra Harding, who is a feminist STS [Science and Technology Studies] scholar once said to me that you just have to begin projects of any kind, with the assumption that you're always already wrong, that somebody has already looked at something in a way that you never would have imagined, that they know something you don't know, and despite this that you have to do the work anyway, even if you know that some aspect of it, there's going to be a gap, there's going to be an oversight. There's always going to be a problem, you're always going to be wrong about something, but that doesn't mean you don't do the work anyway.

Clair: And being wrong is the first step to being right. I don't think I've ever talked to an undergraduate on their very first day of university and they've been like "Yep, I already know everything." And in a similar fashion. I mean, you know, K.J. and the precursors of the Homosaurus created something that was essentially like entirely new, they scoped an entirely new field of knowledge and there's always prospecting to be done. And you know as was actually just put in the Zoom chat, you know, considering there are no rigid borders for queerness and the board that comes after us, just like the board that came before (before, as in, the original creators of the Homosaurus), they're always going to be disagreements and those disagreements are ultimately healthy and they keep the queer community vital and on the right track.

K.J.: Yeah, and I think that even the fact that we're having this conversation is a testament to the transformational power of queer Information Studies work. It's bringing people together. It's having us reflect on our community language practices and the politics and the implications of those practices: how we can contribute to the more ethical, more accurate, more just circulation and consumption of information resources and knowledge. It's such a huge project that we are contributing to, and we're continuing an important legacy; and then we are contributing to that legacy and being able to have these conversations and do this work together—it is so much fun.

bri: For our future readers, I would like to conclude by inviting you to get in touch via the website (http://homosaurus.org/contact) if you notice anything that could be added, things that are missing, or if you want to work with us to put together workshops. Oh, and if anyone very, very rich is listening, or rather, reading this, and would like to sponsor this work, definitely let us know.

Reflections

Reflective Coda—

Clair: I really do hope that we can find happy mediums between the insane pace at which language evolves and how its impacts on individuals (especially marginalized individuals) shifts. The idea of a living, breathing Homosaurus, and other vocabularies like it, for and by communities, is an essential first step. Moving it further into the linked data sphere and utilizing it in community archives, LGBTQIA+ forums, etc., is where we are (hopefully) going. I would love to see a day where LGBTQIA+ people can access materials from hundreds of archives, libraries, etc. in an integrated manner. There are so many difficulties accessing LGBTQIA+ material in so many places, and I do see the Homosaurus as a tool to make that accessing just a tidbit easier.

Jay: As I have gone through and reread our transcripts and made edits, one thing I am a little sad we didn't get to talk about more is the joy of editing the Homosaurus. This abridged transcript mentions a few times that the process and work is fun, but none of us dig into that more. In the recorded conversation, one thing I brought up was the inherent silliness, and sometimes awkward nature, of discussing terms while at work. The pandemic mitigated this a bit, but depending on each of our working environments, it isn't always possible to have our video meetings privately. When I was first brought on, I was told stories of people having to whisper coded references to terms, such as line number, because the terms were things like "Anal fisting." Or, for example, when I have shown colleagues the Homosaurus terms, "Anal beads," "Anal fisting," and "Anal sex" are right near the top alphabetically. I'm sure a few tech services people (or family members!) have gotten flustered overhearing our meetings or looking at the vocabulary.

And I find joy in that. These are human behaviors. (Really fun ones.) They deserve to be represented in a vocabulary, cultural institutions, and scholarship. I think it's fun to talk about erotic body parts or BDSM at work. Let's talk about cataloging porn! Let's talk about archiving leather culture! Let's talk about sex work! In some sense, it's a way for me to be unapologetically queer at work. To quote the miniseries, *A Very English Scandal,* "I was rude, I was vile, I was queer—I was myself!!"

K.J.: There are some traces of joy that you can glimpse in our conversation—bits of banter and laughter—but you are right on point, Jay, that we didn't fully capture how fun this project has been. There's something so powerfully delightful in having a group of queer folks come together to build a queer resource together. We've cohered as a group. We have fun together and we get work done. The Homosaurus is a world-making project that we've already seen is having measurable impacts on the discoverability of queer resources. And we take such pleasure in being able to transform information landscapes on that scale.

bri: That is so well said, Jay! I've written elsewhere about this (so I'm riffing on it here), but I really feel like one of the things that I've not read about are positive and affirming reasons for participating in what K.J. referred to as "worldmaking," and what I'd also call "word" making from the beginning:[13] conversations about intersectionality (rightly and accurately) focused on how having multiple marginalized identities further limits and marginalizes the people with them. This is absolutely true, but I think that intersections can also be generative, in that they allow those individuals a unique perspective: understanding and interpretation of systems—especially systems that divide and classify people. One reaction to this is to become highly critical of the system to the point where the continued use of it is anathema—something apparent in the early queer classifications and thesauri. That reaction is absolutely valid, and I don't want to malign it—I also do it!

I believe that our *word*making engages with dominant structured systems (i.e., thesauri, SKOS, linked data, etc.) from a position of marginality and, ultimately, that is an act of optimism, hope, and, yes, worldmaking.

Bibliography

Adler, Melissa A. "The Case for Taxonomic Reparations." *Knowledge Organization* 43, no. 8 (2016): 630–40. https://doi.org/10/gft38p.

---

13. Kimberle Crenshaw, "Mapping the Margins: Intersectionality, Identity Politics, and Violence against Women of Color," *Stanford Law Review* 43, no. 6 (1991): 1241–99, https://doi.org/10.2307/1229039; Kimberle Crenshaw, "Demarginalizing the Intersection of Race and Sex: A Black Feminist Critique of Antidiscrimination Doctrine, Feminist Theory and Antiracist Politics," *University of Chicago Legal Forum* 1989, no. 1 (1989): Article 8, https://doi.org/10.4324/9780429499142-5. It is worth emphasizing that Crenshaw discusses this from a Black perspective that cannot, and should not, be disentangled from the theory.

———. "Transcending Library Catalogs: A Comparative Study of Controlled Terms in Library of Congress Subject Headings and User-Generated Tags in LibraryThing for Transgender Books." *Journal of Web Librarianship* 3, no. 4 (November 23, 2009): 309–31. https://doi.org/10/fvxmwg.

Adler, Melissa A., and Lindsey M. Harper. "Race and Ethnicity in Classification Systems: Teaching Knowledge Organization from a Social Justice Perspective." *Library Trends* 67, no. 1 (2018): 52–73. https://doi.org/10/gfw9tz.

Adler, Melissa A., Jeffrey T. Huber, and A. Tyler Nix. "Stigmatizing Disability: Library Classifications and the Marking and Marginalization of Books about People with Disabilities." *The Library Quarterly* 87, no. 2 (April 2017): 117–35. https://doi.org/10/gft4b3.

Bechdel, Alison. *Fun Home: A Family Tragicomic.* 2015.

Caswell, Michelle, Marika Cifor, and Mario H. Ramirez. "'To Suddenly Discover Yourself Existing': Uncovering the Impact of Community Archives." *The American Archivist* 79, no. 1 (June 2016): 56–81. https://doi.org/10/gfc3hf.

Christensen, Ben. "Minoritization vs. Universalization: Lesbianism and Male Homosexuality in LCSH and LCC." *Knowledge Organization* 35, no. 4 (2008): 229–38. https://doi.org/10/ggcjs6.

Crenshaw, Kimberle. "Demarginalizing the Intersection of Race and Sex: A Black Feminist Critique of Antidiscrimination Doctrine, Feminist Theory and Antiracist Politics." *University of Chicago Legal Forum* 1989, no. 1 (1989): Article 8. https://doi.org/10.4324/9780429499142-5.

———. "Mapping the Margins: Intersectionality, Identity Politics, and Violence against Women of Color." *Stanford Law Review* 43, no. 6 (1991): 1241–99. https://doi.org/10.2307/1229039.

Dobreski, Brian, Jian Qin, and Melissa Resnick. "Depicting Historical Persons and Identities: A Faceted Approach." *KNOWLEDGE ORGANIZATION* 47, no. 8 (2020): 668–79. https://doi.org/10.5771/0943-7444-2020-8-668.

———. "Side by Side: The Use of Multiple Subject Languages in Capturing Shifting Contexts around Historical Collections." *NASKO* 7 (2019): 16–26.

Drabinski, Emily. "Queering the Catalog: Queer Theory and the Politics of Correction." *The Library Quarterly* 83, no. 2 (April 2013): 94–111. https://doi.org/10/f4rjgb.

Furner, Jonathan. "Dewey Deracialized: A Critical Race-Theoretic Perspective." *KNOWLEDGE ORGANIZATION* 34, no. 3 (2007): 144–68. https://doi.org/10/gfrgjg.

Greenblatt, Ellen. "Homosexuality: The Evolution of a Concept in the Library of Congress Subject Headings." In *Gay and Lesbian Library Service*, edited by Cal Gough and Ellen Greenblatt. Jefferson, NC: McFarland & Company, 1990.

———. "The Treatment of LGBTIQ Concepts in the Library of Congress Subject Headings." In *Serving LGBTIQ Library and Archives Users: Essays on Outreach, Service, Collections and Access*, edited by Ellen Greenblatt, 212–28. Jefferson, NC: McFarland & Company, Inc., Publishers, 2011.

Watson, Brian M., Chloe Noland, and Amber Billey. "The Homosaurus." *Catalogue and Index*, no. 202 (March 2021): 44–47.

Preserving Our History, Building Our Futures: Design, Naming, and Queering Library Systems

Danielle Maurici-Pollock and W. Arthur Maurici-Pollock

Keywords
Design, misnaming and misgendering, reclamations of queer history

Dr. Danielle Maurici-Pollock is an Assistant Professor at Simmons University, where she is a member of the Information Science & Technology faculty. She has a master's degree in information science from the University of Missouri, Columbia and a Ph.D. in communication and information from the University of Tennessee. Her career has included work in public, academic and special libraries.

W. Arthur Maurici-Pollock has been working in libraries for over ten years, with experience in public and academic libraries. After many years as non-degreed staff, he has recently completed his masters in library and information science at the University of Maryland, with a focus in archives and digital curation.

Conversation

Danielle Pollock-Maurici: So, what made you interested in being a part of this conversation?

W. Arthur Pollock-Maurici: Well as a queer library professional, I've given a lot of thought to the experience of queer people working in libraries. I know when I was looking for information on queer library professionals and supporting them, there wasn't a lot. There is a lot about helping patrons, which is great, but we are also on the other side of the desk and we need to talk about how to make the library a good space for queer staff and professional or non-degreed staff either way. What about you?

Danielle: Something I was looking at is the design of library systems and services and how friendly they were not only for queer patrons, but also for us as library workers. What I was finding was that there has been a lot more published about meeting the needs of LGBTQ patrons and a lot more about programming, collections, cataloging and classification, all of which is wonderful, but there were fewer things where we have actually turned the camera lens back on ourselves.

In particular, what I found missing was the voice of non-degreed or paraprofessional staff, which was interesting to me, because that was how I got my start in libraryland. Having worked in several different types of libraries, those are the folks who are often on the ground directly interacting with our users.

Arthur: Yeah, I know. I also got started as non-degreed staff and navigating that has been very interesting. I got really lucky with where I was hired to start with. I know at my one job I came out by friending my supervisor on Facebook.

When I went to my full-time job, my hope was to only be out to the people who absolutely needed to know, but that got a little thwarted by technology. They had set up stuff for you to put in the right name and everything, but they hadn't set it up so that it would actually change the name in the system for faculty and staff—they'd only set it up for students. It's just one of those things that, until cis people have to deal with it, they don't think about it. So that was a bit of a battle. Luckily, my boss was super on my side, so we basically were just like, 'Please change this,' until they changed it.

What about you, how out are you in your jobs?

Danielle: Trying to think all the way back to 1999; it was one of those things where a lot of the colleagues that I was working with were working in circulation and I was at a stage where I wanted to read all the queer books, so I assumed people knew.

Then when I first started to join professional organizations, one of my first homes was what is now the ALA's Rainbow Roundtable, so that information is all over my CV. And my feeling was always, if there is an organization that wouldn't hire me because of that, that's probably not a place I want to work.

One of the things that one of my early mentors said to me was, "If you are a visible minority in any sort of library community, be prepared to be on every committee because they'll want one of you, so if you have the choice to be visible, keep that in mind." That person was not wrong.

Oftentimes we are asked to do a lot of the work related to our own identities, and particularly if we happen to be non-degreed or junior within the organization, we are asked to do this without a lot of the institutional power to be able to make decisions.

Arthur: Yeah, I read Stephen Krueger's *Supporting Trans People in Libraries*.[1] He does talk about how you shouldn't expect your trans staff to do all of the work for changing the organization to be better for them. You want to make space for them to say things because, obviously, if there's a problem, they're the ones experiencing it, but you also don't

---

1. Stephen G. Kruger, *Supporting Trans People in Libraries*, (Denver, CO: Libraries Unlimited, 2019).

want to be like "This is your responsibility because you're this identity," which is true for all identities, really. I can't speak for trans women; I especially can't speak for trans women of color. So, if I'm the only trans person working in a library and they're like, "You have to fix all of the problems with trans people that we have," I can't do that on my own. It's a group effort of the whole organization because it's the whole organization's problem.

Danielle: I know the thing that has come up for me with technology design, I have told people and I tell my students, that if you make me design, for example, this website on my own, I'm going to design it for people who think like me, who have my life experiences, and who are using my exact same computer, my same monitor, and my favorite browser; it's just the importance of not relying on a single input, but getting community input. Not only is there a thing about having people in the room, empowering people to make decisions, but also having to look around and see who's not in the room and why and get their input as well.

Arthur: Yeah. I'm working on research right now for a paper specifically on retention of diverse staff, and I think that ties in with this conversation very well. If your library is in a community that is very diverse, and you're looking around your table in a meeting and there's not that much representation of your community around that table, you really need to be having that conversation. First among yourselves, but also more broadly, to find out what's going on.

It's not just recruitment. If you're bringing in staff who are queer, and you haven't confronted whether there's a culture in your organization that is detrimental to them in some way, you're not going to retain that staff and you're just going to be back at square one. It's an ongoing process.

Danielle: It's not, like, one effort and everything is fixed.

Preserving Our History, Building Our Futures: Design, Naming, and Queering Library Systems

Arthur: Yeah. I think that's especially true now. For trans people we find a lot of our information by going online, looking at websites or forums built by and for fellow trans people, or we find their YouTube videos or whatever. There are a lot of conversations going on online, so a lot of things are changing rapidly. I think there's an extra level to having that ongoing learning process and making sure your organization is doing it. With the way that the Internet facilitates rapid shifts in some ways, I think that that ongoing process has an extra level to it.

Danielle: That makes total sense. My research has always focused on research-oriented communities. I'm not just looking at the way queer people, or different communities and user groups adopt different technologies, but also looking at the way the people in charge of developing library systems and services have adopted new ways of looking at sexuality and gender identity and whether we're actually reflecting that in our systems and services. One of the things I'm interested in is the way that things like the library system's core software can be really, really hostile to that retention experience.

Arthur: Yeah, I know there are a lot of conversations going on that I've seen. I've gone to a few, like, Trans 101 panels for library staff. They're conversations about whether libraries need to have people's legal names on file. If yes, why? If not, why can't trans people just put whatever name they want in their system?

A lot of times, like, I was talking before with them about not setting it up for anyone but patrons; that's something that I think sometimes gets overlooked in those conversations. Your staff is there and if they have to go into their record, or if they have to go into a system that is tied to their legal name, they're like, "Well, my work day just tanked."

Danielle: That's something I want to make sure people are aware of at the very beginning stages of design. If you've got employees, there are probably reasons for retaining legal names, but just be careful that the system is always calling people what you want it to call them.

One of the things that I run into is finding a resource that's very good technically, but will deal with things like gender in an odd way. One of the online tutorials I use for beginning web design has an example of form design with gender as radio buttons: Male, Female, Other.[2] I can remember this tutorial from way back, and I think it used to just ask for male and female.[3]

Arthur: That's an interesting thing, how you were saying they used to have just male and female as the options. I just talked about how the Internet moves fast, but sometimes it doesn't, because the people doing the programming have their biases and don't think about some things.

Danielle: Sometimes it's like we're using a legacy system where somebody a long time ago decided, 'I'm going to use a Boolean for gender,' and it's just going to take a while to fix. I think sometimes if you're just not asking those questions at the beginning of the process, then it's "We've always done it this way," which is a well-known plague of libraryland.

Arthur: Oh, yeah. When I was doing my initial personal research on trans history, I was like, "I will search this term that everyone uses now," and then, of course, the cataloging and the metadata don't use that term, or they use that term and others, and some of them we don't use anymore, and you're never sure which one is going to be used for which book.

Danielle: Controlled vocabularies also move slower.

---

2. W3Schools, "Form with Radio Button Input", accessed June 11, 2021, https://www.w3schools.com/html/tryit.asp?filename=tryhtml_form_radio.

3. See W3Schools, "Form with Radio Button Input." 2 January 2016. Internet Archive. https://web.archive.org/web/20160102142158/http://www.w3schools.com/html/tryit.asp?filename=tryhtml_form_radio. Also note that in the older version, the option "male" is checked by default.

Arthur: Which can be frustrating. For patrons, if they're searching something using terms that they know, then they don't find it because the terms that are used for the cataloging are different. If I'm dealing with a patron who's looking for some sort of queer history, and I have to be, like, "Well, it looks like that's catalogued under 'super offensive term'" and then that kicks me a little bit, and I don't know if the patron's also queer, but if they are then it probably kicks them, too.

If we're used to searching in the library systems, we have a slight advantage on patrons who aren't. It can be kind of frustrating when you're like, "I'm going to see what books on trans people are in my library system. I'm good at searching in the library system because I work here," and you have to go through like eight different keywords to find anything, and the one that finds the most options is super offensive.

Danielle: What are some of the things we want cishet people to know?

Arthur: I guess a big one is, like, we can't speak for the entire umbrella. Just because you have one queer person on staff doesn't mean they know everything about what it means to be queer in all of its different intersections.

Danielle: I am going to add, pay people, compensate people. If you're already compensating them and they're salaried, make sure that that work is acknowledged and taken into account in promotion and tenure.

Arthur: You were saying earlier about the advice you got where, if you have the choice to be a visible minority, that's important to consider, too. I think that ties into the idea that queer people must take on the burden of fixing everything for queer people. Absolutely, representation is important, but you also don't want to make it so that your queer staff has to out themselves if they don't want to.

Danielle: Yeah, that's been a big concern that I've had. I want to make sure that we're never ever putting that burden on anybody, at any point ever. Even little things, like normalizing introducing yourself and saying what your pronouns are, are very good things. Requiring people to say what their pronouns are, that might result in somebody having to misgender themselves, or out themselves in a situation where they're not comfortable, can be an unintended negative consequence.

Arthur: There's discussion sometimes with name tags and including pronouns on name tags, and it should always be optional. Sometimes people might not want to or might not really know their pronouns yet, or maybe they're in a situation where they're not comfortable being out at all.

Danielle: We are recording this in the time of COVID-19. People are using Zoom across all kinds of contexts, and the system does not prompt you to change your name before every meeting. So, if you go by a different name in two different contexts, or if you're not out in a context, I really get concerned about that type of context collision.[4]

I think about those things when I think about required fields on forms. What information do people need to know? What options do we give them?

Arthur: Krueger talks about forms and he encourages, if possible, to have it so they can write it in themselves. I'm honestly 100% behind that one because there are so many different options, not just for pronouns, but also for, like, titles. I had a professor who said, "I got my doctorate so no one would ever call me Miss ever again." I respect that.

---

4. While as of this writing, challenges for identity management across contexts still exist, in June 2021, Zoom added a new Pronouns feature. This includes both an optional field for users to add their pronouns to their profiles and options for controlling if and when those pronouns are displayed during meetings. Users can opt to be asked if they would like to share the pronouns in their profile at the beginning of each Zoom meeting and webinar. See Ronnie Dickerson Stewart, "New! More Easily Add and Manage Your Pronouns in Zoom." June 22, 2021. https://blog.zoom.us/zoom-pronoun-sharing/.

Danielle: You know, I didn't think it was gonna be a big deal; I really didn't. Then, when I got the doctorate, I realized I had a title now and that I could use "Dr." It wasn't so much what that said, but what it didn't say, and it felt good in ways I cannot describe.

Arthur: So much about English is built around these perceived binaries that we built up over time. We want to categorize everything. We have this need for everything to be able to be catalogued and categorized. Look at the platypus; nothing about that animal fits into any of our boxes, but we stuck it in one anyway. That's a thing that happens, not just to trans and non-binary people, but to all queer people. Even within the community, there are arguments about what things mean. That's why having those fill-it-in-yourself options is such a good idea, because we can't know all of the permutations and possibilities, because humans are complex.

Danielle: Have you read *Sorting Things Out* by Bowker and Star ?[5]

Arthur: I have not.

Danielle: The introduction is titled "To Classify is Human." That idea that sorting things out, giving things names, putting things into categories, is something we can't help. Some of us make a career out of it. You make choices when you're imposing a point of view upon the universe and saying, "This is how this should be structured."

Arthur: Yeah, it's something I think about a lot with regards to archives. There have been a lot of conversations in the past year about how we talk about historical queer people and do we use modern queer terminology to refer to them.

One of my big examples is Dr. James Barry who lived his entire life, what we have a record of, as a man, but according to a servant who

---

5. Geoffrey C. Bowker and Susan Leigh Star, *Sorting Things Out: Classification and Its Consequences* (Cambridge, MA: The MIT Press, 1999).

disobeyed his wishes at death, he was assigned female at birth. So, history has labeled him the first woman surgeon. The question that comes up whenever people talk about this is, do we call him a trans man? Or because trans wasn't a category when he was alive in the late 1700s to mid-1800s, do we not do that?

I think about that a lot with my goal to be an archivist. Obviously, you want to have accurate information when you're archiving something, but there's also the question of if someone's looking for information on this person who was, as far as we are aware, assigned female at birth but lived as a man. I, as a queer person now, would say, "Yeah, that sounds like a trans guy."

When it comes to wanting to archive queer history, I don't want to lose the facts of these historical figures who were, as far as we can tell based on their letters and their lives, not cis or not straight. We don't want it to become ahistorical, but we also need to acknowledge that, just because they weren't using our terms doesn't mean that we can't apply them ourselves.

Danielle: You're asking some of the big questions. It's something I think about even going through things like historical survey data. The most I can say is that this percentage of people identified as these categories based on the categories they were given, because we really don't know what information they would have given us if they had been presented with other categories, other ways of talking about themselves.

Arthur: A big reason that this is something I think about so much is that often, for trans men, it's easier to be invisible, so trans male history tends to get erased or stuck into women's history. There are feminist blogs that will talk about Dr. James Barry and be like, "She was the first woman surgeon," but no one really talks about the fact that he did not stop living as a man after he left the military, which a lot of women who disguised themselves as men to fight did. It's very disheartening to be, like, this person who lived a life very similar to my own in the gender sense, and they keep getting called by the wrong pronouns, pronouns that he did not use for himself. I hope in the future I'll be able to do more research on things like the ethics of cataloging people from history.

Does thinking about things through a queer lens change how you think about database design?

Danielle: It does. Very early on in the class I'm teaching on database design, we read articles on inclusive design. Some talk about asking people what we really want to know and making sure we're collecting information that doesn't feel intrusive. That makes our systems friendlier. If it doesn't impact you, and if it hasn't ever impacted anybody you know in your community, you might not necessarily think about things.

Arthur: There's so much diversity out there, and you're not going to be able to have 100% representation all the time.

In one of my courses, we read an article on cultural competency,[6] the idea being that you work to gain a better understanding of cultures beside your own. But you don't become culturally competent, you are constantly working on your cultural competency. If you're working on your cultural competency and you're aware that you have blind spots, you might not know what they are, but you're aware that you have them and being aware is a really important step.

Danielle: Yeah, that's something we definitely talk about. A new class that I co-developed is called Intersectionality, Technology and the Information Professions, and it's something we talk about all the time.

Arthur: That sounds like a really important class. My diversity class is an elective, so it's not part of our core, and I really think it should be. It feels so odd to me to have diversity courses elective.

Danielle: One of the big things that I know my colleagues and I have been talking about is that this should not just be an elective or separate

---

6. Patricia Montriel Overall, "Cultural Competence: A Conceptual Framework for Library and Information Science Professionals," *The Library Quarterly* 79, no. 2 (2009).

from the core. I'm talking about queer identities when we're talking about basic HTML forms because when you're designing websites, that matters.

Another thing I've seen is that when we talk about services to diverse users, often we're talking about public libraries, or we're talking specifically about students. These issues also apply if you're in a special library; they apply when you're dealing with just library staff or with faculty.

Any final thoughts that we want to end on?

Arthur: Being supportive of your queer staff, in particular, and diverse staff generally, is a complicated process, but it's a process. We have to constantly be working to support an organization that is positive for these people and these identities.

Danielle: Yeah. Things are going to change, terminology is going to change, so the work is never done.

Arthur: The work is never done, and honestly, I don't think that the work is ever going to be done. If you're constantly working to be better, then you're constantly going to be getting better, but there's no finish line for this race.

Reflection

Reflecting back on our conversation, one of the things that strikes us is how much our own experiences as queer professionals, including our coming out processes, has been shaped and continues to be shaped by the design of technologies and the categorization, access, and use of digital information. Scholarship on sociotechnical systems can illuminate the values and assumptions that have often been literally encoded within those systems. For example, when considering gender, the assumption is that gender is binary, or that it is a single value that remains fixed throughout a person's lifetime, or—considering the historical scope of Arthur's research—that understandings of gender itself remain the same throughout time and across cultural contexts; or even the assumption that gender is a necessary field at all.

These assumptions are often embedded, not only in our library systems, but in the ways we learn about them. Since our conversation, we have gone on to do additional work examining the identity-management practices of queer library workers and how these are impacted by the design of physical and digital library spaces. The next stage of our continuing research begins where this conversation ends: exploring the ways in which queer issues are discussed in LIS curricula, not just in courses related to diversity, but in all courses, including those in the core and those focused on research data and information technology.

Our identities as queer library workers shape our experiences of the world and can inform the problems and challenges we notice. Our conversation touched upon, but did not name, the practice of participatory design. Involving trans stakeholders throughout a design process, for example, can help us avoid creating a system that misnames and misgenders people. However, queer library workers cannot take on the work alone, nor--given that no individual can speak for an entire community--would it be effective for them to do so. The values and assumptions that shape the way the work of equity and inclusion is framed, measured, acknowledged, and rewarded is perhaps a whole other conversation.

Along similar lines, we also found ourselves lingering on the idea that this is work that doesn't end. Arthur mentioned how cultural competence is a process rather than an end result, and we believe this ties into our discussion in two ways: first, the concept is often applied to patron experience, but it's just as important to consider how it may benefit staff. Culturally competent workplaces are going to be better workplaces for diverse staff. Second, it's vitally important that management and directors understand that there is no one way to make a workplace more welcoming or create a better experience for diverse staff. It is and will always be a continuing process, and we must be prepared to be in it for the long haul.

Bibliography

Bowker, Geoffrey C., and Susan Leigh Star. *Sorting Things Out: Classification and Its Consequences*. Cambridge, MA: The MIT Press, 1999.

Kruger, Stephen G. *Supporting Trans People in Libraries*. Denver, CO: Libraries Unlimited, 2019.

Overall, Patricia Montriel. "Cultural Competence: A Conceptual Framework for Library and Information Science Professionals." *The Library Quarterly* 79, no. 2 (2009).

Stewart, Ronnie Dickerson. "New! More Easily Add and Manage Your Pronouns in Zoom." June 22, 2021. https://blog.zoom.us/zoom-pronoun-sharing/.

W3Schools. "Form with Radio Button Input." Accessed June 11, 2021, https://www.w3schools.com/html/tryit.asp?filename=tryhtml_form_radio.

W3Schools. "Form with Radio Button Input." January 2, 2016. Internet Archive. https://web.archive.org/web/20160102142158/http://www.w3schools.com/html/tryit.asp?filename=tryhtml_form_radio.

Steeping in Community

REPRESENTING THE YONI, THE SELF-NAMING &
SIGNATURE FILES

Polly Thistlethwaite and Morgan Gwenwald

Keywords
Early lesbian feminisms, photo-documentation, lesbian community

Polly Thistlethwaite is a librarian at the City University of New York who worked with the Lesbian Herstory Archives 1987/8- 1996. Polly is honored to have been the "subject" "of portraits by Morgan Gwenwald made in the late 1980s and early 1990s to fight lesbian invisibility and to document queer erotics.

Morgan Gwenwald is a Librarian at the State University of New York at New Paltz where she is the Head of Special Collections. She has also taught in the Women, Gender, and Sexuality Studies Program on campus. She was the Executive Director of In the Life (the PBS LGBTQ TV series), worked as an MSW (at Fountain House, Columbia University, Senior Action in a Gay Environment and Stony Brook University) and also worked at the Gay and Lesbian Alliance Against Defamation. She is an established photographer (widely published in the Women's and LGBTQ press) and has served as a volunteer coordinator at the Lesbian Herstory Archives for over forty years. She is working on a major digitization of her archive of negatives of the women's, lesbian and LGBTQ communities.

Conversation

Morgan Gwenwald: When did we meet? Any idea?

Polly Thistlethwaite: Oh, gosh. Well, you were at the Lesbian Herstory Archives when I got there. I moved to New York in '86. It was '87 or '88 that I started coming up for work nights. I left a message, and I said, "This is Polly Thistlethwaite, and I've heard about Lesbian Herstory Archives, and I'd like to join your work nights." The very next day I got this message from Joan Nestle, and she was cracking up. She's like, "Helloooo, Polly Thistlewhistle…"

Morgan: [*laughs*]

Polly: "… You'd be welcome to join the Lesbian Herstory Archives." Then she gave me these very specific instructions to get there—you know, this secret lesbian handshake at the door, how to get here, and "Don't be alarmed, because it's a private residence." So then I started to turn up. When did *you* come? When did you start with the Archives?

Morgan: I wrote down some dates, because I don't remember anything. And I never have. So it's not a new thing—it's just *my* thing. Um… 1979. It matches my photo collection because that's when I have my first picture of the archives banner in a gay pride march. I kind of follow my life by when photos are taken. That's basically how I know where I was, when.

Polly: You've got some deep lesbian feminist roots, Morgan.

Morgan: Oh, I was riding the crest of the second wave. I'd been living in D.C. with my collective of Flo Hollis and Dorothy Allison, and we'd moved up from Tallahassee after attending the Sagaris feminist institute held in Putney, Vermont. My God, who's turned up at Sagaris: Rita Mae Brown, Bertha Harris, Harmony Hammond, and it just goes on and on and on. We all learned how to be better feminists—and meet girls.

Polly: Was it a festival?

Morgan: No, it was a study time actually. Every day, you had courses you were signed up for, and you'd go to lectures and talk about it. And then there were all sorts of things going on, but it was an institute—basically turned out to be lesbian summer camp but with a lot of politics in it.

Polly: Was it just that one summer?

Morgan: Yeah, it crashed and burned. There was a big split: Ti-Grace Atkinson kind of engineered a big issue in the second session. There were two sessions; I stayed for both. I just didn't want to leave. Dorothy and Flo went back down to Tallahassee—we were all in a collective, the three of us.

Polly: You were in a collective, but how would you describe your relationship with Dorothy?

Morgan: Well, first we were lovers, and then I was lovers with Flo, and then they were lovers with each other and we were really trying to work it; we really were. It didn't last very long. And I was always assuming it was going to get larger, but it never got beyond the three of us... And at that point we're like, "Well, yeah, we don't have any decent jobs in Tallahassee—let's go to D.C." So we all packed up and moved to D.C. and landed at an old Furies house. I think JEB and Rita Mae Brown lived in it when it was a Furies house. We merged all of our monies.

Polly: Oh my god. All three ways? That's a *collective*. Were the Furies co-related to Sagaris?

Morgan: No, no, no—strictly a D.C. group. Sagaris was out of Putney, Vermont, and New York City.

Polly: Oh, dang. See? My history is weak, so I'm so glad you're talking about it.

Morgan: Well, no one knows about that anymore. It was such a long time ago.

Polly: Yeah, but we should know about such things. It's a good thing that we're doing this.

Morgan: "Daughters" was the title of the feminist press that was working out of Putney, and there were some people connected to that, like Bertha Harris and Blanche Boyd and Rita Mae Brown. I think they all published under that name; that's what kind of gave us the connection to decide to move to D.C.

Polly: So the Furies were happening in D.C. and—

Morgan: They were pretty much over by the time we got there. We rented from someone locally.

Polly: When was the D.C. move? Do you remember?

Morgan: We would've moved there in '76, I think, 'cause Sagaris was '75. And then I went to Stony Brook because a couple of people from Sagaris talked me into getting an MSW, which seemed like a good idea at the time. Flo and Dorothy stayed in D.C., and I went up for the year, then to Stony Brook for two years and got my degree. Flo decided she didn't want to be in the collective anymore while I'd been away, and Dorothy was like, "I need to live in New York 'cause I want to be a writer." And I thought, "Well, I got my degree in New York. I know more people in New York. I'm fine with that. Let's move." So Mary

Farmer, who ran Lammas books—she was JEB's partner then. And the three of us and a few others were in a coven in D.C.—

Polly: You changed it from a collective to a coven?

Morgan: Oh, no no no no no. This was a whole separate thing. There was a Dianic coven that we started.

Polly: You know, at this point we're going to have to insert a charge. [*laughs*] A Dianic coven…

Morgan: Almost all lesbians. But "Dianic" means "all women," as in the goddess Diana. A mess of us had gone to a conference up in Boston called, I think, "Through the Looking Glass," and Mary Daly was a big organizer of it. When we got back, we decided, "Let's all meet and keep this work moving in some way, talk about what we've done, see what we want to do." So we had a big group meeting of people that wanted to meet, and it's split into two groups. Now, I always thought it was very interesting. The one group wanted to do, oh, maybe ESP kinds of things. The other group wanted to do rituals and things like build fires and that's, you know…

Polly: That sounds like more fun.

Morgan: That's what *I* wanted to do. But almost all of the ex-Catholics were in the other group because they were not comfortable with this ritual stuff.

Polly: They were communicating with the other side, while you were… conjuring? What's the difference?

Morgan: We were doing traditional Dianic coven things. Rituals. We made a lot of our own. And we'd go out in the country sometimes and, you know, spend the night and build fires and have fire leaping, and people would make up their own little rituals. And in the city, we would meet and celebrate the various seasons and things.

Polly: Oh my gosh, Morgan, that sounds like such an awesome, awesome time. Now I'm going to ask you, you are ageless to me. I have no idea. You are…?

Morgan: I was born in '52.

Polly: I was born in '60, so you're a mere eight years older than I am, and yet your life is so much richer in the lesbian feminist way. How did you walk into your first "lesbian thing"? Like, how old were you, and what did you do?

Morgan: Well, it wasn't a bar. My center, my community, has almost always been through volunteer work, like the Archives.

Polly: All of this—Sagaris and the houses in the collective—I had no idea about that until I met you. You and people like you. When did you start your photographic career? Your photography?

Morgan: I think of it really starting when I borrowed my mom's Polaroid camera and took pictures of the old blacksmith shop that my grandfather and uncles had run. So, that was probably junior high, maybe earlier than that. So, it's always been there. When I went to college, I didn't have any idea what I should major in, and I realized, "I don't memorize languages very well… I will major in photography—and I won't have to take a language requirement," which was a plus.

Polly: I was so in awe of you when I met you, both because of your photography skill and because of your lesbian cred. I remember I thought about changing my name, and I must have mentioned it to Deb Edel, and she told me that *you* had changed your name… like, "Really? Morgan changed her name?"

Representing the Yoni, the Self-Naming & Signature Files

Morgan: [*laughs*] It doesn't sound like a made-up name.

Polly: No, I never imagined that it was a made-up name. I thought a little bit about what would be the consequence of changing my name when I was, you know, twenty-eight years old or something, and since I'd already started in libraries, I decided to keep my crazy name.

Morgan: You have a great name. I like your name.

Polly: Well, it's super femme-y, you know? I thought about changing it to, you know, PJ or Pol.

Morgan: Names are important, too.

Polly: They are, but I never changed it. I wish I had gone with PJ right at the start. You know, "If I'd done like what Morgan did, then I'd have this way cooler name and people wouldn't do a doubletake with me at the reference desk." But then I'm like, "Well, the doubletake at the reference desk is kind of interesting." Almost all of the queers, and even the non-queers, in my professional circles now have in their signature file, "he/him/his, she/her/hers, they/them/theirs." And I'm like, "I'm not going to do that. I don't want to do that." Because it seems like my thing has always been with this crazy name and a mixed-gender appearance. You know, people are startled when they see me in the women's room, but to me, that was the power. If I made it clear, if I went around announcing my gender identity (provided I was clear about it myself), it would let people off the hook. They wouldn't have to do the work anymore of reckoning with a person who has a non-binary gender appearance; I would be doing the work for them—making them feel more comfortable. That's the way I figure it. But now, you're also 'sir'd," depending on how long your hair is, I'm sure.

Morgan: Yeah. I have a lot of issues with that, because I think a lot of that effort erases the reality that I grew up in. And I did not grow up like a little girl. I did not want to be a little boy, but I didn't want to be a little girl, either—not what little girls were. But that's a different reality than now.

Polly: How is that reality different?

Morgan: I don't feel like I'm a cis female. You know, I've never wanted to alter my body. I would like to have smaller breasts—it would be easier to do certain things—but I've never wanted to be in a different body. But I've never identified as a female in the way that every other female around me seemed to until I fell into the lesbian community.

Polly: I totally get you. I totally get you, sister. When I started in librarianship, my first job was at Yale University, and I was trying to follow my dress code from grade school, like, "Okay, I'll wear skirts." I started having a little affair with one of the super butch, cool library workers, and she said, "Polly, come on. Don't do it. It's painful to see you in a dress. We're all looking to you." And so, I threw the skirts away. I was like, "You are so right. I don't have to do this."

Morgan: So, it's like part of our story is totally lost in this pronoun discussion. And I was just in a meeting, and people were doing the pronouns, and I said "she, her, hers—for now."

Both: [*laugh*]

Morgan: I just thought, fuck it! There's no rhyme or reason with what's going on with this. It doesn't speak to my reality anyway.

Polly: Do you put anything in your signature file, Morgan?

Morgan: I've never gotten around to it. I don't know; it's so complicated. And it requires getting to know someone and having conversations. Labels have never worked for us.

Representing the Yoni, the Self-Naming & Signature Files

Polly: Yeah, the gender thing—it's kind of passed us over.

Morgan: It's passed us over because how we move through the world in our identities wasn't against who we were. It didn't make us feel not in our skin. I think for many people going through what I went through, that might not have felt good at all, and if they wanted to be a male or a trans male, wherever on that continuum, that would not be a comfortable identity for them.

Polly: I don't find our particular effort to insist that the *other* people do the work of gender negotiation is much articulated or recognized in this historical moment, with the signature files and pre-meeting pronoun check-ins. Lesbian feminism, too, was all about celebrating the feminine and, you know... [*holds up hands in diamond shape*] It was kind of viewed as a rejection of the phallus. And as an embrace of the...

Morgan: Yoni.

Polly: It was kind of like that was the dichotomy.

Morgan: Yeah, and then there was the big breakout of that around the Sex Wars, where we weren't just simultaneous-vanilla-orgasming lesbians, but we were also SM activists. We were just this whole range, which was a huge issue in our community in the '80s. Think of the Barnard Conference on Sexuality. And the book, *Pleasure and Danger.*

Polly: Did you go to that conference? You would have been able to.

Morgan: Oh, yes; I photographed it. I have pictures of the picketing out front. And we went to the Archives afterwards and hung out. Someone had posted an Instagram picture taken from an archives page of the gathering, with Pat Califia sitting on the sofa with Gayle Rubin and Madeline Davis—they're all sitting there together with other people. It was a very big issue, but that fight in the feminist community broke apart that idea of what lesbian sex was like—maybe in the '70s, '80s, to a degree, that more vanilla kind of thing—and said, "No, we are all these other things. And that's okay." The anti-porn people were saying, "But it's not okay because it's patriarchal" and how you've been duped. "You've been socialized to think that stuff's good. You're not really deciding that."

Polly: "You're too in love with the phallus" or something.

Morgan: Right. So I think all of that was a similar kind of thing around gender issues now, in a way—about people claiming the space to be who they said they were.

Polly: Well, we see the tension set at the Michigan Womyn's Music Festival where "safe space" is defined as a "women-only" space—and then you have to define "what is a woman?" And that gets complicated, and everybody's essence gets threatened by it that way.

Morgan: I have been so proud of the Lesbian Herstory Archives for not doing that and instead saying, "This is women's only night—if you define yourself as a woman, come on in. You decide if you belong here or not."

Polly: There were a few rough spots when I was there. It was not always an enlightened place. It was rougher.

Morgan: It's very different if you come up with those assumptions. That community barely existed when we were coming up.

Polly: Yeah, I was in charge of the periodicals, and we collected FTM news because—

Morgan: That's our community.

Polly: Yeah, those are our people. Ed Varga was an intern, and *Stone Butch Blues* came out at that time. And Leslie Feinberg crossed the community lines pretty fluidly, and so did Ed. And then it started to get a little bit harder when trans men started to define themselves against lesbians, or with lesbians defining themselves against trans men.

Morgan: At the point I knew Leslie, Leslie was not using he or they/them pronouns but was passing, for sure. But it just wasn't that refined in that way.

Polly: Yeah, people hadn't defined themselves against each other as much.

Morgan: For some people, truly, it was if they were living that life 24/7. But in our community…

Polly: There was a lot of fluidity.

Morgan: Yeah, that's a good word.

Polly: But there was some point where I was thinking, "If I change my name or if I change identification in some way, then I'm betraying the yoni." That argument resonated with me at the decision-making process in my twenties.

Morgan: Right now, it doesn't seem like there's any problem at all about being a queer librarian.

Polly: Well, you're living the life, too—what do you think?

Morgan: I don't think there is.

Polly: Librarianship has always been very gay, right? There is still a lot of closet in the upper echelons of libraryland, though.

Morgan: I was the only dyke when I landed at SUNY New Paltz.

Polly: Did you have out dykes on the faculty?

Morgan: A couple. Not a lot. But I was kind of shocked because I, having lived in the city, assumed that, easily, a third of any library would be queer. I think you've got an amazing career; your mentoring is a huge important gift you've given to probably everyone that works with you. But certainly, the queer and outsider librarians that work with you, and I just wonder if you could talk about your feelings about that contribution some.

Polly: You know, I just lost a colleague (Scott White) last week. I never thought he would be a librarian; his is a story about becoming a librarian when you don't fit—you know, leading with your heart. That's the mentorship story that's up in my mind right now. He wasn't queer, but ours was a queer little mentorship story. Mentoring is being in a community of people; it's being in a conversation. The conversation is not always among people who identify the same. And Morgan, you're self-archiving in a way that's very Lesbian Herstory Archives. I mean, you are one of the few artists who have also participated in creating the archive of your work. You've been creating documentation. You are a primary archivist of the lesbian feminist East Coast movement.

Morgan: I don't have as much archival training as I'd like, and as many people coming up do now, but I have been documenting our community. A lot.

Polly: It kind of brings us to that photograph a little bit, too. I was so flattered and honored when you wanted to do a little photo session with me. You did my first professional headshot.

Morgan: [*holds up photo*]

Polly: And it just happened to be that at the NYU Bobst library, then, the HQ 76s were in aisle 69! And, about the other photo, well, like my name and my gender identity, it's not the first impulse that I have to put my naked body out in public. I get my mojo from the way I wear my clothes. It's always a shirt or a pair of pants or jacket that makes me feel good and hot. I have never been comfortable without clothes on—comfortable without clothes on in public. Or...

Morgan: With someone pointing a camera at you.

Polly: Well, yeah. Obviously, I had some level of comfort, and I also respect your artistry for a lot of reasons, tons of reasons, but one of them is that you give power to your subjects, which is not legally required. You allow me to control that provocative photo, right? You do that all the time, with all your subjects.

Morgan: Well, like talking about this photo now: It's cropped.

Polly: You cropped it. But I wanted to talk a little bit about it. In the uncropped version, I had my jacket on but pants off.

Morgan: It was showing, but that's kind of it. It was very shadowy.

Polly: Do you think it leaves them guessing, like the lack of "they/them/theirs" in a signature file?

Morgan: Hmm, I don't think so. I don't see enough with a penis, to really say. But I think you would see a flesh part, there—the appendage.

Polly: Morgan, don't go telling my secrets. I am trying to talk *around* it.

Morgan: Oh, well, I think that's a very brave photo.

Polly: Well, why is it brave? Because maybe I should do it with pants on, though. Why do I have my pants off?

Morgan: Why are the pants off? Because that makes it more in your face. Part of what we're talking about in those images is eroticism.

Polly: Can you just see that photo circulating on the CUNY libraries listserv? You know, it's better that it's an older picture than a current one. Anyway, I hear what you're saying, and I respect it, and I can see things that way. I just feel like, in terms of my eroticism, I've always presented by not exposing my private bits, you know? Remember when everybody was taking their shirts off at the pride marches? Did you take your shirt off?

Morgan: No.

Polly: No. Me, neither.

Morgan: I have no problem taking my clothes off. It's just I wouldn't do it at a march when I'm working and stuff. You might need it for some reason—your shirt.

Polly: Okay, so your reason for not taking a shirt off in the marches is that you're working, which I get. My issue—it's more like I feel like I have better erotic power if I keep 'em guessing, just like the lack of a name file, you know?

Morgan: What's under the clothes, you mean?

Polly: Yeah.

Morgan: I think clothes themselves—the idea of being covered, drapery—can be incredibly erotic because you want to get underneath it. You want to see what's there. It's very evocative in a way.

Polly: We do have very brave models who are in explicit sexual positions. Beautiful, beautiful. You're, like, fighting the Sex Wars in your whole oeuvre. I see your point for that picture. But I guess the other thing is, yeah—job, career. If a naked picture comes out, and it bounces around, you almost have to be in a certain business in order not to get any blowback for that.

Morgan: And that's the conversation I always have with my models, especially about "Do you want your face in it or not?" I would always say, "Well, what if you have kids and you're head of the PTA in ten years? What if the FBI gets this and takes it to your parents?" All of those what if's that happen. So many people were like, "Oh, no one's ever going to see it. It's just in lesbian stuff."

Polly: But it's changed so much.

Morgan: The whole thing has changed. Totally.

Polly: But I think you were really anticipating it. You've done that— you've reversed the legal structure by prioritizing the model. Your artistic freedom is not compromised. By also considering your model, it's made stronger, Morgan.

Morgan: Well, I *am* a feminist. At the end of the day, I don't want to use someone in a way that's going to hurt them. It kind of destroys the whole collaborative effort of what we're doing, anyway.

Polly: You *are* a feminist; you've always presented it as a collaboration. And that's not very porny of you.

Reflection

Wow, that conversation works better on paper than I thought it would (with acknowledgments and thanks to the editors)! I barely changed anything. I am almost newly enlightened, in re-reading this, to see how intertwined were our activism and our professions. Documentation of lesbian lives, particularly of lesbian erotics, was not compatible with librarianship in the 1980s. The Lesbian Herstory Archives (LHA), that drew both Morgan and me to meet there, was defined against the mainstream libraries that failed to collect and refused to name the archives of queer subjects. LHA compensated for the lack of archival representation by collecting and naming queer subjects. Morgan's photography of lesbian and queer people, places, acts, and objects expanded the archive, literally, by making photographs. Such audacity! Boldness! Honoring the subject of the photo, allowing the subject of the photo to determine its publicity and placement, is a signature queer move, one under-recognized by theorists. Allowing the subject to name oneself, is a precursor to the self-definitions and public pronouncements we see in the signature files of our younger colleagues, even as I resist participation in that audacious act. Queer photography and gender pronouncement at once challenge the viewer to accept a self-definition as it challenges the subject to define her-, their-, or himself.

—Polly Thistlethwaite

ARE YOU FAMILY? MAPPING THE GENEALOGY OF BLACK QUEER LIBRARY WORKERS

Zakiya Collier and Steven G. Fullwood

Keywords
Archives, ancestors, intergenerational, queerness, visibility

Zakiya Collier is a Black queer archivist and memory worker. Both in her research and in her work, Zakiya explores the archival labor, methods, and poetics that are often necessary to render perceptible both the material and immaterial artifacts of quotidian Black life. She holds an MA in Media, Culture, and Communication from New York University, an MLIS from Long Island University, and a B.A. in Anthropology from the University of South Carolina.

Steven G. Fullwood is an archivist and writer. He is the cofounder of the Nomadic Archivists Project, an initiative that helps individuals establish, preserve, and enhance collections that explore the African Diasporic experience. Fullwood is the former assistant curator of the Manuscripts, Archives & Rare Books Division, Schomburg Center for Research in Black Culture. He is the cohost of *In the Telling*, a podcast exploring the global Black family experience.

Grabbing Tea: Queer Conversations on Archives and Practice

Conversation

Zakiya Collier: Why is it important to map our Black LGBTQIA+ information legacies?

Steven G. Fullwood: I think that our LGBTQIA+ information specialist ancestors were dreaming of us. They laid the groundwork for us, making it easier to find them even if it was just a bio line, like Audre Lorde saying she was a librarian. As a result, we are, in some cases, more ourselves in the workplace.

I live in Harlem near the building where queer Black archivist and historian, Alexander Gumby, had a studio. He created over 300 scrapbooks about the Black experience in the early 20th century.[1] Gumby also hosted salons during the Harlem Renaissance with folks like Langston Hughes.

Zakiya: As I try to think about how we even came to proposing this topic, I think the best way that I can think of it is by saying, "We're family." When I think about you, I'm like, "That's my family." When I think about the queer community and that question of "Are you family?" I'm trying to figure out do I relate to you? I'm getting this sense that I'm relating to you in terms of, "Are you visibly Black?" Okay. "But are you queer?" Okay. If not, you're *still* family but, like, are you *family*? For you and I, that's a given. But when we think about expanding, I think it's so important to understand more about our future and our present by understanding our past. Doing this Black queer library and genealogy work, it just feels rich and warm. Like you said, their visibility, and sometimes their decision to not be visible, still informs the way that we are able to show up, and/or not show up, as LGBTQIA+ today.

Steven: I love "Are you family?" When I came out in 1995, I was a children's librarian at Mott Branch Library in Toledo, Ohio. Mott was a safe space. My non-queer co-workers were supportive. My father supported

---

1. Alexander Gumby collection of Negroiana, 1800-1981, Columbia University.

me. The community, by and large, supported me. So by the time I came to the Schomburg, I was already formed in a way because I was out in the workplace, a luxury many LGBTQIA+ people might not feel today.

Zakiya: Yeah, thinking about how we wear or don't wear our queerness in the profession; the way that we show up and make ourselves visible is just so important. That was in '95, just a year after I was born. So, another integral part of this conversation is that this is an intergenerational conversation. I'm thinking about the way that you embrace your identity and the boldness with which you approached your work and the profession after that. That made space. When I was entering the profession by way of library school in 2016, I had no thoughts about whether anyone was going to question my identity or whether my identity as a queer person, a Black queer person, would impact my ability to get a job. I think you and others like you, and our Black LGBTQIA+ ancestors many, many years before us, made space for that.

Steven: How do we affirm our own existence through mapping Black queer presence in librarianship, archives and other information specialists in an honorable way? Many ancestors might not have identified as LGBTQIA+ professionally, or in life. People have asked me, "Why does your sexuality have to be in the workplace?" Because it *does*. It's our duty to bury our dead as many times as needed. In her essay, "Burying our Dead Twice,"[2] Barbara Smith describes being at James Baldwin's funeral in 1987 and that no one mentioned him being queer. So she and other Black queer folk held their own ceremony. We have to honor our dead *our* way to prevent erasure.

Zakiya: Yeah, I really like that you brought up this concept of burying our dead two and three times over, honoring with the fullness of their experiences and the fullness of our own. As time goes on, language

---

2. In Barbara Smith, *The Truth That Never Hurts: Writings on Race, Gender, and Freedom* (New Brunswick: Rutgers University Press), 2000.

changes. We learn more about ourselves, and *ourselves* being the mix and combination of all of us that have existed before us. I like to think that with the information that our Black LGBTQIA+ ancestors, and our ancestors more broadly had, and the time period that they were living in, they were making space and opportunity for us to have new ways to identify and new language. So, I like to think that our ancestors were doing the work to make the space for us to have these questions, to have more options in our language, to not have certain identities and certain roles conscripted for us or on us.

I think it's okay to claim and reclaim; to say "Okay, maybe this is not how you identified in 1950. But I'd like to think that if you were here with us in 2020…" In a really Black sci-fi, ancestral way; if Audre was here with us in 2020, what would that look like? How would she identify and what scenes would she be a part of, if at all? It's all speculation, of course, but I think it's still important to ask the questions, if nothing else; just asking all the questions we can think of.

Steven: Beautifully put. You made me think about the precarity of Black LGBTQIA+ life, culture, and history. So, the conversation that we're having is about *ancestry*: connecting, having questions, and doing imaginative work that is critical for archives and for who we are in this world. I came of age, for example, in the age of AIDS, right? Scores of people died. Those lives and lineages need to be resurfaced. When I was collecting material for the In the Life Archive (ITLA) at the Schomburg Center,[3] I learned a lot. Many men and women active in the 1980s and 1990s, who maybe published a poem or short story in an anthology, just vanished. But the traces are there, something to follow and map. Having this conversation about surfacing a Black, queer, information specialist genealogy is not just an affirmation for us, but for them, too. We're clear that somebody else is coming and *needs* this. And no doubt they will take what we're doing much, much further.

---

3. Formerly known as the Black Gay and Lesbian Archive.

The ITLA got me thinking broadly about what's at stake here when we don't actively collect, preserve, or honor our heritage. We lose. We collude in our destruction. *We disappear ourselves, willingly.*

US citizens are amnesiatic; you're supposed to exist in a disconnected state. Be a subject of the empire. Be capitalist or consumer. Family *only* when it works for the economy. And so, here we are, "Are you family?" We *are* family—ancestry means everything.

Zakiya: I think it's precarity from so many different angles; like the precarity of being Black, of being LGBTQIA+, of being those two things *and* in the library profession. We now have these diversity residences, but we have always been there. If you aren't vocal in spaces (not that you have to be), or invisibilized in library spaces, then it's very easy for you to be forgotten. I could imagine that we have some Black LGBTQIA+ library ancestors who may have passed away from AIDS and we don't know. We just don't know, and that is a legacy that we would have to unearth, like Alice Walker did for Zora [Neale Hurston], recreating that grave, burying another time, one time over, bringing the flowers.

I also want to think about this work of digging through and understanding the precarity, but also understanding where that intersects with someone not identifying as queer or LGBTQIA+. And does the identity start at the time you identify, or what if you never identify as such?

Steven: When we spoke prior to this conversation, you mentioned something about non-linear identities; like, when does queerness start? Does it start when you come out? Is it before that? I think that suggested fluidity allows me, personally, to wrap my arms around people who have identified at some point, right? Maybe not in the workplace, but maybe later on in their lives, privately. Also, what about the folks who hadn't, didn't, or couldn't? I want to mention Darryl Stevens, a former Schomburg employee, who left before I arrived in 1998. I remember his name because my brother's name is Darryl, and my name is Steven. [*both laugh*]

I never met him. When I got to Schomburg, many people asked me if I knew him. I was told that Darryl died of AIDS complications, maybe in the late 90s. People would tell me that he was a wonderful guy. He worked in acquisitions. Most people didn't know he was queer, even as he was actively working on a Black gay and lesbian bibliography. So, for me, he's an ancestor, a forefather. He was, in a sense, waiting on *me*, you know? He's somebody who was doing the work that I came to do, right? Which was to highlight, identify, and make available to the public Black queer culture and history at the Schomburg.

One of the first Black gay collections that came to the Schomburg was the Joseph F. Beam Papers, donated by Joe's mother, Dorothy Beam. When Joe died, Mrs. Beam's friends told her to throw all his stuff away; it was only going to make her sad. But she ended up doing the opposite. Not only did she keep Joe's stuff, she sat down and wrote to all the people that had submitted work to Joe's second book-in-progress,[4] and said, "We're going to do the book, don't worry." She invited Essex Hemphill and his cat to live in her duplex to complete the book. After the book was published in 1991, Mrs. Beam gave her son's papers to Schomburg. As a result of her diligence, she got a better sense of Joe's writings and activism. Mrs. Beam became a self-described gay activist, HIV and AIDS activist, and supported parents who had queer children. In addition, she participated in a number of documentaries.

The reason why I bring up Mrs. Beam is because even though she didn't identify as a queer woman, she made sure that we knew Joe. I think about people who don't identify as queer, folks who supported us, the cultural folks who were writing about us and archiving our experiences. I hold those people close to my heart.

Zakiya: Uh hm, uh hm. Extended family. [*laughs*]

Steven: [*laughs*] They're extended family! They're at the picnic, right? We cannot forget the brilliant Ellis Haizlip, who created and hosted Soul,[5]

---

4. That book project became *Brother to Brother: New Writings by Black Gay Men*, edited by Essex Hemphill, conceived by Joe Beam, and the project was managed by Dorothy Beam, 1991.

5 "Soul!" was a pioneering performance/variety television program showcasing Black arts and literature in the late 1960s and early 1970s.

which was on PBS for five years. After the show ended, Ellis came to Schomburg, bringing his talent, influence, and vision, which developed the Center's public programming. He was an out Black queer man. So, although he wasn't a librarian or archivist, he was making those inroads there for Black queer folk, as well.

So this queerness, in the most expansive sense, illuminates us and our extended family who helped make our collective road easier to find and walk. It's incumbent upon us to do good work while we're here. The call is to make someone else's life better. I take it very seriously.

Now, tell me about Audre.

Zakiya: Yeah, I always want to talk about Audre. So, it's December 2016. I'm sitting at NYU's Bobst Library in Greenwich Village, and Audre lived there. I'm sitting in spaces of Black queer history and the gay Rights movement history, just by being in Greenwich Village. And I'm also reading *Sister Outsider* for a Black Feminist Theory class.

I'm also applying for library school and really thinking, "Why do I feel so called to libraries at this moment?" I have always felt called to libraries, you know? I worked in the media center in elementary and middle school. In undergrad I found myself applying to Public Library jobs (and not getting them, which I'm still bitter about). [*both laugh*] Richland County Public Library in Columbia, South Carolina, y'all missed out! Love y'all though, because y'all helped me to get where I am.

But I had this moment like, all right, "Audre has made herself apparent to me in this way, in this moment, for this purpose." So, as I'm writing this application essay, like, "Libraries have always been this to me, but it's also been this violent place for Black people. So, I love the library but also, there's a lot of policing of Black people, myself included. There's this surveillance and it doesn't feel welcoming, including sometimes in libraries in Black neighborhoods." So just like I'm writing about that, I'm also bringing in this spirit of Audre as I'm reading *Sister Outsider*, and going back and forth between the two things.

Later on down the line I learned about her time as a librarian. I learned that she got her library degree in '61 and then worked in libraries in New York from 1955 to 1968. I learned this through the work of Professor Ethelene Whitmire who's done this research into Audre's life as a librarian—going through papers at the Lesbian Herstory Archives in Brooklyn and her papers at Spelman College trying to understand who she was as a librarian—because that's still a part of her identity.[6]

But I do find it interesting that when she decided to quit being a librarian, she also ended the relationship with her husband and started dating women. It's like, okay, so she was *straight* when she was a librarian? What was that experience like for her? Is it like when you cut your hair off when your relationship is over? For us, speaking from her future, *can* we claim her as a Black lesbian librarian if that's not how she identified between '55 and '68? Like, if we speak from the end of her life and just list all the things that she was, and still is to so many of us, the words "Black," "lesbian," and "librarian" are going to be in there. So, I feel like we can claim and reclaim that over and over again and celebrate the fact that this particular figure, who means so much to so many people, was a librarian. So, we have a shared experience in that way, and that feels special. I feel like I can hold on to that, and like no one can take that away from me. Like, no one! [*both laugh*]

Steven: I need Audre! I don't need a nuclear family. I need everybody. We need everybody!

Zakiya: We need everybody! "Are you family?" [*laughs*]

Steven: Let's talk about how we are finding our ancestors. For Audre, she told you in her work. My elders have been critical in identifying people, Black queer lives, in context. There's a difference between visible and being out. People *knew*, but it wasn't necessarily something that you led with. For example, one of my elders told me that you either had to be

---

6. Stacy Torian, "Audre Lorde was a world-famous feminist and poet. Did you know she was also a librarian?" *The Route 3 Blog*, April 2, 2020, https://storianblog.wordpress.com/2020/04/02/audre-lorde-was-a-world-famous-feminist-and-poet-did-you-know-she-was-also-a-librarian/.

Black or gay. At professional library conferences, if folks saw you going into the gay Caucus meeting, it could mean, at the extreme, losing your job. People had a right to be afraid of being "out."

We've always been here. I believe that once you put it into the universe that you want to know something, that's when the stories come. When I told a friend of mine about our conversation, he said, "Oh, I'll ask around." Questions come back to me: "Do you know about such and such?" And then comes a little biography. And then maybe, "Oh, I don't think she has any papers anywhere, but I know her sister."

I love "Are you family" because it hits 360 for me in so many different ways. It feels like, "Oh, we've been waiting on you."

Zakiya: Yeah, I think you made so many great points along the way in talking about how you think about doing this work, and the beautiful thing about this particular format and this book chapter. This book is so beautiful in that it builds on a practice that already goes on in our world. I would say that our communities keep things in conversation, and, like, you don't always find it on a physical document but someone knows that information—the oral tradition, which is so important to Black people; it's this shared importance with the Black LGBTQIA+ community. Like, even if it's not written down, somebody knows it. And so all you have to do, like you said, is put that seed out there, like, "Oh, I'm interested in learning about this person." And it's like, "Okay, I don't know that. But I know this, this, and this," and then, before you know it, you're in a conversation four hours long in some parking lot after you're supposed to have been gone, but you are now having this conversation about all these connections.

The oral tradition will always be one of our best tools because it's the conversation that leads us to the papers, but how do you know where to look? There are efforts to silence and erase our histories and our experiences. And so, thinking about these queer memory worker ancestors who have done this work, and we think about these things, and we come to these answers through conversation. Some of the things that we don't necessarily look for that we can start to look for are, who were the people? Assuming that queer folks attended the library programs, who were the folks who may not identified as LGBTQIA+ themselves, but were family? Could we have found answers by making sure that we were in the room and a part of the conversations? Who were the people making sure that those collections were preserved, whether they made sure they came into the building or just worked with people to preserve their own materials? These are some of the stories that we may only get by way of conversation. We can start to look at the work, have this lineage of labor, and have this family that comes through the shared experience of doing the same type of work.

Steven: The Black Caucus of the American Library Association's (BCALA) 2nd annual conference in 1994 was my first professional library conference. My colleagues and I presented on Mott's thriving against the odds. We had high circulation and great attendance at our programs. It wasn't surprising to us. We had great service, a great selection of materials, and great programming. BCALA was my first exposure to a Black male queer information specialist's presence. I was invited to lunch with a group of these men. I've maintained friendships with a number of these men over the years.

I remember reading the conference program and looking at everyone's headshots. These were smart, bookish people. I was a fanboy. *Family.* Printed materials like this, as well as newsletters for Black and queer roundtables, could be useful to us as we search for our people.

Zakiya: Going back to something you said earlier about the clarity you experienced when you were first going to these conferences, this security, and financial security around if you go to the gay and lesbian section meeting, then there becomes this separation of your identity. It feels like you have to be Black or you have to be queer. Or you get your Black card snatched if you go to that. Even now, I don't personally participate in the LGBT sections of things because I'd rather go into a Black space and have the chance of bumping into another queer person than go to the LGBTQIA+ section meeting and not bump into a Black person.

I saw this thing on Twitter the other day that asked, "What is your academic genealogy?" And they were really just sharing. Like, "Who was your dissertation advisor? Who was their advisor?" I think we could do something like that and ask, "Who were your mentors and who was your mentor's mentor? Were they Queer? Were they Queer-affirming? Who influenced you?"

My first librarian mentor, Shawn(ta), is a co-editor of this book, and I had the distinct pleasure of being her mentee. Alice Walker so beau-tifully talks about the importance of having models for herself as a writer. And I think for us, it's Black LGBTQIA+ information professionals. I have Audre. I had her application day—day one. But it's also important to have present models. I applied to what at the time was the Association of Research Libraries' Initiative to Recruit a Diverse Workforce (IRDW), now called the ARL Kaleidoscope Program. For the mentorship component, they had this form where it asks you "What are your mentor preferences?" And so I'm like, "Black! Queer! Hello? Please!" And I was fortunate that they were able to make that happen. And so they do this little introduction like, "Here's Shawn(ta), your mentor." And I'm reading her bio and looking at her website, and I'm like, "Yeah, oh my gosh, this is gonna be amazing! She's a librarian. She's an archivist, and she's Black. She's queer. She's an artist. She's a writer." And I'm just like, "This is dope! I've struck gold!"

I credit her hugely with how quickly and how comfortably I felt just making a space for myself in the profession and feeling comfortable in being a part of spaces that I never would have even known existed. She invited me to the Lesbian Herstory Archives and gave me a personal tour of what goes on and how things work in a community archive, and she invited me into other library events and conversations. They weren't always Black/LGBTQIA+ specific, but most times they were, and she just made sure that I felt welcome. She made this space for me and made it okay for me to be Black, Queer, and visible and just really emboldened me to be this person that's here today.

Steven: So as you were waxing about our beloved Shawn(ta), a couple thoughts came to mind. My librarian/archivist career was primarily shaped and supported by Black heterosexuals, primarily Black women, who trained and taught me about the politics of saving global Black culture.

Zakiya: Mm hmm.

Steven: They saw something in me, and I really appreciated it. They knew I was ambitious. I can be really bullheaded if I want something. I just go after and get it, stumbling the entire way!

Zakiya: Come on, Capricorn!

Steven: When I was in library school at Clark Atlanta University, I had an opportunity to go to the ALA conference in San Francisco in 1997. All I wanted was to meet Howard Dodson, director of the Schomburg Center. That was it. When I got there, I searched for him, resume in hand. I didn't know what he looked like, so I just went to all the Black booths in the exhibit hall (Johnson Publications), and they said, "Oh yeah, he was just here," or "He went that way." Finally, I found him. Dr. Dodson was kind; he took my resume and gave it to Diana Lachatanere, my boss, mentor, and champion for over fifteen years.

At the time, Ms. Lachatanere was the curator of the Manuscripts, Archives and Rare Books Division and the assistant director of Collections and Services at the Schomburg Center. Her guidance and support encouraged me to start and develop the Black Gay & Lesbian Archive, known now as the In the Life Archive (ITLA). Diana taught me how to develop the ITLA and how to be a thoughtful, ethical archivist.

I was in the right place at the right time. The Black queer community *built* the ITLA. They understood the endless impact of having our culture preserved and were happy to be part of the ongoing conversation about freedom work here in the U.S. and abroad.

Zakiya: Right.

Steven: I speak fluent *community*. I speak fluent *Black*.

I noticed that we haven't talked about love, specifically, which is critical. I'm a loved person, so I assume certain things when I walk into a room because I bring the self I want to bring, the one I like rather than code switch for the sake of safety.

Zakiya: Being loved and trusted are incredibly important. And as we think about the pursuit of mapping out this legacy of Black queer librarianship, there's so much hurt there around how people are treated in spaces; and that is the gist of kynita's piece—not feeling welcomed and not being able to feel whole in these spaces.[7] And so, I think in library spaces it's so important that this process is conducted from a genuine place, to not misgender and mislabel, but really, a place to know more about ourselves and understanding that there may be some missteps along the way.

Zora Neale Hurston, for example, never identified as queer, at least not that I've seen, but I've seen her name on every famous LGBT Black people historical list. But we still don't have any information fully, and that's okay; I'm going to go ahead and claim her, too, especially because, for a very short period of time, she was a librarian, which most people don't know. When I say short, I do mean short. She worked on the Patrick Air Force Base in Florida and actually disliked her duties as a librarian.[8] She was a librarian to have a stable paycheck and a salary, and so that's a bit different from someone who's like, "Yes, this is for me. I'm going to go to school for it. I love it." But I think about this concept of whom we can embrace in this lineage and add to this map or this roadmap for future generations. We have Zora and she didn't like her work and was

---

7. kynita stringer-stanback, "kynita stringer-stanback: Blaq (Black & Queer) in the Library, Part I," *WOC+lib* (blog), September 18, 2020, https://www.wocandlib.org/features/2020/9/18/blaq-black-amp-queer-in-the-library-part-i.

8. Valerie Boyd, *Wrapped in Rainbows: The Life of Zora Neale Hurston* (New York: Scribner, 2004), p. 426.

fired from her job because she was too educated. I want to claim her, and I like to think that, in 2020, she would be an amazing librarian or archivist as a collector of stories and a memory worker.

Steven: I also think about Ann Allen Shockley, former librarian and oral historian at Fisk in the 1970s, who does not identify as queer or lesbian but wrote a novel about Black lesbians in 1974.[9] She's family. So it's not simply you're Black and out, no. There's so much to discover just through talking about the constellation of our Black queer information specialists ancestry.

Zakiya: Uh huh.

Steven: We gotta put it down.

Zakiya: I think just continuing to do this work and digging. Digging back into time, digging side by side, is just so necessary. I just want to read out the quote from *WOC +Lib* called "kynita stringer-stanback: Blaq (Black & queer) in the Library, Part I" and this, this is just the closing paragraph:

> Black, LGBTQ, gender non-conforming/non-binary folks have been part of our libraries since they've existed. Have we been able to organize? Where do we gather? How do we articulate our experiences and help one another move through our careers—being able to bring our entire selves to work everyday? It's hard enough being Black. It's hard enough being LGBTQ. Add non-binary articulation of gender to the workplace and, well, the Black unicorns understand. We are not free. We are restless. We are unrelenting. We must tell our stories. Eventually, they will have to listen.[10]

We could not have said it better ourselves. Invoking Audre Lorde, again, with the Black unicorns. But, to reiterate, we just, we have to tell

---

9. Ann Allen Shockley, *Loving Her* (Indianapolis: Bobbs-Merrill, 1974).

10. stringer-stanback, "kynita stringer-stanback."

our stories and find our stories. And they will listen, and we'll have the pleasure of listening to each other.

So shout out to all the Black LGBTQIA+ non-binary, gender nonconforming folks that we work with, and love and the light in the library profession. Just a shout out.

Steven: Yes. Shout out to librarians, archivists, information specialists, and memory keepers, the ones we know, the ones we will meet, the ones to survive us. To Shawn(ta), Reginald Harris, Alexis Pauline Gumbs, Christopher Stahling, and Lisa C. Moore, a publisher who recently became an archivist. I like to wax about these people and their brilliance.

Zakiya: The lineage.

Reflection

This conversation brings up an abundance of emotions for me. Mostly, I overwhelmingly feel blessed and grateful to have so much Black queer love within the information profession. I am truly indebted to my Black queer ancestors and colleagues—my family—for where I am today and for the successes I've had in my work thus far. And like our dear ancestor, Toni Morrison says, "The function of freedom is to free someone else."[11] So I feel the responsibility to make space for those coming after me in the same way that folks like you, Steven, and Shawn(ta) made, and continue to make, space for me. Any chance I have to speak to Black queer library students, I approach them with warmth, openness, love, humility, and transparency about where we are as a profession. Through conversation, there's so much to learn about ourselves and our Black queer ancestors and descendants.
—Zakiya Collier

---

11. "The Truest Eye," *O, The Oprah Magazine,* November 2003, https://www.oprah.com/omagazine/toni-morrison-talks-love/all.

After rereading and editing this wonderful conversation, it occurred to me how new we Black queer folks are, *in this moment*. That is, being out in libraries and archives and preserving our history and culture. And we now bear the responsibility of making it easier for those coming after us. Visibility is political. We must engage in work that delights in community-building, creating unique archival initiatives, innovative programming, imaginative art works, and whatever else we need to help us love, breathe, create, and help manage information and information systems. Cultural worker Toni Cade Bambara's famed novel, *The Salt Eaters*, begins with the only question anyone ever had to ask anybody, and that is, "Are you sure, sweetheart, that you want to be well?"[12] Black queer artists and activists continue to answer that call. We want to be well, and there's a lot of weight in getting us to well.

—Steven G Fullwood

Bibliography

Bambara, Toni Cade. *The Salt Eaters*. Reissue edition. New York, NY: Vintage, 1992.

Boyd, Valerie. *Wrapped in Rainbows: The Life of Zora Neale Hurston*. Reprint edition. Princeton, N.J.: Scribner, 2004.

Hemphill, Essex, ed. *Brother to Brother: New Writing by Black Gay Men*. First edition. Washington, D.C: RedBone Press, 2007.

Shockley, Ann Allen. *Loving Her*. Open Road Media, 2014.

Smith, Barbara. *The Truth That Never Hurts: Writings on Race, Gender, and Freedom*. First Paperback Edition. New Brunswick, N.J.: Rutgers University Press, 2000.

stanback, kynita stringer-. "kynita stringer-stanback: Blaq (Black & Queer) in the Library, Part I." Blog. *WOC+Lib*, September

---

12. Toni Cade Bambara, *The Salt Eaters*, Reissue edition (New York, NY: Vintage, 1992): p. 3.

18, 2020. https://www.wocandlib.org/features/2020/9/18/blaq-black-amp-queer-in-the-library-part-i.

O, *The Oprah Magazine*. "The Truest Eye." Accessed July 6, 2022. https://www.oprah.com/omagazine/toni-morrison-talks-love.

Torian, Stacy. "Audre Lorde Was a World-Famous Feminist and Poet. Did You Know She Was Also a Librarian?" Blog. *Storian Blog,* April 2, 2020. https://storianblog.wordpress.com/2020/04/02/audre-lorde-was-a-world-famous-feminist-and-poet-did-you-know-she-was-also-a-librarian/.

"It's a Friendship, It's a Kinship, It's a Relationship"

Steven D. Booth and Tracy S. Drake

Keywords
Black queer archival networks, community support, mentors

> **Steven D. Booth** is the Archive Manager of the Johnson Publishing Company Archive for the Getty Research Institute and Smithsonian National Museum of African American History and Culture. He is a founding member of The Blackivists and has held leadership positions in the Society of American Archivists. Steven earned an M.S. in Library Science from Simmons College and also holds a B.A. from Morehouse College.
>
> **Tracy S. Drake** is the Director of Special Collections and Archives at Reed College and founding member of The Blackivists. A native of Chicago, she currently resides in Portland, OR. She is a graduate of Eastern Illinois University with a B.S. in African American Studies, an MA in history from Roosevelt University, and an M.S. in Library and Information Science from the University of Illinois at Urbana-Champaign.

Conversation

Labels

Tracy Drake: We started to have this conversation before; about how you identify and just how complicated that can be. The spectrum is so wide and encompasses a lot of different things. So I've been, at this point in time, calling myself a Queer Black woman. But lately I've been thinking about that in terms of what it means to just say, "Lesbian." Essentially, that's where I am. I'm exclusively dating women, but using the term Queer as a way to have language that is responsive to heteronormative behavior.

Steven Booth: I identify as a Gay Black man, and it's funny that you bring up being Queer. It's nice to see how we as a community have redefined what that means. There's no longer a negative connotation to it—depending on who you talk to, and what age they are, and what era they grew up in. I like that, and it's a nice encompassing term when you think about trying to bring together everyone in the community. In thinking about this and our identity, how have you created or found community in this predominantly white profession?

Community

Tracy: I found that really tough at first, even for somebody who got involved with the American Library Association's Rainbow Round Table.[1] I was around the LGBT community, but within that community I was still the only Black person. It was a little disheartening because I know those folks exist, but it was like, "Where are they?" It's funny, sometimes

---

1. "Rainbow Round Table History Timeline," accessed July 14th, 2021, https://www.ala.org/rt/rrt/about/history. The Rainbow Round Table (RRT) of the American Library Association (ALA) was founded in 1970 as ALA's Task Force on Gay Liberation. It is the nation's first gay, lesbian, bisexual and transgender professional organization.

we as Black folks, Black and Queer folks, just kind of gravitate to each other when we see each other out in rooms.

So even if folks weren't Black, what I've found through working with the roundtable is that finding other Queer folks of color has definitely been a great experience for me. I was able to seek those people out, and in the end that's how I found you, Steven!

Steven: Word of mouth!

Tracy: Yeah! That's how you build. You get your first connection to that world and then that person introduces you to another person, and from there, that's how I've created a community. You know, I'm sure other folks have a very different experience, though.

Steven: I remember going to my first Society of American Archivists annual meeting, which was in 2008 in San Francisco, and I went to the business meeting for the Lesbian & Gay Archives Roundtable.[2] I remember going into this room, looking around, and I was the only person of color. I was also probably the youngest person in the room. It was predominantly white older men—even some Lesbian women. I don't think I stayed for the entire meeting because I honestly felt uncomfortable. I didn't feel like it was a space where I belonged.

It was either at that meeting, or maybe at ALA that summer, where I met Harrison Inefuku. We immediately clicked. It was like, "Oh hey, that's my people!" I think it's easier to find community at professional association meetings because you get to meet people from all over versus being in a workplace where you're probably the only one. So,

---

2. "Diverse Sexuality and Gender Section," accessed July 14th, 2021, https://www2.archivists.org/groups/diverse-sexuality-and-gender-section. The Lesbian & Gay Archives Roundtable was founded in 1989 by members of the Society of American Archivists (SAA) who were concerned about LGBTQIA+ history and the role of members of this community in the archival profession. The group promotes the preservation and research use of records documenting LGBTQIA+ history and serves as a liaison between LGBTQIA+ archives and the SAA. It was renamed the Diverse Gender and Sexuality Section (DSGS) in 2017.

after meeting him, I met others and eventually the circle grew. While it has grown, it hasn't gotten that much bigger.

Tracy: It's still not as big in numbers as we would like for it to be.

Steven: Yeah, it's interesting. I'm grateful for you and for being in community with other folks. These relationships have really helped me stay focused and centered and feel supported, especially while working in predominantly white workplaces. But I wish there were more of us. I'm not sure why there aren't. One thing we've done when we go to conferences is try to make ourselves available and approachable to others that might be in attendance.

Tracy: I'm glad that you made that distinction between the professional associations versus the workplace. It's possible to feel very isolated and alone in these workplaces. Often in various workplaces I have been the only one. I worked in a predominantly Black institution where most of the folks looked like me. But they didn't share all of the same identities as me, which presented its own difficulties.

Donor Relations

Steven: If you're not the only one, there might be this unspoken rule that "discretion is the greater part of valor," which is something that I was told in college. Feeling isolated in a Black workplace is something we rarely discuss. How has your identity influenced and impacted relationships with either donors, colleagues, or institutional leadership?

Tracy: It's been a mixed bag for me. I'll give a couple of examples:

I once had a donor that I really, really struggled with, who made both homophobic and sexist comments. It was problematic. One time he made me so uncomfortable that I had to tell him without making it personal, "What you're saying is not right, and because you're of a certain age and grew up in a certain time period, does not excuse your behavior." It's a delicate conversation to have with any donor, especially prominent people, because you don't want to ruin the relationship that the institution has built. You want to correct the person's behavior, or at least acknowledge that it is problematic. But then also not ruin the possibility of your institution acquiring a collection. I find that to be difficult.

Steven: Was the donor receptive to the correction?

Tracy: So, he did say that he understood, but later down the line he made another comment. Each time he said something, I corrected him again, "Sir, those comments are inappropriate."

Steven: I'm glad you were able to maintain a level of professionalism without it coming across as being personal, even though it is and was a very personal situation.

Tracy: I started to realize just how important it is for us to bring our whole selves to work and what that can mean.

There was a potential donor I had a conversation with over the phone. We set a date for them to visit the library. When they arrived, I noticed they had another person with them. We introduced ourselves and they said, "Oh, this is… I didn't know if it was okay. I brought my partner with me, can they come in the room too?" That part stuck with me, "I didn't know if it was okay." It wasn't about her wondering if it was okay. It was whether or not people were going to be accepting and comfortable.

When we got into the conference room, they sat down and she started the conversation again. She told me that she'd come across my Twitter account and had seen a tweet that assured her it was okay to bring her partner. I told them that, in fact, it was okay because I'm also a part of the community. Once I revealed myself, I was able to shift the mood of the conversation, which made them feel comfortable. I still talk to that donor, even though I'm no longer at that institution. Being in a space where you can bring your whole self and what that means, not just for me but also for the donors and the public that we interact with, matters. We have this kinship. We are family. This is a community.

Steven: Going from a public institution to an academic one, how have you been able to continue to bring your whole self to work at your current institution? I'm thinking about your work with students. What is that like?

Tracy: When I was involved in the Rainbow Round Table's Stonewall Book Awards Committee,[3] I had a student who had a really traumatic experience, and I recommended one of the books to them. The student sat there and read it within an hour. After they finished, they told me, "You know, this was a really powerful book for me to read and I saw myself in it." And the student started crying; we had a moment where we hugged, and it was special. At that moment, I thought, *"This is why I'm here.* This is why it's important for me to be here, in this archival space, this very white space; to be able to connect with other people in ways that are meaningful.: And whether that's through archival material or human connection, it's important.

Collections

Steven: That's really dope. So, thinking about archival material, does Reed College have a large LGBTQ+ collection, and if not, is that something that they're interested in adding to their collection development policy?

---

3. "Stonewall Book Awards," accessed July 14th, 2021, https://www.ala.org/rt/rrt/award/stonewall. The Stonewall Book Awards, sponsored by the American Library Association's Rainbow Round Table, is the first award for LGBTQIA+ books. It was first awarded in 1971 to Isabel Miller for *Patience and Sarah*. The award is announced in January/February and presented to the winning authors or editors at the American Library Association (ALA) Annual Conference in June. The award winners each receive a commemorative plaque and $1,000.

Tracy: We don't. My spiel to students, faculty, and staff is that we shouldn't only encourage students to visit the archives for class assignments. It's equally important for people to see themselves in archival material. They've done a lot of work collecting the materials of old straight white men. So, we definitely have some work to do as it relates to decolonizing the archives and making sure that it is encompassing everybody's story. I'm the first trained archivist they've hired, and I've started to do some of that work, but it's going to take some time. It's a process that I'm committed to for the long haul.

Steven: I'm glad they have someone there, like you, who really cares about that. Oftentimes it takes one person to really shift the culture. So, it's nice to know that Reed, as an institution, is receptive to this criticism and they want to rectify it as much as possible.

Respectability Politics

Steven: I have been really fortunate to have great mentors throughout my career and so I've tried, as best as I can, to pay it forward and also give back. I've noticed that the younger Black queer professionals don't subscribe to respectability politics, and I absolutely adore and admire that. In thinking about my own experience, I've been able to get as far as I have because I know how to dress and speak well. I felt as though if I did that it was okay to be a Black Gay man. I'm glad to know that now people can, as you say, "bring their whole selves" and not have to live under this shadow or this cloak; we don't have to closet ourselves.

Tracy: Have you seen folks that maybe didn't buy into respectability politics and maybe they haven't been as accepted into the professional organizations, or the archiving world?

Steven: I think about that in a different way: who were the people who thought about entering this profession and did not because they didn't see any representation of themselves? Who started their library school programs but decided somewhere along the way that they didn't want to do it because they didn't see themselves? I would like to know who those people are and to hear about their experiences. I've been really fortunate. So, I don't know what the other side of that looks like.

Tracy: Now that's interesting. I guess we'll never know. It's sad to even think that that's a possibility. Or that they didn't stay because they may have had negative experiences and not the connections that we were able to grasp onto early on.

Steven: As long as you have a community, you can survive. Having a support system makes a world of difference.

Tracy: That's how we survive. My first SAA was two years ago. And it was an unforgettable experience. I had a Lena Waithe pin, of her wearing a rainbow flag at the Met Gala.[4] Someone stopped me to ask, "Where did you get that pin from?" We struck up a conversation and before I knew it, I was surrounded by a whole community. And I was like, "this is Love." It was amazing to see and be around other Black folks, and also be in a community where people love you just because.

Steven: It really is a big-ass family reunion. It is nice to see how much it's grown. For a while it was the elders, the Simmons College squad, a few people from The HistoryMakers Fellowship program,[5] and maybe

---

4. "The Costume Institute," accessed July 14th, 2021, https://www.metmuseum.org/about-the-met/curatorial-departments/the-costume-institute. The Costume Institute Benefit, also known as the Met Gala, is an annual fundraiser for the department's exhibitions, acquisitions, and capital improvements. Each May, the gala celebrates the opening of the spring exhibition. The gala is a star-studded charity event bringing together attendees from the fashion, film, society, sports, business, and music industries.

5. "The HistoryMakers Fellowship, Mentoring, Training and Placement Institute," accessed July 14th, 2021, http://thehistorymakersfellows.blogspot.com/p/imls-fellows-2011-2012.html. The HistoryMakers offered two year-long fellowship opportunities, 2011-2012 and 2012-2013, for African American archivists and other archivists interested in working with African American archival collections. The fellowship was made possible by a grant from the Institute of Museum and Library Services (IMLS).

one other person. So, for many years that was just the core group. But then it started to grow, and now it's to the point where I can't keep up. I don't know who's who anymore! It's nice not knowing all the Black people. I absolutely love that.

Elders

Tracy: Since you brought up the elders...are there any Queer Black elders in the profession past or present who have influenced your career, and how?

Steven: My idols are Brenda Banks, of course, who was a powerhouse. She was the first Black woman president of SAA who was also a Black Lesbian and an alumna of Spelman College; so I had nothing but love for her. I met Brenda while I was working on the archive of Dr. Martin Luther King, Jr. at Boston University and she was consulting with the Atlanta University Center Robert W. Woodruff Library. We met at a meeting in New York City at the Mellon Foundation. I'd heard so much about her because Brenda mentored my advisor and mentor, Dr. Tywanna Whorley. What I loved the most about her is that she really poured herself into the younger archivists, especially the Black ones. I remember the last time I saw her was in New Orleans at SAA. Brenda had been ill, but she came to that conference. She talked to me and Derek Mosley in the hallway for a bit. It was just such a beautiful moment, "Y'all keep doing what you're doing, I'm following your career. Let me know if you need anything. Where are you now... you need to leave that place because it ain't shit..." She kept it real! So, Brenda Banks is one. Kerrie Cotton Williams at DC Public Library, she's absolutely brilliant and amazing, and Steven Fullwood, of course, who was at the Schomburg Research Center in New York.

Steven was the first person I saw that I felt was a reflection of me. And it made me not only want to continue to be involved, but also to continue doing the work. He has been, over the years, nothing but gracious with his time, advice, and guidance. So, while I consider him my mentor, he's also a close friend.

They've all done significant things in their career. So, my hope is that someone too will speak of me in a similar way one of these days. But if not, I'll keep doing the work, because you never know who's watching. I appreciate them all deeply for just being who they are and being out and proud and not shying away from that. I think that has given me a lot of comfort and freedom in knowing that I can do the same thing. How about you?

Tracy: Since I'm fairly new to the archival profession and really starting to build that community, I would honestly say, you. As you were talking and you were like, "I hope that somebody thinks of me that way," and I'm like, "I do!"

When you speak about the folks who helped build you, I can tell it comes from a place of love. They not only taught and mentored you, but they also gave you love. In our interactions together, whether that's on a professional note or a personal note, I feel that's what you exude. The advice you give comes from this place of definitely having the understanding of the field, the profession and having that knowledge. But it's also centered in this place of love, because the people who helped you along the way put that into you. So, when I come to you, I know that I'm going to get that back. I might get some hard truths, too, but it comes from a place of love. That's one of the things I love about you.

Steven: I'm grateful for this divine connection because I don't know how else we would have connected. I mean, eventually, right? But the way it happened and how quickly our friendship developed, I'm so grateful for that. It's been such a joy. What I truly love is that you have this no-nonsense attitude. You operate in a space of a radical honesty and empathy. Those are the lessons that I'm learning from you. Because it's rooted in wanting the other person that you're in relationship with to be a better version of themselves. So, I appreciate you for pushing me in a lot of ways, and for keeping me on my toes.

Tracy: I love the beauty in the relationship that we have because, as Black Queer folks on a very basic level, we are able to work together in various capacities.

With The Blackivists, we get to do work outside of our institutions. But we've also been able to create partnerships within the existing frameworks at our institutions. And then there's the personal side of what we have together. There are family members where I'm like, "I know you're a professional hairdresser, but either you gonna be my cousin or you gonna be my hairdresser because you can't be both!" [laughs] And with you I feel like I have all of it! We have this kindred bond that nobody can break.

Steven: Nobody! That's what I enjoy most about being in this profession; a lot of my colleagues really are my friends. So, it can be challenging to introduce people that I work with. For example, when you presented last year and people asked me, "Oh, do you know, Tracy?" Yeah! That's my friend; we don't know each other because we're Black. We hang out. That's the beauty of being involved in this field, you make long-lasting friendships that just grow because of your mutual love and respect for archives and each other. It blossoms and flourishes into something so much more.

Self-Archiving

Steven: What's one thing or something that you're going to include in your archive?

Tracy: My Radical Dreams Pin collection. It's representative of all my identities and all the people I admire. I have a James Baldwin pin, who I know is your favorite. I have a Fannie Lou Hamer pin, with a quote from her. I love her! So, my pin collection definitely has to be included.

I sent you some things I've been finding at my mom's house. She reminds me when I visit that I don't live in Chicago anymore. So, I need to get all my stuff. I've been going through stuff and just finding things from different parts of my journey. Pictures from undergrad with my little baby locs. The pictures really document the journey of me becoming who I am now, starting from early young adulthood into my forties.

Steven: I can't wait to dig through your archive someday. You have the best pictures!

Tracy: What are you going to have?

Steven: One thing that I would like to have would be my text messages. I've had some really great conversations with a lot of people over the years. Also, my personality really shines through text messages and someone can learn so much about me and all of my different identities from reading them.

Tracy: Even some of those voice notes…

Steven: Yeah! I would love for my laugh to be in the archive and the different variations of it.

Tracy: That's one of the things that I find the most beautiful about you. I love when you laugh. It brings so much joy to my heart. It doesn't matter what is going on in the world, the fact that we laugh is beautiful.

Steven: I enjoy it so much. Most shit is hilarious to me and I can't help it. I've been this way all my life. A few years ago, at Thanksgiving, I was visiting my father's family. My uncle started laughing and I turned my head so fast, because I thought it was me! We both have the same laugh. I actually have a picture of us laughing together. So, that's something I would want to accompany: my voice messages of laughs in the archive.

Tracy: I knew you were gonna ask, "What's in your archive?"

Steven: I love that question because I think that, as archivists, we're so focused on doing the work that we forget to do it for ourselves. Black archivists also have great stories. There's so much behind-the-scenes about our work that we don't talk about or share.

So, with that, what does it mean to be Black, Queer, and free in the archives?

Tracy: For me, being physically visible and able to see myself in archival spaces, collections, and metadata. Because of respectability politics, we sometimes let people's identities get lost in the matter, which is unfair. I feel if people lived their lives "out and proud" we should also account for that in the way we archive, document, and preserve them and their stories after death. Or even while they are still alive because not all our donors are dead. Visibility in all aspects of archival work is so important.

Steven: I agree. In a lot of ways it looks like us and all the other beautiful Black Queer archivists and memory workers who work within and outside institutions doing archival work. We're fortunate to be able to live in and experience this moment and movement in archival history. I'm curious to see what it will look like three years from now.

Tracy: I think that's important too. When we consider the next folks that will join the profession, we can say, 'This is what we were able to do, here's still what needs to be done.'

Steven: You're right, friend. Passing the baton.

Reflection

After reflecting on our conversation, we spent time thinking about what major takeaways we wanted the reader to walk away with. We knew that whatever made it to final print, you (the reader) should have a sense of our admiration, respect and unabashed queer Black love for one another. We wanted you to understand the value and power of friendship, love, and community in the cultural heritage profession. Our friendship began with mutual respect for the work each of us was doing to care for archival materials but quickly developed into an affinity and appreciation for each other as Queer Black archivists and individuals. This kinship is built on a foundation of radical empathy and radical love.

Radical empathy, a theory highlighted by Michelle Caswell and Marika Cifor in their article "From Human Rights to Feminist Ethics: Radical Empathy in the Archives" at the core asks individuals to "understand and appreciate another person's feelings and experiences."[6] Within this context, archivists are seen as caregivers, bound to record creators, subjects, users, and communities through a web of mutually affective responsibility. Building upon Caswell and Cifor's theory of mutually affective relationships, archivist and scholar Holly Smith expands upon this work to include a fifth affective relationship of archivists to each other.[7] According to Smith, "our multi-layered and intersectional identities can be just as layered and complex as the collections we steward and we must be cognizant of how we support, challenge and advocate for each other professionally and personally."[8] As evident in our own lives, this theory, in practice, can help information and cultural heritage professionals create inclusive communities made up of shared values, increased visibility, and honesty. In her 1977 essay, "The Transformation of Silence into Language and Action," Audre Lorde, faced with her mortality, helps us to understand the connection between building a strong community and the ability to claim our full selves as Queer, Lesbian, Gay, Bisexual, straight, Black, white, etc. Lorde urges us to move

---

6. M.L. Caswell and Marika Cifor, "From Human Rights to Feminist Ethics: Radical Empathy in Archives," eScholarship, University of California, August 4, 2016, https://escholarship.org/uc/item/0mb9568h, 25.

7. Holly A. Smith, "Radical Love: Documenting Underrepresented Communities Using Principles of Radical Empathy," *Journal for the Society of North Carolina Archivists*, vol. 15 (2018): 1-10, doi: http://www.ncarchivists.org/wp-content/uploads/2019/02/jsnca_vol15_smith.pdf.

8. Ibid., p. 4.

forward in creating communities of care because they are necessary for our survival.⁹ As Black Queer individuals and professionals, visibility also makes us vulnerable to judgment and discrimination. However, it is our visibility that gives us the power to fully live our lives and be our whole selves.

Another component of building inclusive communities is the concept of radical love. We believe that radical love asks us to act with intention, speak honestly, provide nourishment, heal and love ourselves and each other, unconditionally. When we free ourselves from the confines of professionalism, white supremacy, and the limitations of gender norms as a community, we can move closer to liberation for us all. In her book, *All About Love: New Visions*, bell hooks urges us to think about love as an action word. hooks also reminds us how "the benefits of living and loving in a community empowers us to meet strangers without fear and extend to them the gift of openness and recognition...The love we make in community stays with us wherever we go. With this knowledge as our guide, we make any place we go a place where we return to love." [10]

As native Chicagoans, in this sense, we are reminded of the words of poet Gwendolyn Brooks in her poem titled Paul Robeson:

> we are each other's
> harvest:
> we are each other's
> business:
> we are each other's
> magnitude and bond [11]

Brooks' poem, a tribute to the singer, actor, poet, and activist Paul Robeson, calls for people to recognize that they are more than mere individuals and are parts of communities that need help to thrive and grow. In this context, Lorde, Brooks, and hooks help us to understand

---

9. Audre Lorde, *Sister Outsider* (New York: Crossing Press, 2007), 40-44.

10. bell hooks, *All About Love: New Visions* (New York: William Morrow and Company, 2000), 129-144.

11. Gwendolyn Brooks, "Paul Robeson," Poet.org, accessed July 14th, 2021, https://poets.org/poem/paul-robeson.

that we need each other for support and that we must create communities of care that are nurturing, loving, supportive, and healing. In a profession and industry that still has so much work to do to become fully inclusive, we fundamentally believe that community is our tool for survival, pending revolution.

Bibliography

Brooks, Gwendolyn. "Paul Robeson." Academy of American Poets. Accessed July 14, 2021. https://poets.org/poem/paul-robeson.

Caswell, M. L. "From Human Rights to Feminist Ethics: Radical Empathy in Archives," June 27, 2021. https://escholarship.org/uc/item/0mb9568h.

"Diverse Sexuality and Gender Section | Society of American Archivists." Accessed July 14, 2021. https://www2.archivists.org/groups/diverse-sexuality-and-gender-section.

hooks, bell. *All about Love : New Visions*. New York: William Morrow, 2000.

Lorde, Audre. *Sister Outsider: Essays and Speeches*. New York: Crossing Press, 2007.

NAT34. "Rainbow Round Table History Timeline." Text. Round Tables, January 25, 2017. https://www.ala.org/rt/rrt/about/history.

———. "Stonewall Book Awards." Text. Round Tables, December 12, 2016. https://www.ala.org/rt/rrt/award/stonewall.

The Metropolitan Museum of Art. "The Costume Institute." Accessed July 14, 2021. https://www.metmuseum.org/about-the-met/curatorial-departments/the-costume-institute.

The HistoryMakers Fellowship, Mentoring, Training and Placement Institute. "The HistoryMakers Fellowship, Mentoring, Training and Placement Institute: IMLS Fellows 2011-2012." Accessed July 14, 2021. http://thehistorymakersfellows.blogspot.com/p/imls-fellows-2011-2012.html.

Society of North Carolina Archivists. "Vol. 15, 2018," February 1, 2019. http://www.ncarchivists.org/journal-of-the-society-of-north-carolina-archivists-j-snca/vol-15-2018/.

Moments of Complication: Navigating the Profession While Queer

Claudia Berger and Claire Fox

Keywords
Graduate school, professionalism, theory and practice

> **Claudia Berger** (she/they) is a graduate of Pratt's School of Information. She hopes to eventually be an academic librarian, and in the meantime is thinking a lot about plants and how colonial science impacts how we view nature.

> **Claire Fox** (she/her) graduated from the Moving Image Archiving and Preservation program at NYU in May 2020. With a focus on audiovisual formats and preservation, her work explores the intersection between consumer technology and queer community.

Conversation

Claudia Berger (she/they): Something I've noticed in library school is that the literature is very obsessed with gender in weird ways. Yes, it is a very female dominated field, with men in managerial positions, but pretty much every class had some reading about feminized labor of the library. But where's the queerness in this? Because I do identify as non-binary. And while I understand the history of the field is very women focused and I'm assigned female at birth, but there's just so much binary language. At its heart, librarianship is about classification and that does mean you are one or you are the other. We need to have conversations in the gray area.

Claire Fox (she/her): I do wonder about that. Like how, or if it's possible, to extend that kind of space for ambiguity and gray area into librarianship and into archives. I really don't have any inkling of an answer for that. Are you in school right now, or did you just graduate?

Claudia: I'm in school at Pratt's School of Information. I'm doing it part time because I work full time.

Claire: I just graduated this spring from a program at NYU called Moving Image Archiving and Preservation, which is an M.A. program in archive studies that focuses on audiovisual preservation. When I started in my program, I came to it wanting to answer questions about queer archiving that I did not end up answering. At the time, I was getting really obsessed with queer Instagram and asking myself, "Where is this stuff going? Who's saving it?" I was also working with a VHS Archives Working Group at the City University of New York (CUNY) that was focused on collections from people who were from the AIDS activist community. That amazing project focused on identifying collections with support from the community to digitize those collections. But where those would go was just "on the cloud." I was applying to school and thinking, 'Are we going to talk about this?' While those conversations weren't built into the program itself, seeking those conversations helped me find the people who were the out queer people on faculty in my program or who were students in my program. Those are people I hope to have long professional relationships with.

Claudia: It's reliant on you building that cohort yourself. I mean, in some ways, it probably is the case, no matter where you go, that you have to find your people. In my intro class at Pratt, there was another trans student and there were like a number of queer students and so we, even weeks where maybe it wasn't necessarily an explicit topic, brought those perspectives from day one. Maybe complicated things more some weeks but...

Claire: I mean, I certainly hope so. Do you have memories of where moments of complication felt like they might be especially good or especially bad?

Claudia: Yes, with knowledge work when you're talking about authority files and how they deal with gender and people. How do you deal with changing identities and locking things in stone? For my final paper that first class, I wrote about digitizing zine collections and the challenges there. These weren't necessarily things that were meant to be widely distributed or seen by lots of people so yeah, there's this other layer of ethics and care of, well, if someone wrote about their transition or their queerness and you just put it on the Internet, like, they might not be out. It's much more personal than, "Oh, I wrote a book and you're creating a catalog entry."

Claire: If you were to digitize a collection of zines that you didn't think should be in wide distribution, what would you be trying to advocate for?

Claudia: There is a queer zines archives project, QZAP,[1] and it's a website that has digitized zines. But one of the big things that they do is they have people submit their work to it. So it's not like someone is going around collecting work and deciding for it. I came to this prior to library school. I made a lot of zines. I was part of that community. I could decide that I want this to be out there and to reach more people, so I could upload my files and it'd be there. That doesn't help with earlier zines that we don't necessarily know who made them and we can't ask. But the self-archiving aspect of that, I think it's just such a big part of

---

1. Queer Zine Archive Project, https://www.qzap.org/v9/index.php.

the queer community. I get to decide whether or not that gets shared. At some point, someone gave a presentation at my work on community archive projects with old queer newsletters and they wanted to digitize them, but there's names, there's photos, there's a lot there, and we don't know if these people were out and if this would be a disservice. And it's so hard. You can do things moving forward, but how do you reconcile this material that already exists?

Claire: Yeah, but even moving forward. There was a project I was working on early in grad school that was about developing a controlled vocabulary to describe queer film collections. I get there and I'm like, I don't know what metadata is; I don't know what a data structure standard is; I don't know what a data content standard is, let alone a controlled vocabulary. And, like, do I want to use authority headings? Do I want to make something totally new? No idea.

Claudia: That's so hard, especially with queer taxonomy stuff; like, it changes. What I come up with today, in two days there can be new terminology. And they're overlapping. It's not like you fall into this and not this. It's like I can be all six of these things and… It's like the antithesis of queer theory is all of classification.

Claire: Yeah, I feel like I have so many questions about where they can go. Have you read Emily Drabinski's article "Queering the Catalog"?[2] I love this model of preserving the past harmful language with the intention of not forgetting the way that things were. And then also knowing that whatever we're working on now will probably become obsolete at some point in the short term/ long term future. And it makes sense to have that be preserved, too, so we can have a historical understanding of how the field changes. And also not make the same mistakes twice, ideally.

---

2. Emily Drabinski, "Queering the Catalog: Queer Theory and the Politics of Correction," *The Library Quarterly*: Information, Community, Policy 83, no. 2 (2013): 94–111, https://doi.org/10.1086/669547.

Claudia: It's just so important to preserve that journey because librarians are fallible. And archivists—we will make mistakes. We will forget or not acknowledge certain things. We need that past to hold us accountable. To be like "we messed up and need to keep trying." I got to take a class with Emily Drabinski. That was such an amazing class because she 100% is there for those conversations of why doesn't this work, and why is this a problem, and where's the power in this situation? But it's still like, if you're in a library, you have to put a book on the shelf somewhere. I think that's where the power of the digital catalog is; you can add those different tags or categorizations. You can have multiple identities in that digital infrastructure. But when it comes down to the physical library, it's like, no, there's going to be one place where it lives.

Claire: What you just said about thinking about these systems and how they fail different people and then figuring out what you can do, like, and that kind of impetus coming from your queerness and being kind of part of our agenda; that's how I feel with a lot of the work that I do. Sometimes, if I'm working on a project where we're doing a catalog and exercise, I'm like, "This is so un-queer." But then, with other things, it's different. When selecting master copies of tapes, for example, we're selecting the one copy that's going to be the preservation master and then we make access copies from that. During that work, you realize that all the tapes degrade. Everything has to be migrated. Then I realized that everything is evolving; I thought, I can get down with this. Nothing is going to be the most reliable thing. Nothing is gonna be something that you can depend on forever. But what you can depend on is the relationships and the connections to other people. And wanting to do our very best, but at the same time grappling with the loss that's associated with the work that we do.

Claudia: I think that makes perfect sense. A lot of our work is focused on rigid states, both in terms of preservation and access. Like, things have to fit into specific things, but everything is so much more complicated; then, too, there's a fluidity between all of these states. I think that is sort of that queerness of "it is preserved and not preserved at the same time."

Claire: Totally. That's something that I think is both fun and difficult about this kind of work. It's so contextual, and the work that we do is so specific. Which is why we all need each other even more. In the moments that things feel hard...like, am I the lone queer person? Am I isolated in that way? And when I start to feel that way, that's when I default to the systems. Do you feel like being able to know more about the existing infrastructure of a place is a way of being able to figure out where you're going to fit as a queer person?

Claudia: Yeah, if you know enough people at enough different libraries, I can probably figure out if there's another queer person there. That's not an irrelevant fact for me.

Claire: Something that I've been thinking about a lot lately is the process of writing collection assessments. I'm thinking of a particular instance when I was working with a queer filmmaker who had been working with half-inch open-reel video in the 1960s and has continued to make video to this day, but the bulk of the collection was 1960s-1980s. As I'm going through his work and I'm learning about him and I'm learning about off-off-Broadway theatre, which is what he was mostly documenting, there isn't a ton of space in a collection assessment to write about that history or to even research that history. It's mostly just like, "This collection has 120 items," ... you know. Trying to find a way to imbue queerness into that work is an abstract project that's on my mind. But just thinking about how research works in general in archives and in libraries, I think is really interesting.

Claudia: I think the ways critical research and queerness do complement each other in a way is that you can't make assumptions about your data and take them at face value; you have to really think about what's in there and what isn't in there. If you have a spreadsheet and it has a gender column, then what does that really mean? Where's that coming from? Is it self-identified? Who is being counted? Who's not being counted in this? And I think a lot of that comes from things that came out of the queer community, where we are invisible and where we are not. I hope that makes me a better data librarian, making sure that scholars are thinking about that and not just taking the data as it comes.

Claire: Do you feel like there are specific readings or people or schools of thought that are guiding you as you determine where the trust is in the information that is going to ground you?

Claudia: Yeah, I think it's Meredith Broussard who coined the term techno-chauvinism as a concept of that male, Silicon Valley tech bro, "just because technology can, it should" type mindset. There are a lot of people now who are writing against that. There's *Algorithms of Oppression* and there's *Artificial Unintelligence*, books that are about the dangers of all of this thinking.[3] It can help show you how a thing that wouldn't even occur to you as being damaging can actually do so much harm. We assume tech is unbiased, but really it directly reflects the biases of those who design it. I'm lucky that I was trained in thinking critically about how the data was collected. Let's think critically about the contexts and it being taken out of context.

Claire: How do we put people first in this environment? How do we make sure this environment isn't just in service of licensing or monetizing or just having some kind of legacy? It's about taking care of people who are present and then also taking care of the people who could have access to this content, who want to know more about their community now and in the future. And that stuff takes a lot of time. This is kind of what drew me to my particular grad program: trying

---

3. Safiya Umoja Noble, *Algorithms of Oppression: How Search Engines Reinforce Racism*, Illustrated edition (New York: NYU Press, 2018); Meredith Broussard, *Artificial Unintelligence: How Computers Misunderstand the World* (Cambridge, MA: The MIT Press, 2018).

to see if I could learn more about technical infrastructure as a way of serving more people.

Claudia: Do you think you did?

Claire: I think that the things that I've learned don't make me feel like an expert. What I've learned is that I have a greater tolerance for spending time Googling things, seeking out answers in specific places, and going to the right message board. This is a kind of a place where queerness happens, too… Just figuring out, like, okay: I'm not going to post on that listserv because those people are unkind, you know, and I don't think that there are other queer people around. But also, maybe there are, and I don't know it, and I should go and check this out and see what I find. And there's your trusted network of people, a cross-institution network of people that you can call up and say, hey, this weird thing just happened to me, has this ever happened to you? And those are the things that I'm definitely going to rely on after school. It's not so much that I learned how to do tech. It's more that I learned how to build a network and support other people and also just know that we're all in this process of learning. These systems are in the process of being built. How do we support each other through this time of building the thing and making it more accessible to more people?

When I was trying to decide where to go to school, I wanted to definitely go to a program that had an AV option. Coming out of a program like that, like, my specialization is digital preservation. Which is something that happened in part because of my fascination with social media and that kind of proliferation of digital format. I started out thinking about web archiving; it's so new and it's so complex.

Claudia: I've been thinking about that now with all the use of proprietary apps, like TikTok and Instagram. What happens to that stuff once those apps bolt? If you recorded a video in-app and you didn't save a file, it's just going to vanish. Like the disappearance of Tumblr, which

I feel was personally very formative to my queer identity. And now, I've gone back and so much of it's just gone, as things have been taken down.

Claire: It's so disheartening looking back at that. I guess the Internet Archive might have done some work to try and just pull down as much as possible. But you go back and look at the Wayback Machine and it's just, like, this isn't what it looked like, you know?

Claudia: How are we going to talk about that very important queer experience?

Claire: But these are questions that are somewhat similar to what we were talking about before, where it's, like, we just have to save the information and figure out how to contextualize it later. Maybe we'll have different tools for conceptualizing the information or rendering it in a particular browser that makes it look better, look more similar. But who's going to tell you what it was supposed to look like? People who are younger? People who are older? like, I don't know. Just thinking about how to contextualize all the information that we're stockpiling right now is very concerning to me.

Claudia: There's so much that disappears from the web. It's inevitable we're not gonna be able to save every single project. If we can find other ways of documenting it, so it's not reliant on a plugin that could vanish and then your whole map doesn't render or whatever.

Claire: Thinking about alternative ways of preserving whatever your work is, whether it's writing, like, having an accessible PDF for the future or something; I think that's really interesting. There was one specific project that came up recently about preserving algorithms, basically. It's kind of like Safiya Noble's work, but in the context of an Emily Drabinski mindset of how do we preserve the harmful algorithms? How do we remember this? Is it just the books?

Claudia: Saving those dangerous algorithms, or the stories there... it's important. We have to learn those lessons, and that requires us to remember the examples and not just have them fade away. So, it's an interesting tension.

Claire: For myself, when I think about what the future is for these kinds of systems, I immediately go to preservation. But then it's like, if you preserve the bad thing, what do you do with it?

Reflection

Claire: There were many things that I appreciated about Claudia's and my conversation, and one in particular is that we didn't do any preparation ahead of our shared Zoom meeting. We both knew that we were students, and that we were both queer-identifying in some capacity, but beyond that, we had a blank canvas. I think that comes through in our conversation: we touch on a few different topics (school, building community, ethics of data collection, and web archiving, to name a few), but we don't dig too deep into any particular area. Rather, we get a sense of the shape of each other's work—and we find out that our work within libraries and archives is actually quite different!

While speaking with Claudia, I realized that there were certain things I didn't have to explain that had to do specifically with being queer. In other words, the time I usually need to take to explain myself to non-queer colleagues was suddenly available to talk about other things. While this was exciting, it also felt somewhat abrupt. What do we talk about next? In this space, we realized how different our work really is and could identify other bridges that we'd need to cross in order to understand one another. I'm so grateful for that time and that realization. I look forward to speaking more with Claudia and other queer colleagues in the future, and finding more of what we have in common and what makes our work in libraries and archives different and complex.

Claudia: While it may not have been the main focus of our conversation, one of the topics that I keep thinking about is how queerness is going to play a role in my professional life beyond my personal presentation. I fully believe in bringing my full self to my work, but I had not thought concretely about how this would manifest in how I do my job. As a student, there was space in my classes to think theoretically, but at some point, it has to be taken from that nebulous space and transferred into my practice. Now that I've graduated and am figuring out what is next, it is something I need to think about, and talk about with my peers, more. How will my queerness be present in my work? As two early career professionals, we definitely did not come up with answers to this question, but hopefully this is the first of many conversations and we can keep returning to it as we gain more experience. We are not the first queer information professionals and there are others we can learn from, although we have to rely on human networks to find much of this information, as most of what is written about queerness and libraries is focused on patrons and not queer staff themselves.[4]

Bibliography

Broussard, Meredith. *Artificial Unintelligence: How Computers Misunderstand the World.* Cambridge, MA: MIT Press, 2018.

Drabinski, Emily. "Queering the Catalog: Queer Theory and the Politics of Correction." *The Library Quarterly: Information, Community, Policy* 83, no. 2 (2013): 94–111. https://doi.org/10.1086/669547.

Fisher, Zoe, Stephen G Krueger, Robin Goodfellow Malamud, and Ericka Patillo. "What It Means to Be Out: Queer, Trans, and Gender Nonconforming Identities in Library Work." In *Li-*

---

4. Zoe Fisher et al., "What It Means to Be Out: Queer, Trans, and Gender Nonconforming Identities in Library Work," in *Libraries Promoting Reflective Dialogue in a Time of Political Polarization* (Chicago, IL: ACRL Publications, 2019), 71–90.

braries Promoting Reflective Dialogue in a Time of Political Polarization, 71–90. Chicago, IL: ACRL Publications, 2019.

Noble, Safiya Umoja. *Algorithms of Oppression: How Search Engines Reinforce Racism*. Illustrated edition. New York: NYU Press, 2018.

Queer Time in Libraries and Archives: Democratizing Personal and Historical Narratives

Julie Adamo and Tanya Pearson

Keywords
Professionalism, white supremacy culture, capitalism, authentic selves, research methods

> **Julie Adamo** is a librarian, musician, and writer based in Holyoke, MA. She is the Head of Collection Development and Management at Smith College. Julie is working on her first book, drawing from her experience as a patient to examine knowledge formation and contested illness within the medical industrial complex. When not working, she is often playing music or enjoying quiet time with her partner and cat.

> **Tanya Pearson** is a Public Historian and Director of the Women of Rock Oral History Project, a collection of digital interviews and written transcripts documenting the lives and careers of (women-identified) rock musicians. *Why Marianne Faithfull Matters*, her contribution to the University of Texas Press' Music Matters Series, was published in 2021. When she's not working, she enjoys writing, rock climbing, playing in her band Feminine Aggression, and watching *The Golden Girls* with her dogs.

Conversation

Tanya Pearson: What does your ideal job look like? Where would that be?

Julie Adamo (she/her): I would say that my ideal library job would be a collections-focused one. I would have loved being a bibliographer, but unfortunately those jobs are becoming extinct. I wish there was a way I could fully be an artist in addition to being a librarian. It's been feeling really hard to make progress with my creative projects when I'm trying to fit them in after hours.
   What about you?

Tanya: I love working on things that I like to do. Pretty much all of my graduate work is based on rock music. And so now I'm just working on my exams, and then my dissertation, which is exactly what I want to do, and it's fun.

Julie: I'm so glad that you found a way to have your interests be aligned with the career path you're on. That was kind of my hope when I decided to become a librarian. I had tried out a few different things. I tried out journalism and publishing when I was in college. I worked in a public library in high school. Ultimately, I liked working in libraries the best. My hope was that a career in libraries was a path to making a living while staying connected to the world of writing, knowledge, and creativity. In some small ways the field has kept me connected in the ways I'd hoped, but I also feel like it has changed so much over the last few decades.

Tanya: Being at Smith and working in Special Collections, I thought I wanted to do something with archives at first. But being in my thirties at the time, I was like, "You know what, I think I'm gonna try to figure out some kind of way to craft my own job or future or career." But I don't know if that would have happened had I been, like, twenty. I just really didn't want to work for a college. I just really want to do what I want to do.

Julie: Yeah, I think that's great. It's very inspiring.

Tanya: I thought about starting my own archive, too. I'm like, I just need a building. Maybe someday. But then there's also this added weight and validity that comes with having your collection housed at a school archive. So, there's that whole thing, too, where it's like, I could start my own archive, but would it carry as much weight?

Julie: Do you feel like it wouldn't look as good on job applications if you had your own independent archive?

Tanya: I definitely don't think it would look as good. I knew that I couldn't just be this random music fan stalking musicians and asking them to do an interview for a collection that didn't exist yet and was in my apartment.

Julie: There's this tension because, in order to get opportunities or to be respected professionally, you have to have these certain affiliations or do things in a certain way. These kinds of things are on my mind a lot: these tensions between being my whole self, or one's whole self, and having a professional job.

I have always been into rock and punk music, and played in bands. And for a long time now, I've also had a number of health issues, and that's another thing that I feel like I can't bring into the professional sphere. Between my personal interests, my sexuality, and my identity, I just feel like I'm always walking this line with my job or my career. I know that there shouldn't be ableism, or homophobia, or suspicion of people who don't follow a traditional path of getting married, buying a house, and having kids. But I do feel like, in my professional context anyway, there are. It's not explicit. It's not like people walk around openly talking about how you're suspect or questionable if you don't do those traditional things. I know that I have so much to offer with my whole self. But at the same time, I have this fear of being kind of barred if I fully express, for instance, my sexuality. The sexuality piece has been better, actually, since I've been working at Mount Holyoke because there are a fair number of gay or queer folks who work there. I'm working on embracing being my full self as a strength. I had actually been really gaining a lot of steam with that. But now that I'm thinking about applying for jobs again, a lot of those fears are resurfacing.

The concept of professionalism, at least as it's currently encoded and understood, is one that I personally have a lot of criticisms of. And as I learn more and more about anti-racism, it's clear that what many of us commonly understand as "professionalism" is actually, at least in part, white supremacy culture.[1]

Tanya: I don't hide that I'm in a punk band anymore. My cohort of classmates have come to shows. I find that when I am my authentic self, it actually invites people to be their authentic selves. I don't know if I'll feel differently when I'm applying for jobs. So far, it's worked out just acting authentically and being myself, which is amazing because I've lived so long not doing that.

I've been working on my dissertation and oral history work and I've been thinking a lot about subjective experience and its place in scholarship, and how experiential histories are inherently queer in this way that they can't be quantified or measured, and how they're sort of antithetical to traditional, "valid," historical sources. And so, I think my tendency as a historian has always been to utilize these provocative methodologies in order to reclaim these marginalized histories. And that's very much rooted in my identity as a lesbian and as a musician and weirdo. But I've been thinking a lot about actual content and how I'm trying to not only give voice to these subjects that have been marginalized in the larger

---

1. Tema Okun, "White Supremacy Culture," retrieved from https://surj.org/resources/white-supremacy-culture-characteristics/. Now available at https://www.whitesupremacyculture.info/ (1999).

narrative, but also how I just have this need to kind of fuck shit up, for lack of a better term.

Julie: Caro, my partner, wrote an article about creative disruption in libraries,[2] and what you're saying reminds me of that. I think one of the positive things about being a fully authentic punk rocker or whatever in a field like archives or academia is that part of that ethos is to raise questions around the status quo toward something better.

I'm curious to hear more about using different kinds of methods?

Tanya: I consider oral history a method for diversifying and democratizing the overall rock narrative. And in many cases, it's the only avenue that's left because somebody has died. I think it's more accepted now as a "valid" method or methodology, but I do feel like it's maybe not taken as seriously as more quantifiable methods. I feel like oral history is sort of feminized and still may be considered a little superfluous, or it's like, "Yeah, that is great for supplementing the narrative." But the more masculine forms of evidence would be, you know, methods that are able to be measured or quantified, or they are already part of the historiography. So oral history has the power to disrupt the entire canon. And I think that that's still very dangerous because you have so many people, scholars included, who are very attached to their canons and to their popular narratives. So, I do think that is kind of dangerous, in that oral history is kind of inherently queer. It is disruptive.

Julie: I didn't realize or know that about oral history. I mean, I know from other spheres that there are these hierarchies of methods. In some disciplines or circles, quantitative methods are treated as much more "valid" than qualitative ones. So, what are the more "valid" or respected history methods?

---

2. Caro Pinto, "Creative Destruction in Libraries: Designing our Future," In the Library with the Lead Pipe, November 2013, https://www.inthelibrarywiththeleadpipe.org/2013/creative-destruction-in-libraries-designing-our-future/

Tanya: You know: archives, papers, the written word. Those kinds of primary sources. The news, existing scholarship.

Julie: A couple of days ago, I was in a workshop where we were learning about white supremacy culture. One of the topics we discussed was the primacy of the written word as an element of white supremacy culture.[3] A lot of what you were just describing was in the vein of what this awesome trainer, McKensie Mack, was conveying about white supremacy culture. Now I just love your project even more because I love the ways that you're filling out the historical narrative about rock and women and underrepresented people and disrupting methodologies at the same time.

I was just looking at the "Queer Time" article[4] that I sent you. I love the word "chrononormativity." I feel like that word/concept could have some interesting implications for historical methods. That article has been in my psyche ever since I first read it because it captures so well some of the topics we're talking about today, around queerness and expectations of what it means to be a respectable person or a professional. The article is talking about "adulting," but I felt like you could substitute "professionalism" or "being respectable" or "elite," and its meaning would hold. In a lot of ways, academia is this elite culture. I was thinking as I was reading the article this morning about how you are supposed to sort of give up things like rock music as you grow up, and then you're supposed to follow this certain path of becoming an adult if you want to be a respectable person or a professional. And then, at the same time, of course, we're talking about queerness, and the article is also talking about how queers, just by the nature of what our lives are like, have these ways that we are able to disrupt that pattern. But I also think that, with music and punk, it's a similar thing. Punk culture, or DIY culture, is another way of talking back to this idea that we have to follow this certain path in order to be "successful." I really need an

---

3. Okun, "White Supremacy Culture."

4. Sara Jaffe, "Queer Time: The Alternative to 'Adulting'," JSTOR Daily, January 10, 2018, https://daily.jstor.org/queer-time-the-alternative-to-adulting/.

alternative word for "professional" that doesn't have the pre-existing meaning. A word for being a person who has work that they care about and that contributes to society, but that doesn't have this loaded meaning of "you will wear certain clothes, behave in certain ways, and compartmentalize your life."

Tanya: Chrononormativity. I had this word written down, too, and then, in quotes, "eccentric economic practices." Yeah, I love that article. I was thinking about my personal experience versus the sort of inherent queerness in all of the people that I interview and in the work that I do. Being a woman-identified musician sort of disrupts the concept of adulting because it is antithetical to the expectations of what women should be or that whole idea of chrononormativity: like, you follow this timeline and you do these things, and you achieve these goals, and then you become an adult somewhere along the line. I don't know if it's when you get the house with the fence or when you have the kid. I don't know when it is. So even heterosexual musicians that I've interviewed are in a really broad sense of the word, I would say, queer, if we're thinking about queer as disrupting the status quo. Rock music in general could fall into this category. And then I was also thinking about my own personal story and narrative. When I went back to school, I was constantly justifying my age by saying, "Oh, my timeline is way off." I didn't do what I was supposed to do at the time, so I'm doing it now.

But I do feel like my timeline has been off since I was, like, six years old, you know? It sort of stems from having had a crush on my female classmate in first grade. And then after that, I was just, like, oh, this isn't gonna work out well for me. Not being able to accept my sexuality led me to become an alcoholic, become a drug addict, and I tried to change that part. I did not want to be gay. I feel like just being queer put me on this alternate path. It wasn't well thought out or planned, but I also never wanted any of the traditional things. I don't know if that comes from knowing that I was a tiny lesbian at six, but I never dreamt of the wedding, the house.

Julie: I didn't either. I never dreamt of any of those things. And I think as I got older that started to be confusing. I wasn't around a lot of traditional people, but when I went to library school at age age twenty-six or twenty-seven, this vortex of realizing, "Oh, going to library school means I'm supposed to be this certain kind of person if I want to get a good job" started swirling in my mind. And also, that was when social media was exploding because it was in the mid-2000s. I think that created a lot more pressure around compartmentalizing because before, you could easily have your life outside of work and then go to work with whatever version of self that was acceptable.

Tanya: Always knowing that I was gay just sort of made the timeline null and void. That's what I was thinking about recently. I think I just never had a chance with the timeline or with achieving those goals because it was never anything that I wanted to begin with.

Julie: I didn't really figure out that I was queer until later, I guess college-ish, but I always knew that I was different. In retrospect, everything made sense. Over the period when I was working paraprofessionally and then in library school, I started to have a lot of health issues. So, I got really freaked out about having disability insurance and health benefits and all that stuff. And that kind of put the pressure on, in an additional way, for me to get a professional degree, a "real job," and to have a successful career. It made a lot of this stuff that we're talking about today infiltrate my mind in ways that it hadn't before.

Tanya: In capitalism, the structure forces adulting upon you. I hate it.

Julie: Yeah, I feel like we should all be able to have the things that allow us to thrive, like health insurance and a good job. And also, I think libraries and archives are super important and they need to exist, and we need people to administer them. But we shouldn't expect people who work in them to be capitalist automatons. I'm realizing, as we're talking, that as I went down the path to have that real job, and health insurance, and do something that I thought was an important contribution to the world, that part of why I became a librarian was because I didn't want to work for the man or be the man. We might not be working for a big bank, but a lot of that culture still infiltrates in terms of what kind of people many libraries expect their employees to be.

Reflection

Just a couple of weeks before Tanya and I met for our conversation in late September 2020, I spent a whole week of vacation in August updating and overhauling my CV and writing a cover letter for the first job I'd applied to in several years. After working at Mount Holyoke College as a research and instruction librarian for eight years, I decided to begin searching for a new job in August 2020, aiming to simultaneously move into a role centered on collections and to serve in a formal leadership role. This is all to say, the tensions Tanya and I discussed around being non-chrononormative weirdos in professional academic roles were affecting me in real time.

I am very happy to report that a few months after our conversation, I began a new job as Head of Collection Development and Management at Smith College. At the time of writing this reflection, I've been in that new position for almost five months. In this role, I've been open with members of my department on a few occasions about wanting to share more of my full self at work and hoping to create an environment where everyone feels comfortable doing the same. In one such conversation where I was espousing my vision for an authentic self-welcoming workplace, a member of my team responded, "But, we need to have good boundaries, too." The comment stuck with me and I've been reflecting since then on the differences, gray areas, and lines between workplace cultures ruled by a toxic version of professionalism (this could alternatively be called white supremacy culture), those with healthy interpersonal boundaries, and those that are truly inclusive and welcoming of employees' full selves. Being one's full self doesn't mean you can say whatever you want at the expense of others, behave in a way that causes harm or prevents others from getting their work done, or dominate the social environment to the exclusion or silencing of others. Ultimately, I believe healthy interpersonal boundaries are a key component of an inclusive "authentic self" workplace culture. In a sense, strong interpersonal boundaries combined with cultural humility and cultural competency are what I imagine a non-toxic version of professionalism might look like. With healthy amounts of respect, humility, self-awareness, and deep consideration of others, our workplaces will welcome library workers' full selves, promote healthy boundaries, and provide an environment conducive to thoughtful work and service to our communities.

In closing, it feels both pertinent and ironic to share that my partner and I bought a house in 2021 and are planning to get married before the end of the year. We had to flee a moldy apartment, while at the same time well-resourced climate refugees and New Yorkers started moving in droves to western MA during the pandemic, drastically driving up rental and real estate prices. We knew if we didn't secure a home for ourselves, we might never have the chance again. I honestly didn't know how good it would feel to own our own house or how much peace it would bring me. As Sara Jaffe says in closing "Queer Time": "...I am, I suppose, 'adulting,' yet queer time still clocks my sense of myself in the world."

Bibliography

Jaffe, Sara. "Queer Time: The Alternative to 'Adulting'," JSTOR Daily, January 10, 2018, https://daily.jstor.org/queer-time-the-alternative-to-adulting/.

Okun, Tema, and Kenneth Jones. "White Supremacy Culture." Retrieved from https://surj.org/resources/white-supremacy-culture-characteristics/. Now available at https://www.whitesupremacyculture.info/ (1999).

Pinto, Caro. "Creative Destruction in Libraries: Designing our Future," In the Library with the Lead Pipe, November 2013, https://www.inthelibrarywiththeleadpipe.org/2013/creative-destruction-in-libraries-designing-our-future/.

QUE(E)RY INQUE(E)RY: REFLECTIONS ON TEN YEARS OF FUNDRAISING FOR QUEER ARCHIVES

M'issa Fleming and Matthew Haugen

Keywords
Que(e)ry, queer spaces, ALA Annual

> **M'issa Fleming** (they/them) is a genderqueer Librarian for teenagers at the New Orleans Public Library. Raised middle class on the east coast, the five years they spent traveling the country in and out of refurbished school buses, frequently balancing people on their feet, were very helpful in broadening their horizons. M'issa is a white able-bodied settler residing in Bulbancha, the unceded territory of the Chitimacha, Houma, and Chahta Yakni nations.
>
> **Matthew Haugen** (he/they) was one of the cofounders of Que(e)ry in 2010 and has since helped organize Que(e)ry events and maintain Que(e)ry's website. Since 2011, he has worked as a rare book cataloger at Columbia University Libraries and has served on several cataloging committees and task groups. They earned an MSLIS from Long Island University. They live on traditional Lenape land in Brooklyn, N.Y.

Conversation

M'issa Fleming (they/them): You're a founder of Que(e)ry, a party that raises money for queer archives and collections. Do you want to first talk about what made y'all start?

Matthew Haugen (he/they): In 2010, Amber Billey, Tara Hart and I were part of the Desk Set, a group of Brooklyn librarians who were doing fundraiser parties.[1] We saw on a librarian listserv that the Tom of Finland Foundation[2] in Los Angeles needed some funds. We pitched a Pride month fundraiser party to the Desk Set, called Que(e)ry.

M'issa: Whose idea was the name?

Matthew: I think it was Amber Billey, but I added the parentheses gimmick. That first party also fundraised for the Lesbian Herstory Archives.[3] We had literary-themed cocktails, card catalog decorations, and an archivist go-go dancer. It was successful, so we started repeating that formula. We had two parties at the Stonewall Inn, and that historic space felt so appropriate. Lydia Willoughby and Nik Dragovic also got involved early on. In 2013 we had a party in Chicago alongside ALA. You started helping with some of our bigger events at ALA Annual, and smaller meetups at Midwinter. The last Brooklyn party was in 2017, but I'd like to bring that back.

M'issa: When did y'all get formal enough to make the document setting guidelines for the kinds of spaces that you're looking for? When I started helping Que(e)ry instead of just attending the events, you had a document that looks like many people took a lot of care to make sure

---

1. Kara Jesella, "A Hipper Crowd of Shushers," *New York Times*, July 8, 2007, https://www.nytimes.com/2007/07/08/fashion/08librarian.html.

2. Tom of Finland Foundation, https://www.tomoffinland.org/.

3. Lesbian Herstory Archives, https://lesbianherstoryarchives.org/.

the party could happen in a place that hit as many of those important points as possible.

Matthew: That venue document evolved out of lessons we learned whenever we had to find a new venue in Brooklyn, or at conferences where we didn't know the local scene, and the same questions came up: "What's the financial arrangement? Is it accessible? Are the bathrooms gendered? Is there a sound system?"

M'issa: I've experienced that challenge firsthand! I was so grateful that there was a list to make sure that I asked the bar owners, "How many of these things can you check off?" My least favorite part about trying to plan a Que(e)ry party is deciding which aspects of the document to prioritize without a way to determine how many people we'll affect.

Matthew: A lot of older queer bars are dives with tiny bathrooms, stairs, or narrow entrances. Newer places might be more physically accessible but can be expensive or exclusive in other ways. It's challenging to find a space that checks all the boxes, but where do we compromise? Outlining our venue criteria along with a mission statement helped to address those sticky points, and to help make sure what we're doing aligns with our purpose.[4]

M'issa: Is the mission statement something that y'all came up with early and then revised, or was this because you were doing the nuts and bolts of moving off of Tumblr?

Matthew: The mission statement had a few iterations. We moved our website when Tumblr started blocking adult content,[5] but things like queer young adult booklists got flagged too. That provoked a conversation

---

4. Que(e)ry. "About Que(e)ry," https://www.queeryparty.org/about.

5. Tumblr. "Adult Content Help Center," https://tumblr.zendesk.com/hc/en-us/articles/231885248-Sensitive-content.

about whether we as queer information professionals have something to say about biased algorithmic content filtering, which helped refine our mission.[6] You weren't around for some of these early conversations, but what drew you to get involved in Que(e)ry?

M'issa: My first ALA was in New Orleans in 2011—I had a lovely time at the Rainbow Roundtable (RRT) social,[7] but most of the fun I had was carousing with people afterwards. There wasn't a Que(e)ry party that year, but I double rode one of the librarians over to a library vendor party on my bicycle. Somebody grabbed the closest librarian to him and started tangoing crosswise through the dance floor, and everyone knew the gays had arrived. It was a beautiful moment, but I definitely would've had more fun if it had been a queer librarian party instead of a small queer invasion of a straight party.

It was really exciting to know that Que(e)ry existed. I love the RRT's social events and I've never felt especially alienated, but as a gender nonconforming person who wants to dance with people who are similarly riled about the same kinds of stuff, I love that having fun can support the growth of things that I've invested in, in the communities that I visit. I very swiftly went from being really thrilled that Que(e)ry existed and that there was a way to have fun while being political and supportive, to wanting to make sure that it continued and flourished.

Matthew: We were planning to co-host a party with the RRT in Chicago, for their fiftieth anniversary and our tenth, before ALA Annual got canceled because of the pandemic. RRT has that history and legacy, but being part of ALA, I don't think they're allowed to fundraise for other groups. That's one thing I like about Que(e)ry being an independent, informal organization. We can choose local libraries to benefit and take

---

6. Que(e)ry. www.queeryparty.org.

7. Rainbow Roundtable of the American Library Association, http://www.ala.org/rt/rrt.

political positions without answering to ALA bureaucracy. That gives us freedom, but it limits us, too.

M'issa: At the very least, we can use this wealth of queer librarians to make sure we leave one element of the community we're visiting stronger than we found it. I also have encountered folks that wouldn't generally go to the RRT social that would go to Que(e)ry parties. I don't know all their reasons, but as a GNC person on the RRT listserv reading some things specific to trans issues, some members have made really intense and objectionable posts that don't really get answered by anyone, or get answered with intense defensiveness. If I didn't already know people at the RRT, I'd maybe assume I wouldn't be fully welcome at a RRT event. A party called Que(e)ry is presumably run by folks that include trans people as a part of who is queer and will probably actively make sure that trans folks are safe and welcome. The Que(e)ry party is deliberately very fun and a break from the intense professional networking of the conference. Que(e)ry is open, not just to the folks that are librarians at a conference, but to anybody that loves archives. That kind of welcome makes a lot of sense to me.

Matthew: I agree, but it's been interesting seeing Que(e)ry take on a semi-professional identity at ALA. Often we schedule it right after the RRT social. Folks coming from that event might actually want to continue networking. Sometimes the ALA President comes and people keep their conference badges on. Other folks seem to want a clearer separation from the conference; later, it usually becomes more of a dance party with non-librarians.

M'issa: When we're choosing to do these parties in bars, mostly gay bars, there is no guaranteeing what their staff is going to be like in terms of checking IDs. That can be such a cultural difference between a gay club and queer space. I try to warn bar owners ahead of time, "I'm going to be putting signs on your bathroom doors that anybody can be in here." I haven't had pushback, but if we did, that would make a bar a no-go for us.

Matthew: Or gendered or racist dress codes are another dealbreaker.

When ALA was in Orlando in 2016, the Black Caucus of the ALA called to relocate that conference after the shooting of Trayvon Martin and because of the "Stand Your Ground" laws in Florida.[8] I was obligated to attend, but between having difficulty finding a venue and learning about BCALA's position, we decided against organizing a party. Then, two weeks before the conference, the Pulse nightclub shooting happened. Que(e)ry helped promote a vigil, and put out a statement.[9] We worked on the crowd-sourced #PulseOrlando syllabus.[10] Que(e)ry started doing more advocacy and producing more resources, like a Black Lives Matter list.[11] Are there other things you'd like to see Que(e)ry do?

M'issa: I'd like to see a shift in our process. We send an email a month or two beforehand asking "Who wants to help?" We're not a large organization; we work with the two or three folks who respond to the email. I'd love party planning to start earlier so we can factor in things we don't often have time for at the last minute. Looking at who comes to Que(e)ry parties, it's folks from the archive we're supporting plus what ends up being primarily white librarians from the conference, and this mix can be less appealing to BIPOC. I know we've addressed this in readily available ways, like hiring DJs of color and prioritizing

---

8. "Joint Statement from the Presidents of AILA, APALA, BCALA, CALA, REFORMA, and ALA." March 28, 2014, http://www.ala.org/news/press-releases/2014/03/joint-statement-presidents-aila-apala-bcala-cala-reforma-and-ala

9. Que(e)ry. "ALA Orlando 2016," https://www.queeryparty.org/about/events/2016-Orlando.

10. The "Pulse Orlando Syllabus" document is no longer active. It has been preserved as part of the 2016 Pulse Nightclub Shooting Web Archive, to which Que(e)ry also contributed. https://archive-it.org/collections/7570.

11. "Black Lives Matter Library, Teaching, Activism, and Community Resource List," http://bit.ly/BLMresources.

QBIPOC archives. I think that, with more lead time, we can contact librarians of color in a town and ask those folks, "Where are you comfortable attending a party?" Not to treat any one BIPOC librarian as a monolithic representation of how all BIPOC feel about a particular bar, but asking seems better than not asking. I'd also love to consider spaces that are not bars—also easier to do with more lead time—because in the queer community there's a long history of alcohol playing a toxic role.

Matthew: Instead of a bar party, maybe a poetry reading or an archive tour? There's an organization for BIPOC library workers called We Here,[12] that does job listings, webinars, and newsletters. If Que(e)ry becomes more official, I could see us doing similar things. Maybe an advisory board could give us more legitimacy. Que(e)ry has been this unofficial side project for ten years but it's still a huge amount of work. How much of that counts as "professional" activity for my résumé or my day job?

M'issa: Right? If it's not going to be part of our paid professional life, how much time and effort can go into becoming a "real" organization? I feel daunted by linear time. Currently, we're too small to effectively stay on top of everything that Que(e)ry might comment on. An action plan around any of these issues would require active community participation. We're volunteer-based and geographically distanced, so we don't have a lot of in-person time to build relationships. If you only get to attend when the conference is in your area, you don't necessarily feel as tied to folks. For Que(e)ry to be effective in our support for wider change in our profession, like a shift away from being majority white, middle-class cis folks, we'd need a stronger and more diverse volunteer base. However, we get volunteers from party attendance, and our attendance reflects this majority—having an MLIS often determines who's eligible to attend conferences—so we are in a kind of representational catch-22.

---

12. We Here, https://www.wehere.space/

Matthew: Building on that, I hope that by being a visible queer presence alongside ALA and engaging with issues like this, we can challenge that stereotype of the white, cis, female librarian, but I think we could do a better job of centering the BIPOC element of that. You mentioned barriers that reinforce whiteness at conferences and in the profession. With all these white librarians gathered in a city that's unfamiliar to them, the conversation about where to have a party can reinforce racist narratives about what counts as a "safe" venue or neighborhood, and whose safety is meant by that. Letting those attitudes go unquestioned is a problem. But how do we engage with that conversation more responsibly and critically?

M'issa: Relatedly, asking a bar how they handle security is a serious question because of the way the police operate with brown bodies, or gender variant humans, or undocumented people. In trying to figure out where we can throw a party, it's this horrible game of compromises, and I feel like we never gain any ground in finding actually unproblematic places to throw events. We have a giant list of places in New Orleans to throw parties, and there are reasons not to have parties at almost every single one of them. This feels extra challenging when thinking about the future of throwing parties in a more responsible fashion. Knowing we're never going to get it perfect is depressing, but I remind myself that perfectionism can be an expression of white supremacist culture. Also, I understand that one of the best ways to ensure that we are going to hear if/when there is a problem is to make sure that there are BIPOC organizers among us so that nobody has to interact with a white person (if they don't want to) concerning a racially sensitive issue. I wanted to talk about consent culture, which makes things even stickier. Gay culture is different than queer culture in a lot of ways, and one of them relates to consent.

Matthew: Having seen how people interact with drag queens and each other in predominantly gay male bars, a permissive, casual attitude towards bodies and touching has been normalized. But the consciousness around consent is changing in those spaces, too. It's something I'd like to see us take more seriously, whether in the form of a code of conduct, or having people trained to intervene, with alternatives to policing.

M'issa: It brings back your earlier point about Que(e)ry being a quasi-professional environment, except it's not part of the conference. Some people have their badges on, but come expecting a cross between a professional event and a public free-for-all.

Matthew: The bar may be open to anyone, but knowing the patterns of harassment in professional spaces, a conference badge isn't a guarantee of a person's behavior either. I also think our events don't need to be prudish to be respectful or professional. We can have burlesque and go-go dancers and other sex-positive queer expressions, while still being clear that that's not license to disrespect consent.

With everything going virtual, I'm also thinking about Que(e)ry's online advocacy. Do I just say whatever I want on Que(e)ry's Twitter, or is there a coherent Que(e)ry platform? Que(e)ry isn't apolitical, but elections or marriage equality aren't in our lane. Other organizations exist who can do that better. Back in 2011, Que(e)ry walked in the New York Pride Parade. In 2019 we instead marched in the Queer Liberation March, which was QTBIPOC-centered and didn't include cops or corporations. That choice felt right, but I'm trying to be realistic about what we can accomplish with our limited time and resources, whether online or in person.

M'issa: Back to the idea that we need more humans to do much more! Even if it's not Que(e)ry, a non-ALA organization of library workers that could make statements or recommendations for advocacy could be really useful. When we put a statement on the website, who's looking at it other than people who are already concerned? If we make an action plan or collaborate with other people to build one, folks can pass it around on social media and support can spread. Sometimes this creates change. Advocacy can be effective. We can imagine these things: we want a world where library staff reflects the global majority, we want a world where all genders of librarians are welcome in all the spaces, not just in special "for-the-queers" library environments.

Matthew: We could have a virtual forum for discussing and brainstorming.

M'issa: Everybody is building relationships this way. It might be a good time to take advantage of virtual events being the norm. I would still love for Que(e)ry to be a fundraiser for queer archives, but maybe a year of pandemic-induced remote socialization will show us what else we can do in the future. Maybe the answer will be that people just really like to come to Que(e)ry parties. That would be fine with me.

Matthew: With our ten-year anniversary and all the changes in the world and ALA, now's a good time to think about where we might go next.

M'issa: Unfortunately, queer archives largely lack systemic support and are likely to require grassroots fundraising to survive, but it does mean we'll always have a reason to throw these parties. I'd love for folks to use the list of queer archives on the website to throw their own Que(e)ry.[13] We could have a wider effect just by making it clear that it's easy enough to support these archives using a cleverly named party. Regardless of whether or not you can get to ALA, maybe you go to your state library conference. I could try throwing one in Louisiana. Que(e)ry, Que(e)ry, everywhere!

Reflections

Matthew: Revisiting our conversation, I see a few questions beneath the surface. What do queer dance parties at a bar have to do with librarianship? Or, why did we start Que(e)ry when other groups and other

---

13. Que(e)ry. "Resource Lists," https://www.queeryparty.org/resources.

forms of fundraising already exist? I didn't originally set out to create an advocacy organization, but in hindsight, I see Que(e)ry as participating in a broader legacy of queer nightlife-as-activism.[14] At a basic level, we provide financial support and attention not just to a queer library or archive, but to the queer venue we're bringing customers to, and to the DJs we pay. Many queer bars are important sites of queer history, and many are vulnerable to financial pressures like those that threaten the queer libraries and archives we support. Lesbian bars in particular are endangered.[15] Seven venues have closed since hosting a Que(e)ry event.[16] If we can't prevent that from happening, I hope we can at least help preserve their history.[17]

I think some of our initial success was due to the "librarian" sensibility and skill set we brought to our events—not just detailed planning documents, but community building as well. This might also have been in part due to the Que(e)ry "brand" and aesthetic that emerged in our decorations and publicity. By using archival images, like lesbian pulp-novel art or Tom of Finland beefcakes, we try to celebrate the queer art and history preserved by the archives we support. Meanwhile, shushing contests, librarian double-entendre party taglines (like Graphic Content, Leather Bound, or Authority Control), and parodies like adding leather daddy gear to the ALA owl logo, were attempts to challenge librarian stereotypes.

---

14. Brandon Tensley, "Fifty Years after Stonewall, What's the Political Role of the American Gay Bar?" *Pacific Standard*, June 28, 2019, https://psmag.com/ideas/the-politics-of-the-gay-bar-50-years-after-stonewall; Robin Kish, "The 'Lesbian Bar Project' Teaches Us that Queer Reveling is Activism," *Go*, June 10, 2021, http://gomag.com/article/the-lesbian-bar-project-teaches-us-that-queer-reveling-is-activism/; Jeremy Atherton Lin, *Gay Bar: Why We Went Out*, Little, Brown, and Co., 2021; Kemi Adeyemi, Kareem Khubchandani, Ramón H. Rivera-Servera, editors, *Queer Nightlife*, (Ann Arbor, MI: University of Michigan Press, 2021).

15. Sarah Marloff, "The Rise and Fall of America's Lesbian Bars," *Smithsonian Magazine*, January 21, 2021, https://www.smithsonianmag.com/travel/rise-and-fall-americas-lesbian-bars-180976801/.

16. Que(e)ry. "Friends of Que(e)ry," https://www.queeryparty.org/about/friends.

17. Lesbian Bar Project, https://www.lesbianbarproject.com/; Last Call: New Orleans Dyke Bar History Project, https://lastcallnola.podbean.com/; Cruising: A Podcast About the Last Lesbian Bars in the U.S., https://www.cruisingpod.com/.

The issues we discussed, like accessibility, consent, racism, policing, censorship, and compensation, obviously weren't new in 2010, but once Que(e)ry started being more intentional about engaging with them, I think we grew from a party into an organization. We didn't get it right overnight. This was a result of tough conversations, lessons learned after something went wrong, or events in the world that brought additional urgency to an issue. Credit also belongs to organizers who shared their experience and set an example for us. I hope we contributed something more than money in return. Maybe we challenged some venues to adopt more trans-inclusive practices for IDs or bathrooms. And, for me at least, the lessons I learned from Que(e)ry shaped how I see similar values at play in library work, organizations, spaces, and leadership. Looking to the future, maybe Que(e)ry can publish a toolkit with party-planning and social media tips or flyer templates, to help others start their own local versions of Que(e)ry parties.

M'issa: I second these emotions! This conversation covered a lot of ground; one of the things I've been thinking on, but didn't mention, are some less-visible ability issues. I know and hear from folks who would appreciate being around other queer librarians and/or want to support queer archives but have a hard time engaging in a loud party. I'd love to prioritize spaces that include a quieter area to allow for easier audibility and less stimulation. I hope that hearing how Que(e)ry formed and what we are on about has a catalytic effect—more volunteers, updates to our queer archives list, folks using our resources to support their own parties, new venue ideas, suggestions for codes of conduct that are simple to implement at rad parties—there are many directions to go from here, and all of them seem well-positioned to further the queered world we want to exist within.

Bibliography

Adeyemi, Kemi, Kareem Khubchandani, and Ramon Rivera-Servera. *Queer Nightlife*. Ann Arbor, MI: University of Michigan Press, 2021.

Jesella, Kara. "A Hipper Crowd of Shushers." *The New York Times*, July 8, 2007, sec. Fashion. https://www.nytimes.com/2007/07/08/fashion/08librarian.html.

Kish, Robin. "'The Lesbian Bar Project' Teaches Us That Queer Reveling Is Activism." *GO Magazine*, June 10, 2021. http://gomag.com/article/the-lesbian-bar-project-teaches-us-that-queer-reveling-is-activism/.

Lin, Jeremy Atherton. *Gay Bar: Why We Went Out*. New York ; London: Little, Brown and Company, 2021.

Marloff, Sarah. "The Rise and Fall of America's Lesbian Bars." *Smithsonian Magazine*, January 21, 2021. https://www.smithsonianmag.com/travel/rise-and-fall-americas-lesbian-bars-180976801/.

Tensley, Brandon. "The Politics of the Gay Bar, 50 Years After Stonewall." *Pacific Standard*, July 24, 2019. https://psmag.com/ideas/the-politics-of-the-gay-bar-50-years-after-stonewall.

Index

#PulseOrlando, 264
#Schomburg Syllabus, 89

2SLGBTQAI 130-3, 135-9, *see also* LGBTQIA+

ableism, 249
acquisition, 120, 204
ACT UP, 83
Activism in the Five Boroughs, 76
Adler, Melissa, 144
AIDS, 9, 22-3, 26-8, 30-2, 82, 85-6, 202-4, 236
AIDS buddy, 22
Alcohol Tobacco Commission, 29
Allison, Dorothy, 184
Ambush Magazine, 31
American Library Association (ALA), 13, 67, 210, 219, 260, 262-4, 266-9
 ALA Task Force for Gay Liberation, 143
ancestors, 88, 119, 200-4, 206-7, 212-3
anti-racism, 250
anti-violence, 137 *see also* violence
Anzaldúa, Gloria, 65
ARL Kaleidoscope Program, 209
Association of Research Libraries (ARL), 209
Atkinson, Ti-Grace, 185
Atlanta University Center Robert W. Woodruff Library, 225

audiovisual preservation, 236
Audre Lorde Legacy Award, 69, 71
authority files, 237

Baldwin, James, 79, 86, 201, 227
Bambara, Toni Cade, 214
Bamberger, Rosalie, 39
Banks, Brenda, 225
Barnard Conference on Sexuality, 191
Barry, James, 175-6
bars, 29, 30, 261, 263, 265-6, 269
bathrooms, 261, 270
BC Gay and Lesbian Archives, 133
Beam, Dorothy, 204
Beam, Joseph F., 204
Bechdel, Alison, 150
Berman, Sandy, 143
Bérubé, Allan, 103
Bibliothèque Nationale de France, 106
Billey, Amber, 149, 260
biracial, 80
bisexual, 80, 139
Black archivists, 229-30
Black Caucus of the American Library Association (BCALA), 208
Black Gay and Lesbian Archive *see* In the Life Archive (ITLA)
Black, Indigenous, People of Color (BIPOC), 46-7, 264-6
Black liberation, 125

Black Lives Matter (BLM), 37, 82, 118, 130, 264
Bois Burk Collection, 97
bookmobile, 53
Boston College, 77
Boston University, 225
Boyd, Blanch McCrary, 186
Brainard, Joe, 108-9
British Columbia, 53-4, 130, 139,
brown, adrienne maree, 116
Brown, Rita Mae, 185-6
butch, 190, 193
butch-femme, 44
Butler, Stewart, 21, 25, 27, 31

Califia, Pat, 191
Campbell, Jeff, 30-1
Canada, 53, 130-2
capitalism, 42, 46, 116-7, 120, 254
Carey, David, 84-5, 90
Carole, L'Androgyne, 106
cataloging, 67, 79, 87, 120, 142-3, 145, 148, 157, 163, 168, 172-3, 177, 258
Charity Hospital, 22, 27
Chauncey, George, 103
Chicana Feminisms conferences, 65
Christensen, Ben, 143
chrononormativity, 252-3
cisheteronormative historiography, 99
Clark Atlanta University, 210
code switching, 211
collective memory, 47
Collier, Zakiya, 89, 200, 213
Colombia, 64-6

coming out, 178
committee work, 169
community archives, 38, 56-7, 69, 109, 121, 163
Conciencia Femenil (ConFem), 65
consented collecting, 59
controlled vocabulary[ies], 141-2, 148, 161, 172, 238
COVID-19, 30, 45, 60, 78, 82, 174
creative writing, 64
Cruising Utopia, 118
Cruz, Celia, 67
cultural competency, 177, 256
Cvetkovich, Ann, 61

Daly, Mary, 187
data, 176, 179, 238, 240-1, 244 *see also* linked data
Daughters of Bilitis, 36, 39, 45, 48
Davis, Madeline, 191
de la tierra, tatiana, 64-72
death, 46, 82-3, 106, 176, 229
deeds of gift, 121
Desk Set, The, 260
Dewey Decimal System, 154
Diagnostic and Statistical Manual of Mental Disorders (DSM), 146-7
Dianic coven, 187
Digital Transgender Archive (DTA), 144-5, 147, 151
digitization, 184
disabled people (people with disabilities; crip person), 152
DIY culture, 252

Dobreski, Brian, 158
Dodson, Howard, 210
donors, 120-1, 220, 222, 229
Drabinski, Emily, 154, 239, 243
Dragovic, Nik, 260
Dureau, George, 25
Dutton, Ron, 54, 57

Edel, Deborah, 188
Egan, Orla, 149
El Divino, 65-6
Elliot, Beth, 36
emergent strategy, 116
ephemera, 37, 52-3, 76, 78, 97, 107, 149
eroticism, 196
estate planning, 106
Ettarh, Fobazi, 57

Facebook, 38, 168
family, 51, 57, 72, 85, 88, 160, 200, 203, 207-8, 212-3, 222
    Black, 199
    extended, 204-5
    nuclear, 206
fanfiction, 149, 150
Farmer, Mary, 186-7
Feinberg, Leslie, 193
fetish objects, 97, 103
film, 29, 56, 238
Finocchio's, 109
folksonomies, 144
Forward newspaper, 76, 84
Fullwood, Steven, 200, 214, 225

fundraiser, 28, 137, 260, 268
Furies, 185-6

Galvinhill, Alice, 149
Gardeazábal, Gustavo Álvarez, 65
gay krew, 23
Gay and Lesbian Association of Kamloops (GALA), 133
Gay and Lesbian Association of Northern BC (GALA North), 133
Gay Liberation Front, 28
Gay Pride march, 184
gender identity, 58, 104, 142, 153, 171, 189, 195
GLBT Historical Society, 97-8, 101, 104, 147
Greenblatt, Ellen, 143
Greenwich Village, 205
Guatemala, 134
Gumbs, Alexis Pauline, 213
Gumby, Alexander, 200

Haizlip, Ellis, 204-5
Hamer, Fannie Lou, 227
Hammond, Harmony, 185
Hammond, John, 28
Hansberry, Lorraine, 86
Harding, Sandra, 161
Harlem, 76, 200
Harris, Bertha, 185-6
Harris, Reginald, 213
Hart, Tara, 260
Harter, J.B., 29

Hartman, Saidiya, 113
hemispheric cultural networks, 66
Hemispheric Institute Digital Video Library (HIDVL), 112, 114, 120
Hemphill, Essex, 204
Henry, Sue, 55, 60
historical emotion, 50, 59
historical imagination, 99, 100
histories, 46-7, 58, 109, 118, 122, 125, 129
    counter, 105
    erasure in, 139, 207
    experiential, 250
    of immigration and migration, 112
    marginalized, 250
    oral, 133
    of queer/trans people, 68, 108
HistoryMakers Fellowship, 224
Hobby Directory, 98, 101
Hollis, Flo, 184
Holocaust, 76, 78
Homosaurus, 142-52, 154, 156-64
Hurston, Zora Neale, 203, 211

IHLIA LGBT Heritage, 145, 148
Impact magazine, 24
In the Life Archive (ITLA), 202-3, 210
Indigenous Peoples, 130-1, 135, 159, *see also* Black, Indigenous, People of Color (BIPOC)
Inefuku, Harrison, 219
infrastructure, 23, 137, 239, 242

Initiative to Create a Diverse Workforce (IRDW), 209
Instagram, 38, 191, 236, 242
International Classification of Diseases (ICD), 147
Internet Archive, 243
intersectionality, 151-2, 164, 177
intimacy, 61, 115, 125-6
isolation, 132, 138

JEB (Joan E. Biren), 185, 187
Johnson, Marsha P., 46
joy, 88-9, 127, 163, 226, 228
Judaism, 58, 76

kinship, 127, 222, 230
Kizzie, Janaya, 149
Krueger, Stephen, 174

La Barre, Kathryn, 148
Lachatanere, Diana, 210
Lammas Bookstore, 187
language
    Arabic, 158
    Dutch, 145, 158
    English, 75, 145, 151, 157-8, 175
Latin America, 66
Latina lesbians, 64, 66-72
legal names, 171-2
lesbian desire, 65
Lesbian Herstory Archives (LHA), 54-6, 159, 184, 192-4, 198, 206, 209, 260

Leslie Lohman Museum of Gay and Lesbian Art, 29
LGBTQIA+, 46-7, 142, 163, 200-3, 207-9, 213, *see also* 2SLGBTQAI
Library of Congress, 41, 66-7, 72, 120, 146-7, 152, 157
Library of Congress Subject Headings (LCSH), 146-7, 157, 159
LibraryThing, 144
linked data, 145, 158-9
Lipton, Lawrence, 24
literary recovery, 40, 47
Lorde, Audre, 40, 46, 65, 69, 71, 119, 200, 212, 230-1
Lost & Found Press, 40

Mack, McKensie, 252
MARC records, 146
Mardi Gras, 23, 29, 32
Martin, Trayvon, 264
Mattachine Society, 39
Medical Subject Headings (MeSH), 147
Mellon Foundation, 225
mentorship, 194, 209
metadata, 114, 172
Michigan Womyn's Music Festival, 192
microaggressions, 79
Missing and Murdered Indigenous Women and Girls, 130-1
Mock, Janet, 40
Moore, Lisa C., 213
Moraga, Cherríe, 63

Morrison, Toni, 213
Mosley, Derek, 225
Mott Branch Library, 200
Mount Holyoke, MA, 250, 255
Muñoz, José Esteban, 52, 119
Muñoz, Trevor, 117-8
Murray, Pauli, 108
music, 67, 248-9, 252-3

National Women's March Against Poverty, 53
Nealon, Christopher, 50
network, 242
New Orleans, 22-33, 225, 262, 266
New Orleans Stop AIDS Task Force, 30
New York City Public Library, 28
New York Historical Society, 76
New York Pride Parade, 267
New York Times, 82
New York University (NYU), 115, 236
  NYU Bobst Library, 195
  NYU Special Collections, 112
Nguyen, Tan Hoang, 50
nightlife as activism, 269
NO/AIDS Task Force, 22
Nolan, Chloe, 149
non-binary, 39, 44, 130-1, 138-9, 175, 189, 212-3, 235

Occupy Wall Street, 37
Okanagan of British Columbia, 134
ONE Archive, 69

Onuma, Jiro, 99
Open Biological and Biomedical Ontologies (OBO) Foundry, 147
oral history, 250-1
Orlando, 264

participatory design, 179
photography, 188, 198
poetry, 24, 42, 65, 71-2, 265
post-custodial models, 121
Prado, Pérez, 67
Pratt School of Information, 236
preservation, 46, 78, 107, 125, 236, 239, 242, 244
pride marches, 184, 196
Princeton University, 96, 109
Princeton University Library, 99
professionalism, 221, 231, 250, 252, 255-6
pronouns, 67, 81-2, 174, 176, 190, 193
Proust, Marcel, 97
publishing, 38, 43, 45-6, 48, 248
Pulse Nightclub, 264
Putney, Vermont, 185-6

Que(e)ry, 260-5, 267-70
Queer Black elders, 225
queer healing, 125
Queer Liberation March, 267
Queer Time, 252, 256
Queer Zine Archive Project (QZAP), 60, 155, 237

Rainbow Book Fair, 26
rainbow flag, 224
Rainbow Round Table (RRT), 218, 222, 262-3
Rawhide, 29
Rawson, Katie, 117-8, 147
Reed College, 222
representation, 58, 99, 100, 115, 142, 170, 173, 223
research guide[s], 39, 78-9, 86, 88
respectability politics, 223, 229
Retter-Vargas, Yolanda, 70-1
Rodríguez, Juana María, 68
Richland County Public Library, 205
Rising Moon Books & Beyond, 55
rituals, 187-8
Robert Duncan in San Francisco, 36
Roberto, K.R., 148
Rubin, Gayle, 191
Rumaker, Michael, 36-7, 40

Sagaris feminist institute, 185-6, 188
San Francisco, 36-7, 99, 210, 219
San Francisco State University, 97
Schomburg Archival Collections, 89
Schomburg Center for Research in Black Culture, 77-9, 81, 86, 201-5, 210, 225
Schomburg, Arturo, 78, 90
Schultz, Katherine, 107
scope notes, 156-7

Serdatsky, Yente, 83
Sex Wars, 191, 197
sex work, 46, 99, 106, 109, 163
Sexual Minority Archives, 159
Shockley, Ann Allen, 212
silence(s), 46, 64-5, 70, 207, 230
Simmons College, 224
Sisters, 36
slowness, 116-7, 123, 125
Smith, Barbara, 201
social media, 37, 242, 254, 267, 270
Society of American Archivists, 219
Sonora Matancera, The, 66, 67
Southern Decadence, 26, 29, 32
Spelman College, 69, 206, 225
Stanford Gay and Lesbian Archives project, 96
Stahling, Christopher, 213
Stand Your Ground laws in Florida, 264
Stanford University, 96, 108
Star Distributors, 109
Stevens, Darryl, 203
Stonewall, 39, 87, 116
Stonewall Book Awards committee, 222
Stonewall Inn, 260
Stop AIDS Task Force, 28, 30
storytelling, 32, 76
Stryker, Susan, 103
Sueyoshi, Amy, 103
SUNY Buffalo, 64

SUNY Buffalo Library, 67
SUNY New Paltz, 194
SUNY Stony Brook University, 186

Take Back the Night anti-violence march, 137
Tallahassee, Florida, 185
technology design 170
The Holy Barbarians, 24
The Ladder, 36
thesaurus, 145, 161 *see also* Homosaurus
Thompson Area Gays (TAG), 133
TikTok, 242
trans, 36, 39, 47, 80, 103, 131, 139, 145, 151, 155, 169, 171, 173, 175, 179, 237, 263
Trans 101, 171
trans archives, 106, 110, 136, 145
Trans Bodies Trans Selves, 39
trans history, 103, 159, 172
trans life narrative[s], 40, 105, 108
trans male/man, 176, 191, 193
trans studies, 102
trans women of color, 29, 170
transgender Afro-Canadians, 154
Transgender Archives (University of Victoria), 136
transgender Buddhists, **154**
transgender movement, 105
transgender scholarship, 136
transgender terminology, 158
transgender women, 99, 159

transness, 153
transsexual, 105, 143, 159
transsexualism, 147
Truth and Reconciliation Commission in Canada, 131
Tumblr, 242, 261
two-spirit, 131, 139, 153

UCLA Archive, 69
UCLA Chicano Studies Research Center, 70
University of North Carolina, Charlotte (UNCC), 55
Urban Archive, 76

Van der Wel, Jack, 145, 149
Vancouver, British Columbia, 53-4, 130
Vancouver Gay and Lesbian Archive, 60
Vancouver Island, 136
Varga, Ed, 193
violence, 100, 113, 117-9, 132 *see also* anti-violence
vocabularies, 151-3, 155-6, 158-9, 162
    controlled, 172
    history of, 144
    linked data, 146, 158
    queer, 143-4, 146
    standard, 145
    subject, 148
vocational awe, 57
volunteers, 28, 57, 265, 270

Waithe, Lena, 24
Walker, Alice, 203, 209
Walker, Walter "Cat", 149
Wayback Machine, 243
We Here, 265
white supremacy, 117, 120, 231
white supremacy culture, 250, 252, 255
Whitmire, Ethelene, 206
Whorley, Tywanna, 225
Wikidata, 158
Williams, Kerrie Cotton, 225
Willoughby, Lydia, 260
Women on Wheels: Rolling Feminist Library, 53
World AIDS Day, 86

Yale University, 101, 109, 190
Yiddish press, 63, 76 *see also* Forward
Yiddish theater, 84-5, 90
yoni, 191, 193
YouTube, 171

zines, 42, 48, 53, 237 *see also* Queer Zine Archive Project (QZAP),

www.ingramcontent.com/pod-product-compliance
Lightning Source LLC
Chambersburg PA
CBHW050301010526
44108CB00040B/1971